2 edition

Counseling and Educational Research

This book is dedicated to:
my lifelong best friend and spouse Carmen,
my cherished daughter Clarissa and
my grandchildren Ian and Soraya, and my
cherished daughter Serena, a future scholar.

2 edition

Counseling and Educational Research

Evaluation and Application

Rick Houser

University of Massachusetts, Boston

Los Angeles • London • New Delhi • Singapore • Washington DC

For information:

SAGE Publications, Inc.
2455 Teller Road
Thousand Oaks,
    California 91320
E-mail: order@sagepub.com

SAGE Publications India Pvt. Ltd.
B 1/I 1 Mohan Cooperative
    Industrial Area
Mathura Road, New Delhi 110 044
India

SAGE Publications Ltd.
1 Oliver's Yard
55 City Road
London EC1Y 1SP
United Kingdom

SAGE Publications Asia-Pacific Pte. Ltd
33 Pekin Street #02-01
Far East Square
Singapore 048763

Printed in the United States of America

Library of Congress Cataloging-in-Publication Data

Houser, Rick.
Counseling and educational research : evaluation and application/Rick Houser. — 2nd ed.
    p. cm.
Includes bibliographical references and index.
ISBN 978-1-4129-5660-4 (cloth)
ISBN 978-1-4129-5661-1 (pbk.)
    1. Research—Study and teaching. I. Title.

Q180.A1H595 2009
001.4071—dc22   2008024298

This book is printed on acid-free paper.

10   11   12   10   9   8   7   6   5   4   3

Acquisitions Editor:	Kassie Graves
Editorial Assistant:	Veronica K. Novak
Production Editor:	Kristen Gibson
Copy Editor:	Bill Bowers
Typesetter:	C&M Digitals (P) Ltd.
Proofreader:	Caryne Brown
Indexer:	Molly Hall
Cover Designer:	Candice Harman
Marketing Manager:	Carmel Schrire

Contents

Foreword

I feel honored to write this brief foreword of Dr. Rick Houser's new and expanded second edition of his classic research text, *Counseling and Educational Research: Evaluation and Application*. I had the privilege of writing the foreword to his first edition, and it was with excitement and anticipation that I read this new edition. In a nutshell, this new edition is exceptional! Dr. Houser has built upon the unique strengths of the inaugural edition, namely the clarity, scholarship, and overall "user-friendliness" of the contents, in fashioning a fully updated, crystal clear, and engaging text. I promise the reader that you will actually enjoy reading this comprehensive research textbook. Some of the unique strengths of this text are as follows:

1. Dr. Houser is a skilled researcher and a master teacher. He has been teaching, modifying, and experimenting with research courses in counseling and education for over 20 years. He understands that many graduate students in counseling, education, and related fields approach their required "research" and "statistics" courses with trepidation. These students want to be counselors, clinicians, healers, and teachers and may not initially see the relation of research, statistics, and math to their "helping" careers. Dr. Houser meets new research students where they are and highlights that reviewing (and, on some level, conducting) research is intimately connected with their work, and that, in fact, they will be better and more ethically informed practitioners through engaging the research process.

2. The book is easy to read for a research textbook. Dr. Houser writes clearly, and engages the reader in every chapter. In reading the text I felt I was being personally taught and mentored by Dr. Houser. The content is highly user-friendly, and even when presenting more complex ideas, such as reliability, validity, experimental designs, and basic statistics, Dr. Houser successfully grasps readers' attention and guides them in processing and understanding the

material. By using actual excerpts from published research articles Dr. Houser demonstrates strengths and limitations of each component of both quantitative and qualitative research articles. Discussion questions at the end of many chapters allow readers to further explore, process, and understand critical aspects of evaluating and conducting research.

3. The book is fluid and very well organized. It successfully engages the reader on the logical journey of understanding their professional identities as "practitioner-scientists," to searching for articles to read using the latest Internet search tools, to understanding key concepts and constructs in basic statistics and quantitative and qualitative methods, to how to evaluate each section of a published article, to developing one's own research proposal. Dr. Houser provides good examples in demonstrating basic statistical methods and various research designs. He has carefully selected published article excerpts to demonstrate critiquing all sections of a research manuscript.

4. Importantly, Dr. Houser includes strong chapters on recent advances in mixed methods research designs, evidence-based research practice, program evaluation, and applying research into our own practice as counselors, teachers, and educators. His coverage of research ethics and his review of the classic Tuskegee syphilis and Milgram obedience studies are in-depth and riveting. In all respects, the book material is very up to date and well referenced, and it is clear that Dr. Houser has an excellent grasp of the research process generally and of research in counseling and education specifically.

5. Finally, two particularly unique aspects of this comprehensive research text relative to the many others in circulation are Dr. Houser's in-depth knowledge and coverage of qualitative research methods, and his sensitivity and competence in considering multicultural and cross-cultural perspectives in counseling and educational research. Many research texts give just a passing mention to qualitative methods and cross-cultural perspectives, yet for those in the counseling and educational fields, the inclusion of qualitative approaches and multicultural perspectives is critical to our work with clients, students, and their extended families. Dr. Houser, thankfully, gives due justice to these two critical topics.

In summary, it is probably clear to readers that I consider *Counseling and Educational Research: Evaluation and Application* to be an exceptional, scholarly, culturally informed, and reader-friendly contribution to the literature. I loved the first edition of this book, and it is clear to me that this new, fully expanded and updated edition is even stronger than the original. I am very excited about using this text for my research courses in counseling and education at Fordham University.

Joseph G. Ponterotto, Ph.D.
Professor, Counseling Psychology
Graduate School of Education
Fordham University, New York City

Preface

The intent of this text is to prepare students in counseling and educational programs to be good users and consumers of research. Our society holds science and decisions based on sound information as crucial, and even uses such standards in determining culpability for malpractice. It is imperative that practitioners embrace research and the research process, which can provide the best and most current practices. This means using the research literature in one's area of expertise, whether it is counseling, education, or both, and systematically evaluating whether the information presented in professional journals is valid and appropriate for the populations for which it is intended. Acquiring necessary skills for systematically evaluating professional scientific literature is critical in functioning as a practitioner. The majority of this text focuses on preparing readers to be good *consumers* and evaluators of scientific literature published in professional journals.

In addition, a practitioner should engage in small-scale research on the job site to test out new ideas. The practitioner is in a unique position to see problems confronting those whom he or she serves, and can systematically develop new strategies to test. The second purpose of this book is to prepare readers to engage in small-scale research projects that are field-based and can be practically implemented.

I have taught research and evaluation to students in counseling and education programs for more than two decades, and I am acutely aware that the majority of students do not look forward to taking a research course. However, I truly believe it is critical that those entering the counseling and educational field must have a solid background as consumers in reading the professional literature. This means developing the skills to systematically evaluate the professional literature with a critical eye, and to use the literature in a responsible fashion. I have found that at the end of a research course, students generally have a more positive attitude toward research and, most important, feel more competent in reading research from the professional literature. Also,

I have had students who, at the beginning of a research course, state that they shy away from research but at the end of the research reported that they actually enjoyed the experience. I believe that learning should be relatively enjoyable, and this typically occurs when there is in an interest in the topic. This textbook is organized in such a way that students are encouraged to evaluate articles in the professional literature using a systematic approach, with specific questions to address. Therefore, I would recommend that students choose articles to evaluate that are of significant interest to them, and not just find any article to analyze.

I see this text being used as an introduction to the research process and useful for those who plan to be practitioners and consumers of research. There are numerous texts that teach students to be primarily researchers, but that is not the intent of this book. Research and the research process are public phenomena, and, consequently, I have found that allowing students to engage in discussions in reviewing articles, typically in small groups, facilitates the learning process. Also, participating in small-group discussions with student peers and potential future colleagues will, I hope, promote habits that will carry over into professional practice—for instance, discussing research in the professional literature among professional colleagues.

I enjoyed writing this second edition of the book, as I did the first edition, because I like the scientific approach, and I enjoy discussing new ideas and using creative problem solving to address practical issues. I hope students find this text a readable and practical guide that will facilitate the practice of their exciting and challenging professions of counseling and education.

Acknowledgments

I have been fortunate in my academic career to work with dedicated and thoughtful students. Students have provided comments and feedback over the past several years about the first edition of *Counseling and Educational Research: Evaluation and Application.* I want to acknowledge the insightful comments of prior students, and I hope the changes that have been made reflect the needs of other students taking courses in research. One student who made a significant contribution to this edition is Ms. Jenifer Hietala. Ms. Hietala assisted in gathering research articles and assisted in typing the manuscript. She completed much of the work while receiving treatment (even while hospitalized) for a serious medical problem. Her emotional strength in dealing with such a personal challenge while completing this work is truly remarkable.

Completion of this book required significant effort, and there are a number of others who have made essential contributions that I want to acknowledge. First, Kassie Graves, the Acquisitions Editor–Human Services for Sage Publications, carefully selected reviewers to assist in the revision of the text. Her supportive efforts and expertise are greatly appreciated. She professionally and smoothly facilitated the completion of the book. Veronica Novak, Editorial Assistant, facilitated the submission process. Kristen Gibson moved the book through production efficiently and in a timely fashion. Bill Bowers, Copy Editor, provided exceptional review and comments. He diligently reviewed the manuscript and made valuable suggestions. Joseph Ponterotto graciously wrote the foreword, which provides a thoughtful summary of the text. His efforts are greatly appreciated. I enjoy the writing process, and it is made more enjoyable with the assistance and help of the highly skilled individuals mentioned above.

I

Introduction to the Research Process

1

Science and the Research Process

Across the centuries there have been frequent attempts to improve the plight of humankind, and frequently these efforts have focused on the use of research to do so. However, most recent advances in science have been most dramatic. Little (2006) stated: "During the last fifty years science and invention have led us further and further from the world that was; deeper and deeper into a new environment. The process of change has been so rapid that readjustment has been difficult. Yet readjust ourselves we must" (p. 54). Science and scientific advances have been purported to be critical in promoting the well-being of individuals and in societal functioning (Frye, 1965; Mendelsohn & Nowotny, 1984). Padgett (2004) noted that "Faith in the scientific method has been the rock solid foundation of technological advances" (p. 1).

The words *science* and *research* have significant meaning in our current world. Our society has had a "love-hate" relationship with science (Padgett, 2004). This love-hate relationship may be found in various aspects of our lives. The entertainment industry provides good examples of this conflicted relationship. Science and research have been depicted both positively and negatively in movies and on television. *Star Trek, The Six Million Dollar Man,* Ian Fleming's James Bond books and movies, and other media presentations have frequently portrayed science in a positive light. Conversely, *Frankenstein* and even *Jurassic Park* are examples of science and research being presented as potentially out of control and creating problems. Al Gore's movie *An Inconvenient Truth* presents how human efforts in science (creating a greenhouse effect through technology) have impacted our world and potentially may lead to major changes in earth's ability to sustain life.

The advent of the telephone, electricity, and computers (the Internet), along with advances in medicine (genetic engineering), are examples of how science has changed and (theoretically) improved our lives. In fact, today there are probably few places you can go or activities you can engage in and not come into contact with advances achieved through science and research. Additionally, decisions in our society made by government and other social institutions are typically based on scientific research outcomes. Finally, you cannot read a newspaper on a daily basis without coming across reports of scientific advances.

Definitions of Science and Research

The term *science* has been defined in various ways, but there are common elements to the definitions. Best and Kahn (2003) defined science as "an approach to the gathering of knowledge rather than a field or subject matter" (p. 6). They further described science as consisting "of two primary functions: (1) the development of theory and (2) the testing of substantive hypotheses that are deduced from theory" (p. 6). Moore (1983) defined research as "an objective, systematic, testable process for obtaining knowledge about our world" (p. 5). Common elements of science include acquisition of knowledge, a systematic approach, and an objective analysis with opportunities for conclusions about how our world may function. The ultimate goal of research and science is to obtain knowledge useful in understating how our world operates. Moore (1983) described different approaches we have in obtaining knowledge, such as personal experience, tradition, expert opinion, authority, and church-state scholarship. He noted that the use of these methods of obtaining knowledge is fraught with subjective bias. The conclusion he suggests that we reach is that using the research method reduces such subjective bias. Salkind (2006) suggested that there are a number of elements of quality research. For example, he proposed that quality research (1) can be replicated, (2) is generalizable to other settings, (3) is based on a reasonable rationale and linked to a theory or theories, (4) is not based upon political beliefs, and (5) is objective.

In our everyday lives we make decisions, some of which are based on scientific information and some that are based on personal sources. Sources of knowledge have been identified, and some are based on the scientific method, whereas others are based on institutional contributions (Ary, Jacobs, & Razavieh, 2002). One frequently used source of knowledge is experience. We may even trust our experience more than what may be presented in scientific journals. A second source of knowledge is authority, and we frequently seek out the advice of those who have particular expertise, such as lawyers, physicians, and others who hold a high level of expertise in a specified body of knowledge.

Gall, Gall, and Borg (2002) suggested that there are four different types of knowledge, and these various types of knowledge can be clearly linked to certain research approaches. The four are description, prediction, improvement, and explanation. Knowledge viewed from a descriptive approach may be interpreted to consist of attempts to describe natural and/or social or psychological events. The key to descriptive knowledge is a focus on assessment, which allows descriptions of identified events to be made. In counseling, this may involve (for example) a description of the specific characteristics of an emotional condition, such as obsessive-compulsive disorder. In education, an example of knowledge from a descriptive view might be how a teacher interacts with children based upon gender in a classroom.

Knowledge based on a predictive view involves developing ways to predict identified outcomes. For example, in education, we may want to predict success in a particular type of educational program, such as an advanced placement course in biology. In counseling, we may want to predict who may benefit most from a particular treatment approach, such as a post-traumatic stress treatment, e.g., a virtual reality technique; we need objective knowledge that allows us to predict effectively.

Another type of research knowledge, improvement, concerns developing information designed to determine the effectiveness of interventions (Gall, et al., 2002). For example, in education we may be interested in knowing the effectiveness of mainstreaming students with disabilities. An example from counseling might be an interest in the effectiveness of a specific counseling approach—the cognitive behavioral approach, for example—with a condition such as a post-traumatic stress.

The fourth and final type of research knowledge, according to Gall et al. (2002), is explanation. This type of knowledge may be the broadest of all and subsumes the others. Typically, researchers frame questions and problems in terms of theories or explanations of phenomena. For example, behavioral theory may be a basis for explaining a child's tantrum behavior and the reinforcement sequence developed within a particular environment. Researchers would use the theory to establish research studies to support or refute components of the theory.

Although the research method clearly does inherently reduce subjective bias, I want to caution against complete acceptance of the notion that research is always objective and never biased. Babbie (1992) noted that there are eight types of errors that contribute to difficulties in making predictions and decisions, and several of these errors may occur in science and research investigations. The eight are inaccurate observation, overgeneralization, selective observation, made-up information, illogical reasoning, ego involvement, premature closure of inquiry, and mystification. For example, inaccurate observation may occur in research investigations, especially if the investigators are not careful in their procedures. Gall et al. (2002) suggested that another potential criticism of research is that inevitably the researcher's own biases and selection of what to observe create problems. This is the error of selective observation. A researcher may conclude the inquiry before all the variables affecting the observed outcomes are identified or fully understood. Researchers have found that we as human beings have a tendency to quickly decide upon a hypothesis and then gather information to confirm it, rather than seek alternative hypotheses (Pottick, Kirk, & Hsieh, 2007; Strohmer, Pellerin, & Davidson, 1995).

The important question to address is whether the research method does provide more objectivity in gaining knowledge about our world. Kelly (1955), a personality theorist, stated that a major motivation for human beings is to be a "good scientist," and being a good scientist involves making accurate predictions about events. A major tenet of psychology is that we as human beings inherently like to predict and control our lives. Scientific and research methods may ultimately provide one of the better ways to be a good scientist and make good predictions. Being a good scientist professionally can be accomplished in part through our ability to systematically evaluate the efficacy of the scientific and research process and the information present in professional journals used in practice.

Practitioner-Scientist

In counseling and psychology, there has been a relatively long tradition of graduate-level training from a scientist-practitioner orientation (Forsyth & Leary, 1997; Gelso, 2006; Hinkin, Holtom, & Klag, 2007; Hoshmand & Polkinghorne, 1992; Lane & Corrie, 2006; Leong & Zachar, 1991; Nelson & Neufeldt, 1996; Stoltenber, McNeil, & Elliott, 1995; Vespia, Sauer, & Lyddon, 2006). Goldfried (1984) suggested that a profession based on a scientific approach is in a better position to be considered legitimate. The scientist-practitioner model was developed by the American Psychological Association in 1947 (Bernstein & Kerr, 1993). The basic concept is that those practicing the profession of psychology, and also counseling (Bernstein & Kerr, 1993), would split their time and focus rather evenly between research and practice. However, as Heppner, Kivlighan, and Wampold (1992) noted, the reality may be a much different ratio, more like 75 percent practice and 25 percent research, based on need and interest. Most practitioners have been dissatisfied with heavy emphasis on scientific methods and knowledge, using the ideal model of 50 percent research and 50 percent practice. Love, Bahner, Jones, and Nilsson (2007) discussed the relevance of research in psychology or counseling: "Research advances knowledge in the field of psychology and often guides clinical practice, yet very few psychologists conduct research after graduate school" (p. 314). Gelso (2006) noted that students entering graduate programs typically are interested in practice and not in conducting research, and this is manifested in the low productivity of research by those who complete graduate counseling and psychology programs.

Manicas and Secord (1983) attempted to differentiate the tasks of the scientist and the practitioner by stating, "The former practices science by creating at least partially close systems; the latter uses the discoveries of science, but . . . also employs a great deal of knowledge that extends beyond science" (p. 412). In essence, they were stating that practitioners use not only science but other forms of information, such as personal information, in the practice of their profession. Consequently, I like the term practitioner-scientist to more appropriately reflect the realities of how many master's-level-trained counselors and educators use and participate in research. The emphasis is on practice first, with the use of research as a foundation for conducting practice. Others also have used the term practitioner-scientist/researcher (Bernstein & Kerr, 1993). As Heppner et al. (1992) noted, the use of science in practice does not need to be evenly split. Practitioners will most likely choose to emphasize practice with science as a source of knowledge for treatment decisions rather than conducting research or being the researchers who gather the knowledge. Hunsley (2007) noted the different terms utilized from the original scientist-practitioner view to include "practitioner scholar" or "clinical scientists."

Heiman (1995) stated that ". . . psychology is as much a science as the natural sciences of physics, chemistry, or biology because they all employ the scientific method" (p. 5). This statement by Heiman can be applied to education also, as long as the scientific method is employed. So what differentiates a scientific approach from a nonscientific approach? The definition of science and several assumptions about science provide this answer.

Assumptions About Science and Research

Heiman (1995) cited several important assumptions about science that may be helpful in understanding the difference between scientific activity and nonscience. A basic premise of research and science, according to Heiman, is that one can find lawfulness in the subject studied (e.g., psychology or counseling and education). Lawfulness in our disciplines, counseling and education, is determined by the extent to which we can find ways to predict and control events. For example, we may hypothesize that when a client in counseling describes a certain psychological reaction, such as an obsession with cleanliness, and is always washing his hands, that he has an obsessive-compulsive personality. Consequently, we can hypothesize and predict to some degree how the person will react in the future. In education, an example may be teaching a child reading with certain methods of instruction, for instance phonics or whole word, and we may predict that one method of instruction will be better than another based on research outcomes.

A second important assumption, according to Heiman (1995), is that nature is understandable. This means that the laws of nature are understandable, and we can explain them in some way based on a theory. Understanding from a research perspective refers back to an explanation, which is a major goal of the scientific approach (Gall, et al., 2002). Gall et al. (2003) proposed that researchers employ different theoretical orientations in the search for explanations. Three orientations may be used by investigators in their attempt to explain natural and/or social and psychological phenomena: mechanistic, post-positivistic, and scientific realism. The mechanistic approach has been a major orientation of scientific research since the 1800s and consists of developing scientific explanations from a cause-and-effect relationship. If a bowler rolls a bowling ball down a bowling alley and it hits the pins, the assumption is that the ball caused the pins to fall. There is a direct relationship between two or more events: the ball rolling and hitting the pins and the pins falling. An example in education may be an adolescent taking an advanced placement course, and consequently she does well on college entrance exams.

The post-positivist approach, according to Gall et al. (2002), involves an assumption that individual perceptions of the social environment and an event influence how they behave: there is an interaction between the person's perception and certain phenomena. To concretely illustrate this orientation, we can go back to the example of encouraging a child to study and complete his or her work, and the result is a high grade. According to the post-positivist view, the child's interpretation and the meaning attached to getting a high grade will have a significant impact on the outcome. Consequently, the explanation for a particular event or phenomenon is not a simple cause-and-effect relationship. Children may interpret a high grade in a different way's; some may consider a "B" a good grade, whereas others may be satisfied only an "A".

The scientific realism view for explaining events states that the world is composed of layers of causal structures. Some of the causal structures are easy to observe, while others are not as easy to observe (Gall, et al., 1996). The job of the researcher is to identify the various causal structures and how they interact to produce an effect. The following interpretation may be made if we again return, using the scientific realism view, to an example of a child studying to receive a high grade. Not only does the grade influence the outcome, but the events prior to studying have influence as well. For example, did the child's parents have a fight prior to the child starting to study? The student may have just received a high grade in another subject, and this motivates him or her to work hard on the current topic. The job of the researcher using the scientific realism approach is to identify the relevant causal structures influencing the event or phenomenon being studied. The scientific realism view is an attempt to move research beyond a laboratory and into the real world, where events are complex and not based on simple cause-and-effect relationships.

Relevance of Using and Applying Skills in Evaluating Research

The importance of using and applying skills in evaluating research is founded on the classic view of the scientist-practitioner model. As I mentioned earlier, if you read a large daily newspaper on any given day, you will find reports and summaries of scientific research studies. However, the newspapers do not publish specifics of the studies or information about how the study was conducted. An important question is, How much credence should you place on the information you read in such sources? Additionally, if you have a copy of the study, do you accept the results unequivocally because they are published in a professional journal? I would suggest that accepting the results of a scientific study without systematically evaluating the methods is analogous to buying something, for instance a car, without ever test-driving it. Few of us would buy a car or a house without first systematically evaluating the quality of the article being purchased. Consequently, I believe we as professionals have an obligation to carefully evaluate knowledge and research results that may be used in the practice of our professions. I am not suggesting that you evaluate each piece of knowledge presented to you in a comprehensive fashion (this would be extremely tedious and probably impossible), but I believe that acquiring the skills to evaluate how knowledge was generated is a key to functioning as a professional and differentiates those with advanced graduate degrees from those who are not so trained. Most recently, counseling and psychology influenced by medicine has introduced the use of evidence-based practice (American Psychological Association, 2006; Tanenbaum, 2003). Evidence-based practice is focused on the identification and use of the best research available in the implementation of services. Love, Bahner, Jones, and Nilsson (2007) concluded that ". . . one of the most important goals of psychological research is to provide guidance and answers for clinicians with practical, relevant, and useful information that will enhance their ability to practice effectively, ultimately providing more sound services to clients" (p. 315). The use of evidence-based practice as a model provides counselors with a foundation for decision making and services that are more systematic and theoretically more ethical. Few people want to see a physician who does not use the most current research to guide his or her practice.

Steps in the Scientific Process

Science and research are based on a systematic approach and proceed according to specific rules. I want to describe the generally accepted steps in the scientific research process and relate these steps to the sections of a journal article. I also want to note that an important step in the research process is that ultimately the procedures used in a study will be presented in a public arena such as a professional journal or a professional presentation, so the methods can be evaluated as to their efficacy. The steps to scientific research are depicted in Figure 1.1.

Step 1	Identify a problem.
Step 2	Define the problem operationally.
Step 3	Develop hypotheses or research questions.
Step 4	Identify and develop the research design (procedures).
Step 5	Develop and/or identify techniques or instruments that can be used to gain knowledge about the identified problem.
Step 6	Collect data.
Step 7	Analyze the data collected.
Step 8	Generate conclusions about the data.
Step 9	Report the data in a public arena such as a professional journal or presentation.

Figure 1.1   Steps in the Scientific Research Method

Purpose and Overview of the Text

A major purpose of this text is to provide a framework for practitioners in the fields of counseling and education to use in systematically evaluating the efficacy of scientific research reported in professional journals so that the information may be used and applied in practice. In other words, one goal of this book is to prepare counselors and educators to be good consumers and users of scientific research. This will be partly accomplished by relating the scientific research method to journal articles and providing a guide for evaluating counseling and educational research. The format of a research article may easily be related to the scientific method through the steps described earlier (Figure 1.1). A research article is typically composed of four major sections: introduction, methods, results, and discussion (Figure 1.2).

Sections of Journal Article	Steps in Scientific Research
Introduction	Identify the problem.
Review of the literature	Define the problem operationally.
Purpose statement	Develop hypotheses or research questions.
Methods Sample	Identify and develop the research design (procedures).
Procedures	Identify the instruments to be used.
Instruments	Collect the data.
Results	Analyze the data collected.
Discussion	Generate conclusions about the data. Report the data in a public area.

Figure 1.2   Relating Sections of a Journal Article to Steps in Scientific Research

A second purpose of this text is to provide the basic skills necessary to professionally practice as a practitioner-scientist from a systematic and, when appropriate, a scientific approach. The completion of this purpose will involve a discussion of how to conduct research. A basic overview of how to participate in and conduct research is presented. Contributing to the professional counseling and educational research literature is an exciting and important role of graduate-level-trained practitioners. This discussion includes coverage of conducting both quantitative and qualitative research.

Another goal of this book is to provide an introduction to program evaluation. Also, I will provide information about program evaluation—how to systematically evaluate interventions used. Steps in conducting program evaluation are discussed, as are various types of program evaluation, such as formative and summative evaluation. There is a presentation of an example of a program evaluation to illustrate the process.

The last goal is to inform the reader of current and future issues confronting those conducting and using research in the fields of counseling and education. As was mentioned earlier, there is a controversy over the designation of training graduate-level practitioners as "scientist-practitioners" or as "practitioner-scientists." Another issue (and this is discussed in earlier chapters) is the use of quantitative versus qualitative research. The last issue addressed is the use and conduct of research sensitive to cultural diversity. We live in an extremely diverse society, and the use of research in a responsible and sensitive manner based on cultural and diversity issues is critical. Ignoring culture and diversity is irresponsible in research and may result in misuse of research.

To accomplish the goals cited, this text is organized around three major sections: Introduction to the Research Process, Evaluating Articles in the Professional Literature, and The Application of Research and Evaluation. Section I, Introduction to the Research Process, includes the first eight chapters. The first chapter is an overview of the research process. Chapter 2 is an introduction to searching for journal articles and the use of electronic online databases. The third chapter is a basic overview of statistical methods. It includes a discussion of descriptive, inferential, correlation, and regression methods. Chapter 4 is an overview of a certain category of research, quantitative research, which is defined in terms of results and data being quantifiable. Most standard research designs may be categorized as quantitative research, and most professional journals publish primarily quantitative research rather than other types of research, such as qualitative research. The argument is that quantitative research is based more on the scientific approach and is more systematic. As part of this chapter, there is a presentation of various research designs that may best characterize this type of research. There are limitations to the quantitative approach, and these are presented.

Chapter 5 addresses another major approach to research, qualitative research. Qualitative research is defined in terms of how data is analyzed and which research designs are used. Data is collected and analyzed using language and descriptive methods rather than numerical methods. Qualitative methods include such research approaches as case study methods, phenomenological, grounded theory, and ethnographic. Qualitative methods provide opportunities for investigators to do more naturalized observations of the actual object of study versus the more experimentally controlled approach used in quantitative methods. Limitations of the qualitative approach are discussed in this chapter.

Chapter 6 discusses mixed research methods. The development of mixed research methods has provided a link between qualitative and quantitative research methods. These two traditions, quantitative and qualitative, have had significant differences over the past 100 years. There have been recent efforts to develop systematic mixed methods designs, which have led to more integration of the approaches. I discuss the benefits of employing mixed methods in research.

Chapter 7 is a focus on evidence-based research practice. As was mentioned earlier, the importance of using evidence-based practice as a model is increasingly being acknowledged as a critical component of becoming an effective counselor (Nezu, Ronan, Meadows, & McClure, 2000; Tanenbaum, 2003). There is a discussion of the strengths and limitations in using an evidence-based practice approach. Lastly there is a discussion of the best way to practice using an evidence-based model (Davison & Lazarus, 2007).

Chapter 8 focuses on ethics in the research process. The primary focus of the discussion is on the appropriateness of interpreting and applying results from one specific sample in the literature to a different group of subjects or in practice. Guidelines for interpreting the impact of research results on the population are presented, and studies from the research literature are used to illustrate how to evaluate ethical concerns. For example, there is an evaluation of the Tuskegee Syphilis Study with African American males, using the proposed guidelines. The purpose of the Tuskegee study was to determine the natural course of untreated syphilis. The researchers in this study used 400 African American males who were left untreated for syphilis, even when effective treatment was available.

Chapters 9 through 15 comprise Section II, Evaluating Articles in the Professional Literature, and provide a foundation for systematically evaluating the efficacy of articles presented in the professional counseling and educational literature. Chapter 9 is the beginning of the major focus of this text: a presentation of guidelines for evaluating the efficacy of research reported in journal articles. Methods for evaluating each section of a journal article will be presented, starting with an article's introduction. To clearly illustrate how to evaluate the various sections of a journal article, there will be examples taken from the counseling and educational research literature. The introduction section of an article includes the development of the argument or the rationale for conducting the study cited; this is frequently accomplished through a review of the relevant literature. Methods for evaluating the literature review will be presented here.

Chapter 10 is a discussion of how to evaluate the purposes and hypotheses statement that is also a part of the introduction section. The purpose statement and hypothesis (or hypotheses) is typically found toward the end of the introduction section, after the literature review. The purpose statement should be clear and concise as to what the study and researchers are investigating, whereas the hypothesis is more specific and gives information about any predictions the researcher is making.

The subsequent chapter, Chapter 11, focuses on the second section of a journal article, the methods section, beginning with sample or subjects used in the study. A discussion is included on how to evaluate the selection procedures used and the appropriateness of the particular sample based on the purpose of the study. Chapter 12 is an examination of how to evaluate the procedures used and described in the methods section. The procedures are a step-by-step description of how the study was conducted. Chapter 13 is a discussion of how to evaluate the third part of the methods section, the instruments. Investigators must decide how to assess the outcomes of the focus of the study and use valid and reliable methods.

Guidelines for evaluating the results sections are the focus of Chapter 14. The results section generally involves the presentation of statistical methods used in the analysis of the study. It is not unusual for students in counseling and education to skip or skim over this section because of an aversion to numbers and math or statistics. The ability to evaluate the results section is not based solely on knowledge of statistical methods, and the evaluation approach introduced here is rooted in general concepts and assumptions that can be reviewed without significant expertise in statistics. Chapter 15, the last chapter in the discussion of the evaluation process of a research journal article, is the discussion section. This is where the researchers summarize the results of the studying descriptive form and attempt to generalize and relate the results to actual practice in counseling and education.

Section III, The Application of Research and Evaluation, is a discussion of how to develop and use research in actual practice for those in the fields of counseling and education. The discussion will be presented from the practitioner-scientist approach.

In Chapter 16, I provide a brief overview of how one goes about developing a research proposal. The discussion includes how to conduct small research studies as a practitioner, with particular emphasis on using the professional literature as a basis of design and implementation. Both quantitative and qualitative research designs are discussed.

Chapter 17 addresses program evaluation. Counselors and educators may be asked to interpret and develop program evaluation. Program evaluation is quite useful to practitioners because the focus is on evaluating the effectiveness of the programs they are implementing and providing justification for continuing such programs. Program evaluation knowledge and skills seem particularly important in recent times of fiscal conservatism and accountability. The purpose here is to provide only an overview of the process of program evaluation and not to provide and in-depth review; there are other texts designed to provide a more detailed explanation (Padgett, 2004; Sanders, 1994; Thyer, 2005; Wholey, Hatry, & Newcomer, 2004).

The last chapter, Current and Future Issues in Counseling and Educational Research (Chapter 18), is a discussion of the current and future issues confronting those conducting, and particularly those using, counseling and educational research. For example, issues of conducting research that is sensitive to cultural diversity is a current dilemma in the field. Another controversial issue is accountability in counseling and education. How can research be done to address such issues?

2

Searching Articles in Professional Journals and Online Databases

A basic skill in the research process, which you may have already mastered, is to conduct searches through various sources. As a user—and even a producer—of research, you need to develop skills for searching various sources. An understanding of the search process can facilitate your searching. Search sources include hardbound journals, electronic journals, databases, online search engines, and metasearch engines. There are strategies that can be used to expedite and refine your search. Once you have identified what you want to search, you must decide how you will search and what sources you will use. After obtaining the search information, you must determine how you will use the information and how you will cite or reference the information you obtained. A key component of using information is the fair and accurate citation of the information. There is a discussion of appropriate methods of citation, issues of plagiarism, and ways to avoid plagiarism.

One of the first steps in using and conducting research is to access sources of information. A starting point in accessing information is to first identify what you want to search. This sounds simple, but if you do not have a clear search topic you will struggle to find usable information that meets your needs. Once you have identified a topic, or someone (an instructor) has identified one for you, you should conduct a brief initial investigation of the topic to find out how broad it is. You can do an initial search through a search engine such as Yahoo or Google and/or a database such as PsycInfo.

There will be a discussion later in the chapter giving more information about using a database like PsycInfo and various search engines. You also can go to your class textbook or various encyclopedias to select your topic. (See www.lib.umb.edu/newtutorial/module1.php.) Your initial investigation gives you information about how large the topic is and what may be some variations on the topic. Once you complete this initial search you likely will need to refine your search because it may be either too large or not quite what you wanted. Keep in mind that you want to be able to manage the information, and if your search topic is too large you may have trouble covering all the information available. After refining your topic, you want to generate key search terms. The selection of your search terms is important because it may result in the search being too large or missing your topic altogether. Various strategies have been suggested, such as organizing a search using a Boolean approach (see http://lib.ua.edu/tutorials/ WebTutorial/modue11/Module1–4.html and http://lib.umb.edu/newtutor ial/module1_4html). A Boolean search involves the use of the following terms: *and, or,* and *not.* The use of "and" results in connecting two or more words in your search.

The result is a narrowing of your search based upon the terms used. The use of "or" expands your search because either term can be used alone. The use of "not" results in the exclusion of identified terms. You may be aware of a topic that is connected to your search that you want to eliminate, so you use "not" to narrow your search.

Database Searches

Once you have identified key search terms, you are ready to proceed with your search strategy. I do not suggest jumping to use search engines such as Yahoo but using a more scientifically based source such as PsycInfo and initially conducting a database search. Databases like PsycInfo are useful because they contain primarily citations of original research that typically are peer-reviewed, so the quality is good. If you go to the university library's Web site and click on "database search" you can begin the process. The databases are listed by topic and alphabetically. The major databases you would search include PsycInfo, Academic Search Primer, Expanded Academic, JSTOR, PsycArticles, PsychCritiques, Sociological Abstracts, and Biological Abstracts. Once you determine the database, you type in your search terms and the Boolean search strategy. Typically the Boolean search strategy gives you the option from a drop-down box. Depending on your initial results, you may want to either expand or restrict your search.

If you receive too many results to manage, you may want to restrict your search. If you receive too few, you may want to expand. For example, you may restrict your search by reviewing sample citations and identifying those that closely match your interests and then using the specific terms found in the citation to further focus your search. Once you find your citations in the database, you may have a choice of an article abstract or full-text options. Most often you want full-text options so you can access the full article. The full-text options may be in either PDF format or HTML format. Periodically an article is available in both PDF and HTML format. You can restrict the years of your search. You also may search by author and publication date.

Electronic Journals

Another format for a search is through electronic journals. If you know the journal title and the publication year, you can locate an article through your university's electronic journals. Electronic journals are alphabetized so you can easily find your journal. Also, there is the option of abstracts or full-text articles (not your choice but the library's and publisher's). The electronic journals are organized by date and publication volume. Once you have an article that fits your interest and topic, you may use the references in the article to gather further journal publications that may be of interest. You may want to determine the impact of a particular topic or article/research, and you can do this through citation searching. There are several Internet databases that provide information about the number of times an article or publication is cited in a particular database. Such citations give evidence of the impact of a publication on the field—the view is that others are using the article or study information as documentation in their work. A primary source for determining the impact of a study is the Web of Science database. A search of the Web of Science database provides information about citations listed in the sciences, social sciences, and arts and humanities.

Search Engines

Before I discuss how to conduct a search through a search engine, I want to review how to evaluate the source in regard to quality. The information on the Internet (aside from that found in electronic professional journals) may or may not be accurate. There is no systematic evaluation of information posted on a Web site. Consequently, you as the reader must determine whether the information posted is credible. Guidelines for evaluating Web-based information include a determination of accuracy, authority, objectivity, and currency (see www.lib.ua.edu/tutorials/WebTutorial/module7/Module7–2.html and www.lib.umb.edu/tutorials/EvaluateInfo/GuidelinesEvalInfo.pdf). The first question is whether the information is accurate and is factual. What is the source of the information? Are there any citations of objective data presented, such as refereed journal publications? (Refereed publications are defined as those publications whose documents are evaluated by experts, and their review is an anonymous review.) Another question is whether the information presented is peer-reviewed and sources are documented. A second criterion for evaluating the source of information concerns authority and whether there is an author identified and what his or her credentials are. Does the author have an expertise and background on the topic addressed on the Web site? A third criterion is a determination of objectivity of the source. Is there any bias expressed in the information provided, or is the site affiliated with a group (e.g., a political group) that has a specific agenda? (See www.lib.umb.edu/tutorials/EvaluateInfo/GuidelinesEvalInfo.pdf.) The fourth criterion to consider when evaluating a Web site is the currency or recentness of the information. Materials several years old may not have current information, and the information may not be accurate as a consequence. (See www.lib.ua.edu/tutorials/WebTutorial/module7/Module7–2.html and www.lib.umb.edu/tutorials/EvaluateInfo/GuidelinesEvalInfo.pdf.) The last question concerns relevancy and addresses the appropriateness of the material for your topic (see www.lib.ua.edu/tutorials/WebTutorial/module7/Module7–2.html).

Once you have completed a search through traditional formal methods such as databases and electronic journals, you may want to expand your search and use a search engine such as Yahoo, HotBot, AltaVista, AllTheWeb, or Google. You also can use a search engine when you have narrowed your search and you are looking for a specific site and specific information. You may find important information through search engines, such as government Web sites that provide information about state, national, and international statistics. Additionally, brief government reports may be available through these Web sites identified through the search engines.

Broader search engines are the metasearch engines such as Dogpile, Mamma, and Vivisimo. These search engines are designed to link to multiple single search engines, and they can provide a large base of information. These metasearches are fast and can find large amounts of information (see

www.lib.ua.edu/tutorials/WebTutorial/module7/Module7–2.html).
However, you need to use search terms that fit their configurations, or you
may miss relevant topics in your search.

Plagiarism

Since the topic of this chapter addresses searching topics and the use of
database citations, it is important to discuss academic honesty, or rather
what is considered academic dishonesty. One type of academic dishonesty
that relates to searches and citation of references is plagiarism. Plagiarism
is committed when someone presents another's ideas or writings as his or
her own. In essence, the plagiarist is not giving the person who actually
wrote the material credit and is attempting to take credit himself or herself.
An alternate form of plagiarism is called "cybercheating" and refers to taking another's work from the Web, copying it, and pasting it into your own
work (see www.lib.ua.edu/tutorials/WebTutorial/module7/Module7–2
.html). Marsh (2007) concluded that "Plagiarists commit acts of petty lar-
ceny, trying to steal or pass off the words or ideas of another as if they were
their own" (p. 31). It is interesting that researchers have found that college
students have difficulty knowing what plagiarism is (Landau, Druen, &
Arcuri, 2002; Roig, 1997). Undergraduates in the Landau, et al. (2002)
study could not identify acts of plagiarism in a text sample. Also, plagiarism
may be unintentional and be a consequence of the person's memory of the
source material (Bredart, Lampinen, & Defeldre, 2003). Bredart, et al.
(2003) defined plagiarism that was unintentional and a result of not
remembering that one obtained the information from another source as
"cryptomnesia." Despite there being a controversy over the ability to detect
or know if one is plagiarizing or whether it is a case of cryptomnesia, col-
leges and universities have increasingly focused on stopping such practices.
(Roig & Caso, 2005).

Roig and Caso (2005) stated: "Many in academia now believe that with
the advent of computers and the internet 'copy and paste' plagiarism has
increased dramatically in recent years" (p. 485). In most instances, the discovery of plagiarism results in a negative consequence for the student that
may involve lowering a course grade or dismissal from the university
(Robinson-Zanartu, Pena, Cook-Morales, Pena, Afshani, & Nguyen, 2005).
So it is important for students to be aware of what plagiarism is and how to
avoid it. There are several ways to avoid plagiarism (Landau, et al., 2002).
One way is to provide appropriate and accurate citation of the work used in

your search. It is acceptable to give a quote a source based on the accuracy of the citation. The citation should include the author, title, date of publication, and location (see www.lib.umb.edu/tutorials/EvaluateInfo/Guidelines EvalInfo.pdf). Another approach is to use methods of reporting on an article or publication through summarizing or paraphrasing so you do not use the exact words used by others, unless you are using a quote. You still need to cite the source of your information; ideas are considered property, and giving credit for ideas is important. Practice summarizing and paraphrasing can help with reducing or stopping plagiarism, along with appropriate and accurate citation of the work. A review of a few samples of paraphrasing and direct quotes may help understand how to avoid plagiarism.

An example of a direct quote is: Olvera, Steward, Galindo, and Stephens (2007) stated: "Group (particularly familial) goals are emphasized by most Latinos; however, American culture emphasizes individual goals" (p. 225). A paraphrase of the same quotation could be: American culture generally highlights individual goals over group goals, whereas Latinos tend to highlight group goals (Olvera et al., 2007). Note that the paraphrase results in the use of different words to provide the same meaning.

Summary

Conducting a search involves first using a relatively reliable source through databases. Further searches may be done through various search engines to help focus your topic and the information you are collecting. An even broader approach to gathering information on your topic is the use of a metasearch engine, which combines the search power from single-source search engines. Once you have obtained the information, you want to be sure that you cite the source of the information accurately and give credit for information that you have accessed, in order to avoid plagiarism. The search procedures you use will determine how useful the information is, so it is important to employ systematic and effective search strategies.

3

Basics of Statistical Methods

To understand and systematically evaluate research, it is first imperative to have an understanding of several basic statistical methods and related terminology. Mendenhall (1983) described statistics as "an area of science concerned with the extraction of information from numerical data and its use in making inferences about a population from which data are obtained" (p. 6). Key in this definition is the statement about extracting information and making inferences about a population. Statistics is primarily focused on making inferences about the population. Before we start a detailed discussion of statistics, I want to point out that whole courses are presented on various quantitative statistical methods, such as analysis of variance and multiple regression. This chapter will consist of a discussion of (a) different measurement scales, (b) descriptive statistics, (c) inferential statistics, and (d) correlational and regression methods.

Measurement Scales

Four different measurement scales have been identified that are used in quantitative research: (a) a nominal scale, (b) an ordinal scale, (c) an interval scale, and (d) a ratio scale (see Table 3.1). Researchers generally differentiate between numerals and numbers. *Numerals* are defined in terms of symbols, such as letters or words (e.g., male and female), and the interval between units cannot be assumed to be equal. Nominal and ordinal scales are considered numerals. *Numbers* are values on which one can perform certain mathematical operations such as adding, subtracting, and so on, and the distance between units is even (e.g., the interval between 101 and 102 is the same as that between 104 and 105). Interval and ratio scales are based on the use of numbers. These measurement types of scales are considered to be somewhat hierarchical in regard to the different mathematical operations that can be performed on them. Nominal scales are considered to be the simplest and ratio scales the most complex. This means that the most mathematical operations may be performed on ratio types of data and the least on nominal types of data.

A nominal scale refers to one in which the researcher has assigned differences in observations or measurements to distinct categories. It is the least complex scale, one in which the fewest mathematical operations may be performed. Examples of nominal data are gender status (male or female) and ethnicity (African American, Asian, Caucasian, and so on). Nominal scale data, therefore, involves counts for each category. Researchers do at times assign values to nominal scales to compute a limited number of mathematical operations. For example, a researcher may assign a value to different ethnic groups (e.g., Latino = 1, African American = 2, Caucasian = 3, and so on) to perform basic mathematical operations such as determining probabilities, but they cannot calculate means or averages, since the value assigned is artificial and a different assignment of values would result in a different calculation of averages.

Ordinal scales involve assigning values to data based on rank or order. This is the second least precise scale of measurement. One example of ordinal data is ranks in the military (private, corporal, sergeant, and so on). Ranks are not overly precise and do not differentiate by equal units. For example, a sergeant is not twice as good as private, but a sergeant outranks a private. Essentially, ranks are not equidistant between points. A second example might be ranking brands of ice cream by taste. If we rank brands A, B, and C, we know that ice cream brand A tastes better than brand B, but we do not know if brand A is twice as good as brand B. Brands A and B may be only slightly different, or they may be significantly different.

Interval scales are the third type of measurement in quantitative research and involve the use of numbers with equal units of measurement. However, even though numbers are used, there is no true zero point on the scale. For example, most psychological and educational tests are based on an interval type of scale. An individual can obtain a range of scores on an IQ test, for example 20 to 200, but can an IQ of zero be measured? Someone could theoretically score a zero, but the true score will not be known, or cannot be measured, because of the limitations of the instrument.

Ratio scales are the fourth type of measurement scale and are defined in terms of equal numbered units, similar to interval scales, but there is a true

Table 3.1   Types of Scales

Scale	Description	Numeral or Number	Mathematical Operations
Nominal	Represents nomination to categories for variables	Numeral	Minimal calculating expectancies
Ordinal	Represents position or order for variables	Numeral	Minimal calculating expectance
Interval	Represents equal units or intervals	Number	Most with operations
Ratio	Represents equal units and has a true zero	Number	Any operation

zero. Weight is an example of a ratio scale, and the measurement starts at zero. Another example is temperature based on a Kelvin temperature scale. The ratio is the most precise of all the scales and the one in which the greatest number of concise mathematical operations can be done. A study can be considered quantitative only when the variables have been operationalized into one of the four scales mentioned.

Common Statistical Definitions

Data set refers to the scores found in a specific collection of scores, generally from a sample of the population. So an example of a data set might be scores of 100 respondents in a sample from a particular study.

Distribution refers to how scores are distributed across a data set.

Frequencies refer to the number times a score is found in a distribution

Median refers to the middle point, where 50 percent of the scores fall above and 50 percent fall below this point.

Mode is the most frequent score in a distribution.

Normal curve refers to a symmetrical bell-shaped curve.

Range refers to the distance between the highest and lowest scores in the distribution.

Scales of measurement refer to the types of scales used in measuring the identified variables.

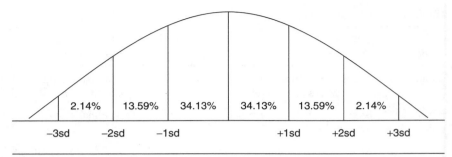

Figure 3.1   Normal Curve Distribution and Standard Deviation

Standard deviation is the way scores vary around the mean and are stated as standard units or standard deviations.

Variance is how scores vary from the mean in a distribution

Descriptive Statistics

Descriptive statistics are used to describe the sample on which the study was conducted (not the population). It was stated earlier that the intent of statistics is to make inferences back to the population. However, descriptive statistics are used to first describe the sample of the study. The statistics associated with descriptive statistics are in part presented based on the normal curve and are identified as measures of central tendency. A good place to start this discussion is a focus on the normal curve. A normal curve is a bell-shaped curve that is evenly distributed on both sides of the mean (and mode). The normal curve is characterized by a specific distribution across a normal curve with related percentages of scores associated with each standard deviation (see Figure 3.1). The distribution is based on establishing a corresponding standard deviation above and below the mean. For example, a mean in a study may be 100, and the standard deviation is found to be 20. One standard deviation above the mean is 120, and one standard deviation below the mean is 80. Just over 68 percent of the scores in a normal curve will fall within these two standard deviations, one standard deviation below and one standard deviation above the mean.

Descriptive statistics have been described as efforts by researchers to systematically summarize the data collected (Urdan, 2005). The idea is for researchers to present data descriptively in a way that is easy to understand and that conceptualizes general characteristics of the sample's responses. Descriptive statistics address the sample only and are in no way connected to

Table 3.2   Characteristics of Descriptive Statistics

Statistical Procedure	Characteristics
Measures of central tendency (mean, median, and mode)	Statistical methods that are used to describe the frequency distribution of scores or the sample. The most frequently used measure of central tendency is the mean.
Measures of variability (standard deviation, variance, and range)	Statistical methods that are used to describe or summarize how scores are dispersed. The most frequently reported measure of variability is the standard deviation.
Tables and graphs (histograms, bar graphs, and so on)	Visual methods that are used to describe the frequency distribution of a data set.
Measures of relationship (Pearson correlation, Spearman rho)	Used to determine the relationship between two variables. To what degree do the two variables covary?

understanding or generalizing back to the population. Generally, descriptive statistics are presented first in the results section, followed by inferential statistics. The actual calculation of descriptive statistics can easily be accomplished using statistical software. Consequently, I am only giving a description of each statistic rather than how to calculate it. Typically, four major types of descriptive statistical measures are used in reported research results: central tendency, variability, tables and graphs, and relationships or correlations (see Table 3.2).

The most commonly used measure of central tendency is the mean, which is the arithmetic average of all of the scores in a frequency. The mean is calculated as the sum of all scores divided by the total number of scores. Another measure of central tendency, but not used as often as the mean, is the mode. The mode is simply determined by counting the most frequent score in a distribution. The median is calculated by adding one to the total number of observations and dividing by two. Based on this calculation, you find the midpoint in the distribution. It is not the actual score but a score where 50 percent fall above and 50 percent below. So if a researcher has 11 scores, the median is the sixth score in the distribution (when the scores are arranged from high to low). The standard deviation is calculated by first calculating the variance, which is the sum of differences between each score in the distribution and the mean.

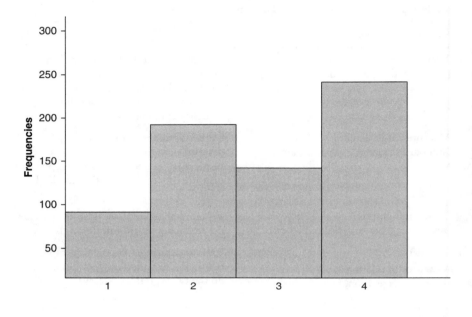

Figure 3.2   Example of Bar Graph: Students by Grade in a Rural Community

The sum of differences is then divided by the total number of scores. This calculation gives the variance, but the variance is not helpful as a statistic, because one cannot compare a variance in one distribution to another. Taking the square root of the variance gives a standard score, which can be converted to a score that can be interpreted on a normal curve.

Tables and graphs are another method that researchers use to describe the sample (see Table 3.2). Tables and graphs are, obviously, visual and can provide the reader with a quick summary of certain descriptive results. Tables and graphs may be used to display frequencies of participant response, percentages, means, standard deviations, and so on. Various types of graphs (e.g., bar graphs) may be used within nominal and ordinal data to illustrate results (see Figure 3.2).

Measures of relationships is a type of descriptive statistics researchers use to present results from the sample (see Table 3.2). Relationships are descriptions of the extent to which two or more variables covary. A relationship between two or more variables is generally defined in linear terms. Correlations may be understood as potentially ranging from a positive 1.0 (a perfect positive correlation) to a negative -1.0 (a perfect negative correlation). Figure 3.3 depicts a positive correlation, but not a perfect one. Figure 3.4 illustrates a negative correlation. Note that when there is a high correlation,

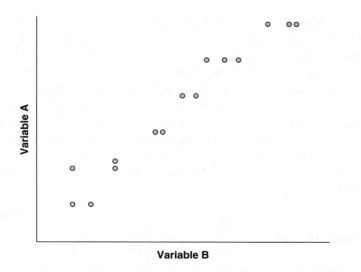

Figure 3.3   Example of a Positive Correlation

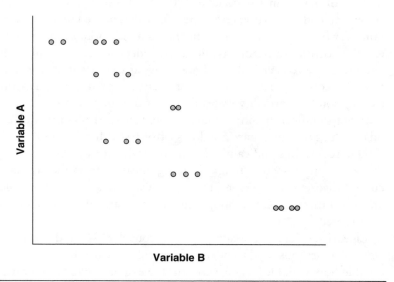

Figure 3.4   Example of a Negative Correlation

either positive or negative, the variables covary closely. For example, a high score on one variable is correlated, in a positive correlation, with a high score on a second variable. When there is no relationship between variables, the correlation is closer to zero. It is most important to remember that a strong correlation, or relationship, is never an indication of a cause-and-effect relationship; it simply means that the variables of interest vary together.

The most frequently used correlation statistic is Pearson's Product-Moment Coefficient, or a Pearson r. The Pearson r can be used only with interval or ratio data. The Spearman rho, or rank-order coefficient, is used with ordinal data but is used much less frequently than the Pearson r statistic because the Pearson r is more sensitive to finding significant correlations. The Spearman Rank Correlation Coefficient is used at times to determine correlations or relationships between two variables when one of the variables is based on rank-ordered data.

Inferential Statistics

Before beginning our discussion of inferential statistics, we must understand several important concepts: (a) four basic assumptions of inferential statistics, (b) the differences between parametric and nonparametric statistics, and (c) level of significance (Coolidge, 2006; Moore, 1983). In considering which statistical methods to use, researchers have determined that it is best to maintain four basic assumptions about the data. The four assumptions of inferential statistics are normality, linearity, independence, and homogeneity of variance. Moore (1983) defined normality as the extent to which a distribution of scores approximates the standard normal curve. Essentially, the assumption for normality states that a set of scores (the scores of a sample) does not significantly differ from a normal curve. There are statistical methods, such as the chi-square goodness-of-fit test (Moore, 1983), to determine if these scores do significantly deviate from the normal curve. A violation of this assumption—scores that deviate significantly from the normal standard curve—theoretically indicates that certain statistical methods should be used and not others, typically nonparametric statistics if a normal curve is not represented.

Linearity, a second assumption to consider when determining which statistical methods need to be used, particularly when the researcher is interested in how variables relate, concerns the extent to which two variables correlate in a linear fashion. Some relationships between variables may be more curved or circular and violate this assumption; therefore, the researcher is required to use appropriate statistical methods, a nonparametric statistical method.

A third assumption, independence, is concerned with whether each score is independent of every other score. Basically, this assumption states that scores must be independent of each other and that individual scores must not influence each other in any way. Violation of this assumption, as with others, requires researchers to use certain statistical methods. For example, if a group serves as its own control and completes pretesting and post-testing, the scores are not independent of each other because the same individuals are responding pretest and post-test. If researchers compare the pretest and the post-test, this violates the assumption of independence.

The fourth assumption, homogeneity of variance, is the extent to which the variances of the groups are homogeneous. There are statistical tests to determine whether the assumption of homogeneity of variance is violated; the *F Maximum test for homogeneity of variance* (Gall, Gall, & Borg, 2003). A rule of thumb is that if standard deviations are three times larger for one group than any of the others, it is likely that this assumption has been violated, but statistical tests should be calculated to be sure. Again, if this assumption is violated the researcher must use certain statistical methods.

No specific number of violations of assumptions has been associated with the decision to use particular statistical methods. Recently, researchers have noted that the violation of one or several of these assumptions does not necessitate using less powerful statistical methods (Coolidge, 2006). When all these assumptions are met, researchers can typically use statistical methods that are more sensitive to differences and thus more powerful in detecting differences.

To interpret inferential statistics, we must understand levels of significance. Levels of significance refer to the probability of accepting or rejecting a null hypothesis. A null hypothesis means there is no difference between compared groups. The level of significance is typically referred to as the p (probability) value or alpha level. Basically, the level of significance is the chance of an error occurring in the rejection of the null hypothesis. For example, a researcher might compare the effects of a stress training program (the independent variable) on reported levels of stress (the dependent variable). The researcher basically wants to know if the program brought about the differences in generalized stress scores between the group that experienced the program (intervention) and the group that did not. The null hypothesis states that there is no difference between the groups on generalized stress scores. In this situation, the researcher sets an alpha (p) value, which reduces the chance of rejecting the null hypothesis but at the same time detects the real differences between the groups as a consequence of the program. So if a researcher conducted 100 studies using the same methods and randomly selected the subjects from the population of interest, he or she is by chance going to make an error in the actual outcome based upon the p value. Specifically, if all 100 studies were conducted there is a probability that a certain percentage, for example, 5 percent ($p = .05$) would result in outcomes not consistent with what actually should be found, the chance of error. There are several explanations for why this occurs. One of the major reasons is that the sample chosen in any one group is not representative of the actual population and therefore their responses on the dependent variable are not based upon the influence of the independent variable but more likely based on personal characteristics that make them different from the population. The chance of making an error in the acceptance or rejection of a null hypothesis has been defined in terms of Type I and Type II errors. A Type I error is one in which the researcher rejects the null hypothesis, although there are in actuality no real differences between the groups. A Type II error is that in which the researcher accepts the null hypothesis, although there is in actuality a difference. A curious phenomenon is that increasing the chances of making a Type I error decreases the chances of making a Type II error. That is, raising the p or alpha value from .01 to .05 increases the chance of making a Type I error while it reduces the chance of making a Type II error. Typically, researchers have determined that an acceptable level of error is .05, or 5 chances out of 100, of making an error and rejecting the null hypothesis when it should not be rejected, a Type I error. The important issue in setting a low level of significance, .05, is that if the researcher finds a difference, he or she is publicly stating so and is creating new knowledge. Consequently, researchers generally would rather make a Type II error, not rejecting the null hypothesis when in reality it should be rejected, than a Type I error, rejecting the null hypothesis when it should not be rejected. Basically the researcher is testing whether the group means (from data dealing with the dependent variable) are significantly different, taking into account the variances within and between the groups compared.

The setting of a level of significance at .05 or .01 is connected to tabled values that are compared to statistical calculations based on the data obtained. Whatever the statistical calculation, numerical values that relate to the levels of significance have been established. The established values are also connected to what is referred to as degrees of freedom. The number of degrees of freedom has been defined as the number of observations that cannot be clearly determined. Specifically, if there are five respondents and there are five scores having to do with the dependent variable, then only one score can be clearly identified once the other four are known. This is a difficult concept to explain and understand. For example, suppose that you know the IQ scores for four participants: 111, 101, 116, and 97. There is only one score left, and you know which participant had the missing score. If there were two scores left, you could not be sure which score was related to which participant. Degrees of freedom are used in the calculation of several inferential statistics and in reading tabled values for levels of significance.

Inferential statistics are used to make decisions or reach conclusions about whether results obtained from a sample can be applied to the target population. All the methods discussed as applications of inferential statistics are associated with quantitative research methods. There are a number of types of inferential statistics, but I want to address the most frequently used: t-test, analysis of variance (ANOVA), multivariate analysis of variance (MANOVA), analysis of covariance (ANCOVA), multiple regression, and chi-square (see Table 3.3). The majority of the methods used in inferential statistical procedures involve making comparisons between groups.

One statistical procedure, the t-test, is intended to compare the differences of a dependent measure between two groups. Data analyzed must be either interval or ratio scale scores. Basically, calculation of the t-test concerns differences between the groups compared to within-group differences. The between-group differences must be significantly larger than the within-group differences before the researcher can conclude that the scores on the dependent measure show a significant difference. The calculation of the t test focuses on determining whether the groups in the sample score more like each other compared to the comparison group or that there is no difference in dependent measure scores within or between groups. Gortmaker and Brown (2006) conducted a study focusing on the perceptions of out-of-the-closet versus not-out-of-the-closet gay and lesbian college students in campus climate. The researchers used t tests to determine if there were any differences between the perceptions of campus climate. The specific question they addressed was this: "Is level of outness related to students' perceptions and experiences on campus?" They described the results as:

Perceptions and experiences of an anti-LG climate. The first variable consisted of a total score of perceptions of an anti-LG climate and sightings of anti-LG graffiti. The perceptions of anti-LG attitudes item used a 1–5 response format (1 = "very little extent," 5 = "very great extent"). Students noted the number of times they saw anti-graffiti on campus using a "0" to "four times or more" response format. (p. 610)

Using an independent t-test and non-overlapping 99 percent confidence intervals, our students perceived the environment significantly more negatively than did closeted students ($t[78] = 3.56$; p = .001).

In this example, the calculated t value is 3.56, and it is significant at the p value of .001. This means that the two groups, those who were out of the college closet versus those who were not, reported significantly different experiences in college climate. Specifically, those who were out of the college closet reported a more negative climate than those who were not out of the college closet. There is only a 0.1 percent chance of making a Type I error, rejecting the null hypothesis, when in fact there are no differences between the groups' perceptions of college climate, which is a quite small chance of error. The researchers in this study can be relatively confident that there are significant differences in perceptions and attitudes given the small chance of Type I error.

A second frequently used inferential statistical procedure is the analysis of variance (ANOVA), which is used to compare groups (it also is referred to as an F test). Two or more groups can be compared with this approach (see Table 3.3). It is used when there is one independent variable and, typically, three or more groups. The dependent variable must be in interval or ratio scale. As with the t-test, the basic function of the ANOVA is to determine whether there are significant differences between groups versus within groups. The larger the difference between groups versus within groups, the more likely significant differences will be found. Luszcyznska and Sobczyk (2007) provide an example of the use of ANOVA in a study on obesity. They describe the results of their ANOVA analysis as:

> Our first hypothesis concerned the effects of the IIP on weight loss and BMI. An ANOVA revealed a main effect of time for body weight, $F(1, 49) = 84.92$, $p < .001$ ($\eta^2 = .67$), as well as a Time × Group interaction, $F(1, 49) = 9.08$, p $< .01$ ($\eta^2 = .18$; post hoc observed power test 0.84). On average, IIP participants lost 4.2 kg (95% confidence interval [CI] = 3.19, 5.07), whereas control group participants lost 2.1 kg (95% CI = 1.11, 3.09). (p. 510)

Calculation of the F ratio is achieved by computing the mean square between divided by the mean square within. The mean square between is determined by calculating the sum of squares between. The sum of square between is generated by calculating the total mean for all groups and dividing it by the degrees of freedom for between. To obtain a significant F value and the difference among groups, the researcher must find that the means differ and the variances between and within the groups do not account for this difference.

Another type of ANOVA is the factorial ANOVA, which allows the researcher to compare different levels of several independent variables and determine if there are any interactions between the independent variables on the dependent variable (see Table 3.3). For example, a researcher could use a factorial ANOVA to compare the effects of a teaching intervention compared to a control group and also compare the students by gender. Such a study would be characterized as a 2 x 2 factorial design, 2 (experimental intervention and control group) x 2 (male and female).

The repeated-measures ANOVA allows the researcher to compare the dependent variable to be measured and compared over several different

Table 3.3   Characteristics of Parametric Inferential Statistics

Statistical Procedure	Characteristics
T-tests (independent), t-tests (correlated)	Involves testing the diff means of two groups.
Analysis of variance (ANOVA)	Involves testing the extent the means differ based upon the degree that variances differ among the means of three or more groups with one independent variable.
Factorial ANOVA	Involves the use of two or more independent variables and two or more levels. Allows for researcher to determine if there is an interaction between independent variables.
Repeated measures of ANOVA	Allows the researcher to compare differences over several different observations or times.
Multivariate analysis of variance (MANOVA)	A statistical procedure to calculate difference among the variances of means of two or more groups with two or more dependent variables. The analysis of the dependent variables is conducted simultaneously.
Analysis of covariance (ANCOVA)	A statistical procedure to calculate differences among the variances of means of two or more groups and simultaneously control for the effects of an extraneous variable on the dependent variable.
Multiple regression	A statistical procedure used to calculate the relationship between a predicted variable and several predictor variables.
Chi-square	A statistical procedure designed to determine whether there is a significant difference between observed versus expected scores.
Structural equation modeling	A statistical technique that is used in theory testing. Relevant constructs are operationalized and instruments identified to test the model. Correlational techniques are used in theory testing.

ɔbservations or measurements (see Table 3.3). This statistical procedure addresses the threat to external validity of novelty or disruption effects (ecological validity) (Bracht & Glass, 1968). A researcher can use a repeated-measures design to assess the effects of the dependent variable over time and determine whether the effects are short-term or long-term changes. Iverson, Brooks, Collins, and Lovell (2006) conducted a study and utilized a repeated-measures ANOVA. The purpose of the study was to determine the changes in neuropsychological functioning after a brain injury over time. Participants were 30 athletes who experienced a concussion during a sporting activity. They described in their results section the statistical calculations, one using a repeated-measures ANOVA: "Repeated measures ANOVAs were used to determine if mean cognitive and symptom scores differed across the four assessments. . . . For the verbal memory composite score, there was a significant main effect for time" (p. 248). The repeated-measures ANOVA gave the researchers the opportunity to determine the impact of a concussion from a sports brain injury over time, four observations.

Multivariate analysis of variance, MANOVA, is another type of inferential statistic (see Table 3.3). MANOVA is similar to the ANOVA, which involves comparison among groups, but includes comparisons for more than one dependent variable simultaneously. There are situations in which dependent variables have strong interrelationships and should be analyzed together, such as when the individual item scores that related to a particular dependent measure are compared between two or more groups. Results reported in the literature using MANOVAs are similar to the way in which ANOVAs are expressed. Henry, Anshel, and Michael (2006) studied various types of aerobic and interval circuit training programs on fitness and body image. They used MANOVA in their study and compared groups and time. They described their results:

> Table 3 presents the pretest and posttest scores for each body image subscale. A 3 (group) x 2 (time) MANOVA with repeated measures on the last factor yielded a significant main effect for time (F (9,61) = 3.54, p = .001) and for time x group interaction (F(18,122) = 2.02; p = .013). The group x time interaction indicates that the three groups differed on changes in body image during the training program. Univariate analyses of variance were then performed to detect which physical fitness variables were responsible for the significant interaction in the overall MANOVA. (p. 294)

The Analysis of Covariance, ANCOVA, is a statistical procedure for calculating differences among the variances of means of two or more groups and simultaneously controlling for the effects of an extraneous variable on the dependent variable. Moore (1983) described the ANCOVA as adjusting the scores on the dependent variable based on the effects of one or more extraneous variables (the use of ANCOVA changes it to a control variable). A study by Culatta, Reese, and Setzer (2006) illustrates the use of ANCOVA in a research study. They described their study as focusing on the effectiveness of an early literacy program that uses skill-based instruction to improve literacy. In the results section, they state: "To contrast performance on the trained versus untrained rhyme and alliteration skills, two-way ANCOVAS (2[Class: AR, RA] x 2[Time: Posttest 1, Posttest 2]) were conducted using each group's pretest performance as a covariate to control for entering performance for each of the literacy measures" (p. 74). So the researchers compared trained and untrained rhyme and alliteration skills. They controlled for beginning performance because they could not randomly assign to groups; they had to take an intact classroom.

Multiple regression is a statistical method that involves the use of statistical procedures that allow one to predict scores on one variable based on those from one or more variables (Rosenthal, 2001; Toothaker & Miller, 1996). The underlying concept in regression is that the variables of interest may covary together in either a positive or negative way. It does not mean that one variable causes the other, but that they vary or covary together. A common example of the use of regression is the prediction of success in college. There may be several predictors of college success, but a few that have been used include high school GPA, admission test scores such as the ACT or SAT, success in advanced placement courses, and high school rank. A college admissions officer may want to know the relationship between college success and these high school sources of information. College admissions officers want to make the best predictions for success, and so a good regression equation would give them valuable information. A researcher may find that high school GPA and success in advanced placement classes are the best predictors of college success, not SAT or ACT scores. It does not mean that high school GPA causes the success in college, but only that one can predict the other. Figure 3.5 illustrates how high school GPA can predict college GPA. A high grade point average in high school is related, or varies in a positive way, to predicting college grade point average.

Klomegah (2007) provides an example of the use of multiple regression. His study focused on predictors of academic performance in college students. He was particularly interested in understanding how variables such as ability, self-efficacy, and goal setting were predictive of course grades. He described his multiple regression results:

Figure 3.5   Prediction of College GPA

To explore the research questions posed above, standard multiple regression was utilized. First, a check of the assumption of multicollinearity showed that none of the independent variables were correlated highly. The collinearity diagnostics performed by SPSS did not show any low value of tolerance in the diagnostic table indicating that the independent variables did not correlate among themselves; therefore the assumption of multicollinearity was not violated. With regard to the normality and linearity of the residuals, the Normal Probability Plot was inspected and found to be in a reasonably straight line, suggesting no major deviations from normality. Upon examining the scatterplot, no cases of outliers were detected as cases had a standardized residual of less than 3.3 or –3.3.

As indicated in the table, the R2 equals .44 meaning that the model (which includes ability, self-set goals, self-efficacy, and assigned goals) was able to explain 44% of the variance and the dependent variable (academic performance). (p. 414)

An important point in reviewing Klomegah's results is the statement that 44 percent of the variance was explained by the predictor variables. This means that the predictor variables are able to predict almost half of the scores on the outcome variable, academic performance. This leaves 56 percent unexplained and results in other factors influencing the outcome that are unknown to the researcher. The explained variance in this example is quite high. The larger the R2 value, the greater the explained variance.

Chi-square is another statistical procedure, and it is considered both a parametric and a nonparametric statistic. However, most calculations with chi-square use nominal data, and therefore it is used in such cases as a nonparametric statistic. The underlying principle of chi-square is that there is a comparison between observed and expected frequencies. The intention is to determine if any significant differences exist between these scores. The calculation is determined by first identifying the expected frequency. Expected frequency is calculated by summing the total number of responses and dividing by 2. So if a researcher wants to know the ice cream preferences of choices between chocolate and vanilla and there are 250 respondents, he or she would divide 250 by 2 and the expected frequency would be 125. The expected frequency would then be compared to the observed, or actual, frequency.

Another statistical method is structural equation modeling. Structural equation modeling is a statistical technique that is used in theory testing. Relevant constructs are operationalized and instruments identified to test the model. Correlational techniques are used in theory testing. Raykov and Marcoulides (2006) noted several different methods of structural equation modeling: path analysis models, confirmatory factor analysis models, structural regression models, and latent change models. Path analysis models may be understood in terms of the models for explaining adolescent aggression, for example. Components of this particular model may also include participation in aggressive video games, experiencing bullying, and experiencing child abuse. The path analysis would seek to find correlations between these variables in explaining the variance of the outcome, in this case adolescent aggression. Also, it would attempt to show how these variables relate to each other—for example, does experiencing bullying interact with playing video games? A confirmatory factor analysis model is focused on discovering patterns of interrelationships among several variables (Raykov & Marcoulides, 2006). For example, multiple intelligences have been identified, and there may be numerous factors that contribute to these different intelligences (Shearer, 2004). For example, two theoretical types of multiple intelligence that potentially interact are kinesthetic intelligence and musical intelligence. Kinesthetic intelligence may include abilities in movement, such as dance or athletic activities. Variables related to kinesthetic intelligence that may contribute to this intelligence may be peripheral vision and eye-hand coordination. Musical intelligence may involve a relationship between pitch and rhythm. Also, these two intelligences may interact, e.g., pitch and rhythm may interact with movement and dance abilities and intelligence. So these variables may be assessed, and a confirmatory factor analysis may be used to look at the relationships and how they interact.

Structural regression models are somewhat similar to confirmatory factor analysis models, but there are indications of directions and relationships that the research has identified and that can be tested (Raykov & Marcoulides, 2006). So if we return to the previous example of multiple intelligences, it may have been found that kinesthetic intelligence is related to the abilities of dance and that musical intelligence of pitch and rhythm is more closely linked to pitch. The structural regression equation would seek to further understand that relationship.

The last structural equation model is the latent change model. This model involves analyzing change over time with repeated measures; it is referred to as latent change analysis (Raykov & Marcoulides, 2006). This model is particularly helpful in determining effects over time, both increases and decreases.

Nonparametric Statistics

Parametric statistics are used when the data is essentially based on normal distributions and meet the four basic assumptions discussed earlier. Data must be interval or ratio for parametric statistical methods to be used. Nonparametric statistical methods are used when ranks or ordinal types of data are used, and this involves violations of the assumptions cited earlier (e.g., normality, homogeneity of variance, and so on). Several nonparametric tests are used in inferential statistical methods. Generally, nonparametric tests are used with nominal and ordinal data or when there is a violation of one or more of the four assumptions cited earlier. The correlated t test is similar to the noncorrelated t test, except that it is used when there is a violation of independence. A researcher may choose to compare the same participants on a pretest and post-test, and the scores are not independent of each other. Consequently the research must use a nonparametric statistics.

Other examples of nonparametric tests include the Wilcoxon signed rank test and the Mann-Whitney U Test (Koronyo-Hamaoui, Danziger, Frisch, Stein, Leor, Laufer, Carel, Fennig, Apter, Goldman, Barkai, Weizman, & Gak, 2002). Both are designed to test differences between groups. These tests are used rather infrequently because most comparisons made by researchers are based on interval or ratio data. Koronyo-Hamaoui, et al. (2002) studied anorexia nervosa and genetic factors like chemical imbalance. In the results section, they stated: "The non-parametric two-tailed Wilcoxon signed rank test was used to compare the distribution of transmitted and non-transmitted alleles derived by HRR (haplotype relative risk) from the family trios" (p. 84). Essentially the researchers were attempting to determine if there was a higher rate of transmission of certain genes to those who had anorexia nervosa and those who did not, a form of nominal data. They also stated: "In the case-control study, allele frequencies and distribution were compared between

Table 3.4   Characteristics of Nonparametric Inferential Statistics

Statistical Procedures	Characteristics
Wilcoxon Rank Test	A statistical procedure used to compare differences between paired ranks, ordinal data.
Mann-Whitney U Test	A statistical procedure used to compare difference between groups when the data violates one or more of the assumptions underlying inferential statistics (e.g., normality, homogeneity).

anorexia nervosa and control groups with the two-tailed Mann-Whitney test" (p. 84). Using the Mann-Whitney U test, they compared those with anorexia nervosa and a healthy control group.

Linder and Bauer (1983) conducted a study focusing on agreement between males and females on their value systems and their understanding of the opposite gender's value systems. They used a Wilcoxon Rank Order Test in their analysis. They stated in the results section that: "Comparisons of males and females at different levels of perspective were made for each terminal value using the Wilcoxon rank-sum statistics. The probability level accepted was < .05. The results are presented in Table 2" (p. 60). In Table 2 in their article, the researchers list different values, such as a comfortable life, an exciting life, and so on. The Wilcoxon rank statistic was reported for differences between males and females based on ranks, and the researchers found, for example, values of 364.5 (a comfortable life) and 528.5 (an exciting life). A difference in rankings by males and females was found for the value of having an exciting life at the .05 level of significance, Wilcoxon rank order = 528.5. (See Table 3.4.)

Summary

Statistics are used to understand and make inferences about the population. The underlying principles of statistics concern determining the probability of obtaining data that is representative of the population of interest. Measurement scales are used in collecting data about the dependent variable, and each type of measure allows the researcher to make calculations based upon the data collected. Descriptive statistics are best understood as a summary of the data obtained from the sample. No attempt is made with descriptive statistics to make inferences back to the population. Descriptive statistics are concerned only with describing the results from the sample.

Inferential statistics are those that are used to make inferences back to the population of interest. Inferential statistics are based on probabilities of the data being representative of the population. There are several different types of inferential statistics, and these include t-tests, analysis of variance, multivariate analysis of variance, analysis of covariance, multiple regression, structural equation modeling, and chi-square.

In cases where the data, particularly the types of data (nominal and ordinal data), are not based upon the normal curve, the researcher must use nonparametric tests. Nonparametric tests are most appropriate for certain types of data and where there are violations of assumptions, such as normality, homogeneity of the variance, and so on. Nonparametric tests include the correlated t-test, the Mann-Whitney U Test, and the Wilcoxon Sign Test.

4

Quantitative Research and Research Designs

To understand and systematically evaluate research, it is first imperative to have a basic understanding of basic research designs and the research process. This chapter will consist of (a) strengths and weaknesses of quantitative research, (b) a discussion of typical research designs used in quantitative research, and (c) examples of quantitative research designs from the counseling and psychology literature.

Quantitative research methods have been considered to be the traditional approach to research in counseling and psychology. Quantitative research is defined as research that is based on measurement and the quantification of data. Whatever the dependent variable of interest in quantitative research, there must be a way to transform it into numbers.

Types of Variables

Before I begin discussing research designs, it would be helpful to understand the relevant variables that have been identified as important in research, and they include (a) independent variables, (b) dependent variables, (c) extraneous variables, and (d) control variables. Best and Kahn (1998) defined variables as "... the conditions or characteristics that the experimenter manipulates, controls, or observes" (p. 160). An *independent variable* is an event, condition, or measured attribute or characteristic that the researcher for the most part controls (there is no manipulation or control of an independent variable that is measured). Manipulation refers to the researcher's having some control over or ability to alter an event or condition of interest for an individual or group (the sample). Ary, Jacobs, and Razavieh (2002) described the independent variable in this way ". . . the manipulation of an independent variable is a deliberate operation performed by the experimenter" (p. 279). There are different degrees to which a researcher can manipulate or control an event, and this affects the quality of the study, which will be discussed in greater detail in subsequent chapters. Additionally, an independent variable must have two or more levels or groups to compare.

Attributes, or measured independent variables, have been defined as those characteristics about a person that the researcher cannot manipulate but are of interest to the research as it affects a dependent variable. Examples of attributes or measured independent variables include socioeconomic status, age, gender, IQ, race, marital status, religious affiliation, and living arrangements. More specifically, a researcher may be interested in a causal relationship that IQ has with coping behaviors during stress. Clearly, the researcher cannot manipulate IQ; he or she wants to understand a causal relationship between an individual's coping and IQ. As independent variables, measurement-type variables must be categorized so that they become specific categories and not continuous numbers. For example, IQ can range from the 50s to the mid-140s. A researcher using IQ as a measurement-type independent variable would need to group the scores because raw scores would make it difficult to use such data—there would be too many groups. The researcher may use average IQ as one category.

The dependent variable is defined in terms of changes in the subject as a consequence of the independent variable. In essence, dependent variables are influenced by and dependent on independent variables. Returning to the stress and coping example, the dependent variable is the subject's level of stress at any one moment of interest.

Extraneous variables are considered to be either uncontrolled or unknown factors that can potentially affect the results or the response to the dependent variable. These are not variables controlled by the researcher, and the results of a study may be called into question if significant extraneous variables are identified and not controlled for in the design. For example, in a study on stress and coping, extraneous variables might be socioeconomic status, age, and health of the subjects (Gallo, Bogart, Vranceanu, & Matthews, 2005). They are extraneous variables because they may impact the dependent variable, which could be the amount of stress reported.

The fourth type of variable is the control variable. This is an extraneous variable that the researcher has identified, and he or she has developed ways to control for its effects. There are several methods of addressing extraneous variables so they become control variables. One method is to build the extraneous variable into the design and thus control its effects. For example, if socioeconomic status is hypothesized to influence stress levels, the researcher may want to select subjects from different, specific socioeconomic groups and assess the effects of IQ on stress levels. The researcher can include analysis of socioeconomic status on stress levels; thus, in this situation a previous extraneous variable becomes an independent variable.

A second method of making an extraneous variable a control variable is to remove the possible effects of the extraneous variable. This may be accomplished by selecting subjects from only one socioeconomic group, for instance, the middle class or lower class. All other socioeconomic groups would be excluded from this particular study. However, the researcher could only generalize the results back to the specific socioeconomic group selected. A third method of controlling an extraneous variable is through statistical methods after the study has been conducted. For example, as mentioned in Chapter 3, there is a statistical method called analysis of covariance (ANCOVA) that factors the effects of the identified control variable into the analysis.

Research Designs

Quantitative research can also be distinguished, for the most part, by the type of research design used. There have been several different ways proposed to categorize research designs, but there is still some common agreement (Gall, Gall, & Borg, 2003; Heppner, Kivlighan, & Wampold, 1992; Moore, 1983). Different designs are frequently associated with either quantitative or qualitative research, but some designs may actually be used in both methods and are then differentiated by the types of data collection done and how the data is analyzed. Major categories of research designs include true experimental, quasi-experimental, pre-experimental, descriptive, correlational, ethnographic, and historical (see Table 4.1). Typically, true experimental, quasi-experimental, pre-experimental, and correlational designs are more closely associated with quantitative research (Charles, 1995). Ethnographic and historical research is more closely associated with qualitative research (Charles, 1995). Descriptive designs may be used with the same frequency by both methods (Charles, 1995). In this chapter, I will address all four types of research designs (see Table 4.1).

True Experimental Designs

Experimental design is essentially a map or systematic plan for conducting the collection of data. Each design results in more or less clarity in the plan, or more or less control over the relevant variables (Heppner, et al., 1992). I will address the amount of control the researcher has over the various methods and the strengths and weakness of each design in Chapter 12, "Evaluating the Methods Section—Procedures."

It is important to keep in mind, as we review the various research designs, that these traditional designs may be modified to fit the purpose of a study. For example, many traditional research designs have had a control group or a comparison group. However, variations may include changing the comparison group to a group exposed to a more traditional intervention, which is then compared to a new innovative method. A study may or may not have a traditional control group but still have a comparison group.

Two criteria are used in distinguishing true experimental designs from other designs: random assignment to groups and manipulation of the independent variable. True experimental designs include a pretest–post-test equivalent group, a post-test-only group, and the Solomon Four-Group Design.

Researchers have developed methods of representing research designs with symbols (Campbell & Stanley, 1966). The symbols used include the following designations:

R = random assignment of participants to groups

X = exposure of the group to treatment or manipulation of a targeted condition

O = observation or measurement of the dependent variable

The pretest–post-test equivalent group design is then denoted as

Group 1: R O_1 X O_2

Group 2: R O_3 O_4

In the pretest–post-test equivalent group design, there is random assignment of subjects to groups, and a pretest is given. The pretest is a measurement of the dependent variable or variables. Group 1 is the experimental group, and the X denotes an intervention or manipulation of a condition or experience of the subjects. The second group, the control group, in this case receives no manipulation. Both groups receive a post-test, again measuring the dependent variable or variables.

Table 4.1   Categories of Quantitative Research Designs

Types of Design	Purpose	Amount of Control by the Researcher Over Extraneous Variables	Characteristics
True Experimental (e.g., pretest–post-test, post-test only equivalent group)	Comparisons of treatment groups to control or traditional approaches	High amount of control	Manipulation of the independent variable and random assignment to groups
Quasi experimental (e.g., time series, ABAB)	Comparisons between groups or the same group at different times	Moderate amount of control	Manipulation of the independent variable; no random assignment to groups; typically multiple assessments of the dependent variable
Pre-experimental (e.g., one-shot pretest–post-test)	Comparisons between groups or within a group, but generally not over time	Minimal control	Manipulation of the independent variable or measurement of an event that has occurred for one group over which the researcher has no control; no random assignment to groups
Descriptive (e.g., survey, causal comparative, observational)	To describe an event or phenomenon	No control over the event or phenomenon	No manipulation of an independent variable; no random assignment to groups

As mentioned earlier, there can be variations of the general designs. For example, the design can be slightly altered and be denoted as

Group 1: R O_1 X_1 O_2

Group 2: R O_3 X_2 O_4

Group 1 in this altered design may be subjected to a traditional intervention, whereas Group 2 may possibly experience a new intervention. For example, if you wanted to determine the effectiveness of a new cognitive approach (X_2) to treating anxiety, you might compare it to a group that received a traditional behavioral approach (X_1). The design still involves the pretest and post-test for both groups, along with random assignment to groups and a manipulation. However, there is no control group, a group that does not receive any intervention.

Another variation of the pretest–post-test research design involves adding additional groups but still retaining the major steps, random assignment, manipulation, and pretests and post-tests. Below is the symbolic representation of such a design.

Group 1: R O_1 X_1 O_2

Group 2: R O_3 X_2 O_4

Group 3: R O_5 X_3 O_6

In this variation of the pretest–post-test design, the researcher is comparing three different interventions. Group 1 may again receive the traditional behavioral approach to treating anxiety. The second group may receive a new innovative intervention, such as a cognitive approach. Finally, Group 3 may receive a combination of a cognitive approach and medication.

Driver, O'Connor, Lox, and Rees (2004) conducted a study using a true experimental design, pretest–post-test (see Table 4.2). The study focused on understanding the effects of an aquatic exercise on the physical fitness of people with brain injury. The experimental condition was the aquatic exercise. The control condition was simply those not participating in an aquatic exercise program who had a brain injury. The researchers stated, "A stratified random sampling technique was used. A pool of participants was created from individuals who were outpatients at a local rehabilitation centre, who were above level six (confused-appropriate) on the Ranchos Los Amigos Scale of Cognitive Functioning" (p. 850). They further described the experimental group: "The experimental group completed an 8-week exercise programme that consisted of 24 exercise sessions (three times a week) each lasting 1-hour" (p. 850). This study met the two criteria for being a true experimental design: random assignment and a manipulation.

A second design is the post-test-only equivalent groups design, which is denoted in the following way

Group 1: R X_1 O_1

Group 2: R X_2 O_2

In this design there is random assignment to groups, and then the intervention is presented to the experimental group. Note that no pretest is given.

Table 4.2   Pretest–Post-Test Design

Aquatic exercise (experimental)	R[a]	O_1	X_1	O_2
		Body composition	8-week exercise program that consisted of 24 exercise sessions	Body composition
		Flexibility— sit and reach		Flexibility— sit and reach
		Modified curl test		Modified curl test
Vocational class (control)	R	O_3	Control	O_4
		Body composition	Vocational class was a reading and writing program for instructional and safety reasons.	Body composition
		Flexibility— sit and reach		Flexibility— sit and reach
		Modified curl test		Modified curl test

Structure taken from: Driver, O'Connor, Lox, & Rees (2004).

After the intervention for the experimental group, both groups are given a post-test. The purpose of using the post-test-only equivalent groups design is to reduce the effects of pretesting sensitivity. I will further explain the effects of pretesting on the validity of a study in Chapter 12, "Evaluating the Methods Section—Procedures." As with the previous design, there can be variations of the post-test-only equivalent groups design. For example, two or more treatment groups may be used:

Group 1: R X_1 O_1

Group 2: R X_2 O_2

Group 3: R X_3 O_3

In the above design, the researcher is comparing three different treatments using the post-test-only equivalent groups design. To maintain the essential format of the post-test equivalent groups design, the researcher must have random assignment to groups and use only a post-test to measure the dependent variable or variables. The post-test equivalent group design is not used as often as other designs, such as the pretest–post-test design.

Park, Chang, and Chung (2005) conducted a study on the effects of a cognitive intervention program on health beliefs in Korean women. The study design was described as follows: "This study used non-equivalent, control group, post-test only design to test the effects of a cognition-emotion focused program. The post-test only design was used because repeated measures of variables such as knowledge and attitudes can result in a testing effect" (p. 291). They further defined their procedures: "After random assignment of the participants to the two groups, the experimental group met to schedule attendance for the group program" (p. 293). (See Table 4.3.)

Table 4.3   Post-Test Equivalent (Group Design)

Group 1	R^a	X_1	O_1
		Cognitive intervention program	Knowledge of cervical cancer
			Health belief
			Self-efficacy
Group 2	R	X_2	O_2
		No treatment	Knowledge of cervical cancer
			Health belief
			Self-efficacy

R = random assignment

Structure taken from: Park, Chang, & Chung (2005).

Researchers are hesitant to use the post-test-only design because without the pretest, they do not have information at the beginning of the experiment as to whether the groups used are truly equivalent. However, when the sample is large enough, significant characteristics should be adequately distributed, ensuring equivalence across the groups with random assignment (Moore, 1983). (Random assignment involves randomly assigning participants to experimental and control groups.)

The Solomon Four-Group Design is the last true experimental design I want to discuss. It may be denoted symbolically:

Group 1: R O_1 X_1 O_2

Group 2: R O_3 $\quad$ O_4

Group 3: R X_1 O_5

Group 4: R O_6

A Solomon Four-Group Design is a combination of the pretest–post-test equivalent groups and the post-test-only equivalent groups designs. There is random assignment to each of the four conditions, and two groups receive the intervention or manipulation. Use of this design is an attempt to control for the effects of testing or the subjects' becoming sensitive to what the researcher is investigating through repeated administration of the dependent variable or variables. Possible variations here include the control groups' simply receiving a traditional method of treatment rather than receiving no treatment. A Solomon Four-Group Design is not used often, mainly because it is expensive to conduct: four groups, and thus more subjects, are required (Bohon, Santos, Sanchez-Sosa, & Singer, 1994; DeTienne & Chandler, 2007; Reid & Finchilescu, 1995; Sawilowsky & Markman, 1990). (See Table 4.4.)

Table 4.4   Solomon Four-Group Design

Control group 1 (15 males, 15 females)	R^a	O_1 Mental task: mathematical computation		O_2 Mental task: mathematical computation
Exertion group 1 (experimental; 15 males, 15 females)	R	O_3 Mental task: mathematical computation	X_1 Exertion: walking as exercise	O_4 Mental task: mathematical computation
Control group 2 (15 males, 15 females)	R	O_3 Mental task: mathematical computation		O_5 Mental task: mathematical computation
Exertion group 2 (experimental)	R		X_1 Exertion: walking as exercise	O_6 Mental task: mathematical computation

R = random assignment

Structure taken from McNaughten & Gabbard (1993).

Quasi-Experimental Designs

A number of different quasi-experimental designs have been proposed (Campbell & Stanley, 1966). The definition of a quasi-experimental design is one in which there is a manipulation that is controlled by the researcher but no random assignment to groups. I want to review three of the more common quasi-experimental designs: the pretest–post-test non-equivalent groups design, the time series design, and the multiple time series design. The pretest–post-test non-equivalent group design consists of no random assignment to groups. Because of the characteristics of the situation, the groups cannot be separated (for instance, intact treatment groups may be used, such as two different day treatment programs for those with chronic mental illness). In this design, a pretest and post-test are administered to all groups involved. The typical design is a comparison between an experimental group and a control group but, as with other designs, there can be alterations with more than two groups used. A symbolic representation of the design would be

$O_1 \; X_1 \; O_2$

$O_3 \qquad O_4$

When the researcher is unable to use random assignment to groups, there are more threats to the internal validity of the study because there are possible differences between the group members prior to the intervention. (Internal validity refers to the reduction of the effects from extraneous variables on the study; this concept will be defined more thoroughly in Chapter 12.)

Farynaiarz and Lockwood (1992) employed a pretest–post-test non-equivalent group quasi-experimental design in a study focusing on the impact of microcomputer simulations on environmental problem solving. Subjects for the study were 59 community college students who were enrolled in environmental science and biology courses. The experimental group comprised those registered in the environmental sciences course, and the control group consisted of those in the biology course. No random assignment to groups was possible because students made their own selection of courses. The investigators stated, "Because there were similar environmental concepts included in both course curricula, the samples were considered to be from a single population" (p. 457). The intervention that the experimental group received involved computer simulations of environmental problems. Students were provided with information indicating the relevant variables to consider in problem solving. The design is depicted symbolically in Table 4.5.

Table 4.5   Pretest–Post-Test Non-Equivalent Group Quasi-Experimental Design

Group 1 (comparison)	O_1		O_2
	Tests of integrated science		Tests of integrated science
Group 2 (experimental)	O_3	X_1	O_4
	Supervised home-based exercise training, high intensity	Environmental imulations (e.g., wastewater treatment)	Tests of integrated science

Structure taken from Farynaiarz & Lockwood (1992).

A second type of quasi-experimental design is the time series design. In this design, there is again no random assignment, but there is a manipulation. One group is used, with assessment or observations taken over a period of time. No comparison group is used. The design may be symbolized as

$$O_1 \ O_2 \ O_3 \ O_4 \ X_1 \ O_5 \ O_6 \ O_7 \ O_8$$

In the time series design, the researcher is looking for changes that occur between observations or assessments four and five (O_4 and O_5), or after the intervention has occurred. Variations of this design may include more observations or measurements. As with the previous quasi-experimental design, there are some problems with controlling for extraneous variables and more threats to the validity of the study.

Mastel-Smith, Binder, Malecha, Hersch, Symes, and McFarlane (2006) provide an example of a time series design. The purpose of the study was to investigate therapeutic life review procedures to determine the effects on depression among senior women. The subjects for the study were 14 older women who received home health services. The treatment or intervention involved the use of a therapeutic life review. A single group was used, and the design is symbolically represented in Table 4.6.

Table 4.6   Time Series Design

Group	Oa	X	O
14 women over 65	$O_1 \ O_2$	Therapeutic life review	$O_3 \ O_4$

a. O = observation of sharing

Structure taken from Mastel-Smith, et al. (2006).

A third type of quasi-experimental design is the multiple time series design. The time series design uses multiple observations with multiple groups. There is no random assignment to groups, but the independent variable or variables are manipulated. The design may be symbolized as

$$O_1 \; O_2 \; O_3 \; O_4 \; X_1 \; O_5 \; O_6 \; O_7 \; O_8$$

$$O_9 \; O_{10} \; O_{11} \; O_{12} \; X_2 \; O_{12} \; O_{13} \; O_{14} \; O_{15} \; O_{16}$$

$$O_{17} \; O_{18} \; O_{19} \; O_{20} \; X_3 \; O_{21} \; O_{22} \; O_{23} \; O_{24}$$

The multiple time series design typically involves two or more groups, all of which receive some form of manipulation of the independent variable. Felce, de Kock, Mansell, and Jenkins (1984) conducted a study that illustrates the use of a multiple time series design. The study focused on evaluating the effects of systematic teaching to severely disturbed and profoundly mentally handicapped adults in residential facilities. Subjects for the study were 24 residents of four community-based programs serving individuals with mental handicaps. Felce, et al. (1984) described the intervention as follows:

> A behavioral assessment is made of the current skill repertoire of the client by care staff, who then meet to decide a realistic goal. The programme-writer (a senior member of the staff) plans a sequence of weekly teaching steps that take the client by small increments from their current skill repertoire to the long-term goal. The teaching strategy is derived by analyzing the target skill into component behaviors and by teaching each with varying conditions of help. (p. 302)

A multiple time series design was employed (see Table 4.7) with six groups. The groups were identified by the goals set with a skills training method.

Pre-Experimental Designs

Campbell and Stanley (1966) described pre-experimental research designs that involve no random assignment to groups with an intervention. They further stated that pre-experimental designs typically did not allow for detection of differences through comparisons with other groups or with multiple assessments of baseline. Baseline is defined as the starting point prior to the presentation of the independent variable or the condition of the dependent variable before intervention.

Table 4.7   Multiple Time Series Design

Group: Skill	Assessment of Skill Demonstrated	Skill Training	Assessment of Skill Demonstrated
Group 1: touching cradle	O_1 O_2 O_3 O_4 O_5	X_1	O_6
Group 2: picks up striker and hits xylophone	O_1 O_2 O_3 O_4 O_5	X_1	O_6
Group 3: client works a jigsaw	O_1 O_2 O_3 O_4 O_5	X_1	O_6
Group 4: client washes hands	O_1 O_2 O_3 O_4 O_5	X_1	O_6
Group 5: client colors pictures	O_1 O_2 O_3 O_4 O_5	X_1	O_6
Group 6: client copies name	O_1 O_2 O_3 O_4 O_5	X_1	O_6

Structure taken from Felce, et al. (1984).

Three types of research designs have been categorized as pre-experimental (Campbell & Stanley, 1966): the one-shot case study, the one-group pretest–post-test design, and the static group comparison. The one-shot case study design involves a single group that receives an intervention followed by an observation or measurement of the dependent variable. This design may be symbolically represented as

$$X \ O_1$$

The use of the one-shot case study design in current literature is minimal because of the severe limitations of the validity of the study (internal validity). Consequently, few journals publish studies conducted with this design.

The one-group pretest–post-test design is composed of a single group receiving an intervention, with a pretest and post-test for minimal comparison purposes. Again, in this design there is no random assignment because there is only one group. This design is rarely found in the professional literature because of the many threats to validity (see Chapter 12). The design may be depicted symbolically as

$$O_1 \ X \ O_2$$

Table 4.8   One-Group Pretest–Post-Test Design

Group 1[a]	O_1	X_1	O_2
	Reading achievement Sense of control over environment School attendance	Classroom management approach: contingency management	Reading achievement Sense of control over environment School attendance

Structure taken from Matheny & Edwards (1974).

Matheny and Edwards (1974) provide an example of a one-group pretest–post-test design. Matheny and Edwards ". . . attempted to bring about certain changes in pupil behavior through specified changes in teacher behavior. The desired changes in pupil behavior were increased proficiency in reading, an increased sense of control over the environment, and improved school attendance" (p. 224). Twenty-five elementary classroom teachers and 757 students in Grades 1 through 7 participated in the study. The intervention was a weeklong teacher-training session in contingency management. In addition, two inservice training sessions were held during the school year to reinforce skills. The dependent variables were reading achievement, a sense of control over one's environment, and school attendance. Note that only one group, elementary school students, was used in the study, with no comparison group. (See Table 4.8.)

The final pre-experimental research design, the static group comparison, involves a condition that a control group has not experienced. There is no random assignment to groups and no attempt to determine whether the groups are similar or are matched on relevant demographic or extraneous variables. For practical reasons, the comparison generally involves an intervention or experience that has already occurred, so the groups cannot be randomly assigned to an experimental or control condition. Thus the use of the term *static* refers to existing groups remaining intact because the intervention has occurred. The static group comparison design may be symbolically represented as

$$X \: O_1$$

$$\overline{}$$

$$O_2$$

The intermittent line indicates that the groups are not randomly assigned, not equivalent, and intact prior to participation in the study.

Table 4.9   Static Group Comparison Design

Group 1	X_1	O_1
52 medical students	Enrichment program	practice choice
Group 2	X_2	O_2
318 medical students	Traditional medical school training	practice choice

Structure taken from Lynch, et al. (2001).

Lynch, Teplin, Willis, Pathman, Larsen, Steiner, and Berstein (2001) con-ducted a study using a static group comparison design in which they focused on participants in a rural scholars program for physicians. Subjects for the study were 52 medical students who enrolled in the rural scholars program and a comparison group of 318 medical students who did not participate in this program. The authors described their methods: "A static-group compar-ison design where postintervention comparisons are made between one group who participated in an intervention and one group who did not, was used to compare scholars with their peers" (p. 38). The independent variable in this study was an enrichment program for encouraging general medical practice in rural settings. The groups are considered static because the researcher can-not assign individuals to medical student groups. The measurement variable or dependent variable was placement of students in specific settings, such as family practice and community hospitals. (See Table 4.9.)

Descriptive Designs

Descriptive research has been noted to include four different approaches: survey, observational, correlational, and causal comparative (Moore, 1983). Descriptive designs involve no random assignment to groups, nor is there any manipulation of an independent variable. Generally, descriptive research is an attempt to describe characteristics or the effects of events for an iden-tified population. A good portion of published psychological research may be categorized as descriptive.

A survey of descriptive design involves the use of self-report to clarify the perception, attitudes, or behaviors of a target group. In survey research, there is no independent variable. Manning and Cheers (1995) provide an example of survey descriptive research. The purpose of their study was to identify how strongly residents of a small country town felt about child abuse and how likely they were to notify authorities when abuse was suspected.

In the methods section, the researchers described the design in the following way: "In a cross-sectional survey design, semistructured interviews were conducted in 1989 with a simple random sample of all people over 18 years in 60 non-Aboriginal living groups in a small remote town in central western Queensland, Australia" (p. 389). The purpose of this study was not to determine the effects of a treatment or an intervention. The methods were designed to gather information about the attitude of a target group, individuals living in a small rural town.

Observational descriptive research is an attempt to avoid problems with self-report (problems with self-report approaches will be discussed further in Chapter 13) and still clarify personal characteristics through observations by others or raters. The sole domain of interest is behaviors of the target group; clearly one cannot observe another's attitudes or feelings. Shore, Lerman, Smith, Iwata, and DeLeon (1995) conducted a study using an observational descriptive design. The purpose of the study was described as an attempt to examine and identify the quality of care in a geriatric setting. Subjects for the study were 104 residents of a proprietary nursing home and the staff who provided their care. In the journal abstract, the researchers stated: "Direct observation was used to examine multiple aspects of care provided in a proprietary nursing home" (p. 435). Furthermore, the researchers stated in the methods section:

> Upon entering the facility, the observer proceeded to each observation area and scored categories of environment condition, resident condition, and staff activity using a time-sampling procedure in which observers recorded the event of interest at the "moment" of observation. (p. 438)

The researchers in this study were interested in systematically identifying certain variables of interest, such as quality of care. The methods used were based solely on observations made by trained observers.

A third type of descriptive design is a correlational approach. Human beings are complex, and oftentimes it is difficult to separate important variables that influence behaviors, attitudes, and perceptions. Consequently, researchers use correlational methods to identify and understand the relationship between multiple variables, or how several variables of interest covary.

Preechawong, Zauszniewski, Heinzer, Musil, Kercsmar, and Aswinanonh (2007) conducted a correlational study investigating the relationship between family functioning, self-esteem, and coping in adolescents with asthma. The researchers described the purpose of their study: "This study examined the relationships of both self-esteem and family functioning to resourceful coping in Thai adolescents with asthma" (p. 25). The researchers used a sample of convenience and adolescents who had asthma, taken from outpatient clinics in four hospitals.

Causal comparative descriptive research concerns attempting to identify the effects of an independent variable after the fact. The independent variable is not under the control of the researcher but is of interest. The researcher therefore compares two or more groups who have had different experiences (the identified independent variables). Hollowood, Salisbury, Rainforth, and Palobaro (1994) investigated the use of teacher and student time when the classroom had students with mild and severe disabilities. The researchers described the research design as follows:

> A causal-comparative between groups design was used. Group membership (independent variable) was determined by the presence or absence of a child with a severe disability or whether a classmate evidenced a severe disability. Students in Group 3 constituted a post-hoc control group. The major dependent variables were allocated time, used time, and engaged time. (p. 245)

Eighteen elementary school students with severe and mild disabilities served as subjects for the study. Group 1 was composed of six students in Grades 1, 3, and 4 with severe disabilities who were enrolled in four different classrooms. Groups 2 and 3 were composed of students without disabilities who were randomly selected from students in Grades 1, 3, and 4. For this study, then, the comparisons were made between three groups, and the researcher had no control over the independent variable, the type of disability.

Summary

Quantitative research methods, the traditional approach to conducting research, may be defined in terms of converting the results into measurable quantifiable units for analysis. Additionally, the researcher typically has control over the variables of interest. Measurement amounts may be categorized as four different scales: nominal, ordinal, interval, and ratio. Four different types of variables are of interest to researchers using the quantitative method: independent, dependent, extraneous, and control.

Research designs most closely associated with quantitative research are true experimental designs, quasi-experimental designs, pre-experimental designs, and descriptive designs. True experimental designs always include random assignment to groups and manipulation of the independent variable. Quasi-experimental designs involve no random assignment but a manipulation of the independent variable. Pre-experimental designs also involve no random assignment with a manipulation; however, the amount of control by the researcher over extraneous variables for pre-experimental designs is the least among the four designs.

Descriptive designs, the fourth general category of research methods used in quantitative approaches, include survey, observational, correlational, and causal comparative. Descriptive designs involve no random assignment, nor is there a manipulation of an independent variable. Typically, descriptive designs are an attempt by the researcher to characterize events or conditions of an identified population.

5

Qualitative Research Methods

The initial use of qualitative methods was first proposed by Descartes and Kant in the 1600s and 1700s (Hamilton, 1992). Hamilton noted that Descartes was responsible for founding the qualitative research approach. Qualitative research approaches have been used in more recent history since the early part of the 20th century by sociologists and anthropologists (Rosaldo, 1989). However, the term *qualitative research* is a fairly recent one and first appeared in the 1960s (Bogdan & Biklen, 2003). Denzin and Lincoln (2000) described qualitative research as follows:

> An emphasis on the qualities of entities and on processes and meanings that are not experimentally examined or measured (if measured at all) in terms of quantity, amount, intensity, or frequency. Qualitative researchers stress the socially constructed nature of reality, the intimate relationship between the researcher and what is studied, and the situational constraints that shape the inquiry. (p. 8)

The goal of qualitative research has been described as "to gain an in-depth, holistic perspective of groups of people, environments, programs, events, or any phenomenon one wishes to study by interacting closely with the people one is studying" (Farber, 2006, p. 368).

In this chapter, I will first address the strengths and weaknesses of qualitative research and its basic characteristics. Second, several approaches or traditions of conducting research within a qualitative orientation will be presented, including the case study method, ethnographic methods, grounded theory, phenomenological methods, participatory action research, narrative analysis, historical descriptive methods, and mixed methods.

Researchers in the social sciences have long struggled with achieving a sense of respectability for the methods that are used (Padgett, 2004). This struggle has been associated with perceptions of how objective and measurable results are. Guba and Lincoln (1992) noted that the social sciences have long been considered "soft" sciences and less quantifiable compared to "hard" sciences like mathematics, chemistry, and physics. This struggle, and the desire to be viewed both externally and within the social science fields as closer to "hard" sciences, have resulted in qualitative methods of inquiry being perceived as less desirable. Sells, Smith, and Sprenkle (1995) have described the historical antagonism between quantitative and qualitative research methods. They noted that in many investigators' views, the traditional quantitative approaches were the only ethically responsible way of conducting research. An added issue for those conducting qualitative research is that the way qualitative data are organized and reported in professional journals is different from the ways used for traditional quantitative research (e.g., the methods section in particular may differ).

Advantages and Disadvantages of Qualitative Research

Several advantages and disadvantages of qualitative research have been proposed (see Table 5.1) (Gall, Gall, & Borg, 2006). One advantage is that the researcher can gain a more detailed understanding of the phenomena of interest than with quantitative research. Second, qualitative research is helpful in understanding or explaining unusual situations that could not be identified through large-scale quantitative methods. A third advantage is that the researcher can adjust data-collection procedures during the process, based on the issues that arise.

The major difficulty with qualitative methods concerns the validity of generalizing results to the larger population (Gall, Borg, & Gall, 1996). By focusing on specific phenomena, the researcher increases understanding of those phenomena but loses a broader perspective. A second limitation of qualitative research involves ethically maintaining the privacy of the individuals studied when the information presented is so specific.

Bogdan and Biklen (2003) have identified five characteristics of qualitative research: a naturalistic approach, the use of descriptive data, an emphasis on process, an inductive approach, and a focus on meaning. A naturalistic approach involves the collection of data from the natural environment. Contrary to traditional quantitative methods, which attempt to control the extraneous variables in the natural environment, qualitative research enters the natural setting to study its complexity. An understanding of the context is critical to observing and being in the natural setting. The second characteristic of qualitative research is the use of descriptive

Table 5.1   Advantages and Disadvantages of Qualitative Research

Advantages	Disadvantages
1. Able to obtain a detailed understanding of a person, event, or phenomenon	1. Limitations in generalizing the results to the larger population
2. A detailed understanding of a person, event, or phenomenon	2. Potential for bias in interpreting data
3. Flexibility in responding to events or phenomena (e.g., can alter flow of interview to address uniqueness of event or phenomenon)	3. Lack of consistency in methods of data collection
4. Generally does not require extensive resources to conduct	4. Potential for loss of privacy for individuals studied because of intensive description of individual cases
5. Helpful in understanding unusual or exceptional situations	
6. Helpful in the initial exploration of individuals, events, or phenomena	

data, which is collected and presented through language and pictures (Bogdan & Biklen, 2003). Bogdan and Biklen (2003) noted that such data may be in the form of interview transcripts, videotapes, notations made, and photographs. Such data collection may be done with exceptional detail and focus on small elements of the context. A third characteristic of qualitative research, emphasis on the process, is to some degree an investigation that is more interested in the way things are done rather than the outcomes or the accomplishments (Bogdan & Biklen, 2003). The emphasis is on how things happen and an understanding of how events or conditions occur. A fourth characteristic is an inductive approach, which is an attempt to explore in a more organic way what comes up, rather than hypothesizing what is there and looking to find support for the hypothesis, a deductive approach. The orientation of the qualitative researcher is one of entering the naturalistic environment with an openness to discovering what can be found, but with a focus on elements of the environment. The last characteristic is the meaning of the experience to those in the context and environment (Bogdan & Biklen, 2003). The researcher is interested in understanding the participants in that environment perspective and view of the experience. In essence, the question is what meaning certain things in that environment have for the person or participant.

Table 5.2   Comparison of Qualitative and Quantitative Research

Comparison points	Qualitative research	Quantitative research
Focus	Quality, which includes the nature and essence	Quantity, which includes amounts
Philosophical Orientation	Phenomenology and interaction	Empiricism and logical positivism
Approaches	Fieldwork, ethnographic, naturalistic, and grounded	experimental, empirical, and statistical
Goals	Understanding, describing, discovery, and hypothesis generating	Prediction, control, and hypothesis testing
Design Characteristics	Flexible and evolving	Fixed and predetermined
Sample	Generally a small sample, which is nonrandom, is used	A large, random sample of the population is used
Data-Collection Approaches	Research is the method of data collection, achieved through interviews and observations	Administration of structured instruments, surveys, and questionnaires
Method of Analysis	Inductive and use of language	Deductive and use of statistics

Adapted from Sorin-Peters (2004).

Sorin-Peters (2004) differentiated qualitative research and quantitative research on specific comparison points. For example, the focus of qualitative research is quality, and the focus of quantitative research is quantity. (See Table 5.2.)

Units of Data Collection

Lofland, Snow, Anderson, and Lofland (2006) proposed a common approach to understanding and interpreting qualitative research through units of data gathering. They proposed that there are nine units of analysis or data collection (gathering) for qualitative research: social practices, episodes, encounters, roles (roles and social types), relationships, groups and cliques, organizations, settlements, and lifestyles or subcultures.

According to Lofland, et. al. (2006), units are arranged hierarchically and increase in social complexity from practices to lifestyles. Social practices are defined as the smallest unit of analysis in social settings and are characterized by repetition of communications and behaviors in interactions. Additionally, social practices are identified by being routine or unnoticeable (Lofland, et al., 2006). For example, rituals may be classified as practices. One ritual that might be studied in counseling is that of initial greetings, such as a handshake or the client calling the counselor Ms., doctor, and so on.

A second type of data unit analysis, episodes, has been characterized as unusual dramatic experiences. Examples of episodes are significant events such as going through a divorce, experiencing a natural disaster such as a hurricane, or experiencing a violent crime. Episodes, according to Lofland, et al. (2006), may involve only a few people, such as a violent crime in which one individual robs another, or may include thousands of people, such as all those experiencing an earthquake. The important issue is that the unit is episodic and not long term. Researchers in the field of counseling might be interested in a number of psychological events that affect a client and have the potential to bring a client into counseling, such as rape, divorce, or the death of someone close. The effects or experience of the terrorist attacks of 9/11 is another example of an episode.

The third category for unit of analysis in qualitative research is encounters, which are defined in terms of there being two or more individuals sharing social space and who are focused on maintaining a mutual interaction (Lofland, et al, 2006). Encounters are well defined and generally involve specific roles and boundaries between participants. The key point is that there is a mutual focus among the participants. An example of an encounter in counseling is a client and counselor meeting for the first few sessions. The interaction is based to a large extent on the social roles each brings to the relationship, and there is a common focus: identifying and understanding the client's problem. Researchers in counseling might be interested, for example, in the meaning ascribed by the client to early counseling experiences (e.g., the client's knowledge of the process of counseling and the roles client and counselor are to play).

A fourth type of unit of analysis in qualitative research is composed of two subcategories: roles and social types. Roles are composed of clusters of behaviors that are connected to a specific position. So, a teacher is expected to behave in a certain way in a classroom, for example, stand in front of the class and impart information, give tests, ask questions, and so on. Social types are considered to be a subcategory of roles and are somewhat more general. Examples of social types may be "bully" or "class clown" (Lofland, et al., 2006).

The next relevant unit of analysis is the relationship, which has been defined as involving two individuals who are relatively connected and to some degree interdependent over a period of time (Lofland, et al., 2006). Examples of relationship are spouses, friends, and supervisors and employees. For counseling researchers, the counseling relationship (beyond the first few sessions) may be interpreted as this kind of analytic unit.

Groups are another type of unit of analysis; they are defined as a number of individuals who interact over a period of time and form a social structure (Lofland, et al., 2006). Work groups and families are examples of groups as units of analysis. Counseling researchers might be interested in how families cope with changes, such as those that occur when a young child attends school for the first time.

Organizations are the next level of social unit analysts suggest for conducting qualitative research. They are defined as systematically formed collectives of individuals with specific purposes and goals (Lofland, et al., 2006). Organizations are established with specific rules and entrance restrictions. An example of an organization is a student club. A counseling researcher might be interested in studying an informal treatment organization, such as Alcoholics Anonymous (AA). There are formal goals for AA, such as maintaining sobriety, and rules for participating in the organization, such as maintaining the anonymity of members (Alcoholics Anonymous, 1952).

Settlements or habitats are another unit of analysis, identified by Lofland, et al. (2006) and these are defined as ". . . complexly interrelated sets of encounters, roles, groups, and organizations, existing within a socially defined territory and performing a range of life-sustaining functions" (p. 129). Concrete examples of settlements are neighborhoods, towns, and villages. The counselor researcher might be interested in investigating the effects of a drug-prevention program on a town or a neighborhood.

Lifestyles or subcultures are the last social unit of measurement category in qualitative research. Lofland, et al. (2006) defined lifestyles as ". . . a mixture of behavioral, normative, and cognitive elements that together characterize the way of life or orientation of a set of similarly situated individuals and that distinguishes them from other groups or aggregations within or across other social units" (p. 131). A counseling researcher might, for example, be interested in discovering how different health lifestyles affect psychological well-being, whereas an educator might be interested in how socioeconomic background influences motivation for learning.

Traditions or Paradigms in Conducting Qualitative Research

As has been mentioned, there are several different approaches for conducting qualitative research. One major approach is the case study. Although all case study research is not qualitative, some case study methods may be (Yin, 2003). Case study research has long had an important history and influence in psychology and education; Freud and Piaget used this approach to developing many of their theories. Case study is an intensive investigation of a single individual in an effort to treat or intervene with that person and/or to make inferences about others. For example, Freud (Spurling, 1989) developed much of his theory of personality development using case study methods (e.g., the cases of "Dora" and "Little Hans"). Piaget employed his own children as case studies, using this method to develop his insights into cognitive development during infancy (Daehler & Bukatko, 1985).

Case Study Approach

The case study approach of qualitative research may be defined in terms of the intensity of focus on a particular case or set of cases and specific phenomena of the case or cases. Case study research is typically, although not always, conducted in a natural setting. Stake (2000) noted that qualitative case study requires establishing boundaries and units of analysis to study in the environment so it is not totally open or undefined. As Stake (2000) stated, "Case study is not a methodological choice but a choice of what is to be studied" (p. 435). Gall, et al. (1996) stated that case studies serve three purposes: to achieve detailed descriptions of phenomena of interest, to develop possible explanations of phenomena, and to evaluate the phenomena of interest. To understand the case study as a qualitative approach, it may be best to have a description of the characteristics of the approach. As Stake (2000) stated, "Perhaps the simplest rule for method in qualitative case work is this: Place the best brains available into the thick of what is going on. The brain work ostensibly is observational, but more basically it is reflective" (p. 445). This refers to the use of strong observational methods in the naturalistic setting to understand the case of interest. Yin (2003) proposed that several different approaches to case study may be distinguished and that there may single or multiple case studies. A single case study clearly involves focusing only on one case. A multiple case study is composed of several single case studies.

Another way to characterize case study research is by the manner in which the data is collected and analyzed. Data in case study research is typically collected in the form of summaries and extensive note taking of the researcher's observations. Researchers may use triangulation in data collection, which refers to using multiple data-collection methods, sources, or observers (Stake, 2000). For example, the researcher might use several other researchers to observe the same phenomena, or use a variety of sources to understand a particular phenomenon or meaning. They engage in continuous contact with the case or environment and revise meanings and understandings over time (Stake, 2000).

The qualitative researcher is generally interested in particular phenomena that may shed light on processes of events, persons, or things (Gall, et al., 1996). Qualitative researchers identify a focus of their attention in regard to the phenomena of interest; they also define the unit of analysis to be studied. If for example, researchers are interested in understanding the counseling relationship as the focus, they might choose the relationship unit of analysis. The case study then would be of single client-counselor interactions. Researchers might choose to study more than one counseling "relationship," but the unit of analysis still remains the same, and the researcher in qualitative research uses the case study approach. The researcher may observe the counseling relationship over several sessions and record or describe the process. Recall that qualitative research is generally conducted in the natural setting, so the researcher might observe through a one-way mirror. Also, the counselor may choose multiple case studies and study several counselor-client relationships.

An example in educational qualitative research might be an interest in the process of interaction between a teacher and his or her students. The unit of analysis might be a group (all those in the classroom). The researcher might enter the classroom as an observer over several days, weeks, or longer. Detailed descriptions would be made of the interactions between the class and the teacher. A multiple case study would involve studying several classrooms.

Stake (2000) described the selection of case study as being unique, and this is based on the particular interest in the specific cases to be studied. He goes on to propose that selection of the case is of critical importance and that a researcher may choose to randomly select from a certain population that is of interest. Despite the limitation of generalizability of qualitative research there remains the intent of offering some effort at generalization. Stake proposes six steps in using a case study approach: (a) establishing the boundaries of the case, (b) identifying themes of emphasis, (c) focusing on specific patterns of data, (d) the use of triangulation in data interpretation, (e) considering alternative views, and (f) determining appropriate generalizations from the case.

Erickson, Hatton, Roy, Fox, and Renne (2007) conducted a qualitative case study to investigate the leaders in the field of early intervention for children with visual impairments supported and promoted literacy in early intervention. The researchers described the procedures as follows:

> The qualitative case study was selected for its strength as a means of exploring, explaining, and describing the contexts within which particular practices are employed. When the unique features of each case are compared with the experiences of others, each of the three cases has important atypical features, relationships, and situations that may be generalizable to other cases (Stake, 2000). Because of the dynamic nature of home visits and the lack of empirical information on this topic, the case study methods were deemed the most appropriate for the research question. The combination of participant observations, teacher interviews, and document reviews provided multiples sources of information, and supported the extraction of as much information as possible about the early intervention practices employed by the participants in the study. (p. 83)

One can see from this description that the researchers used several approaches to gather data, including triangulation of data gathered from several participant observers and interviews.

Ethnographic

Ethnographic research methods involve intensive study of the characteristics of a given culture or distinct group with their own worldview from a naturalistic, firsthand experience (Tedlock, 2000). Like many other qualitative methods, the ethnographic approach was initially developed by anthropologists. Tedlock (2000) described the benefits of an ethnographic approach as ". . . ethnographers can better understand the beliefs, motivation, and behaviors of their subjects than they can by using any other approach" (p. 456). Shimahara (1988) identified three characteristics of ethnographic research: (a) focusing on investigating cultural patterns in behavior and commonalities of a given culture, (b) determining how members of a culture define and derive meaning from the experiences and events occurring within that culture, and (c) studying these cultural behaviors and patterns in their natural environment. Thus, for those using the ethnographic approach to research, defining characteristics are to focus on culture or a particular group. Gall, et al. (1996) stated that the goal of ethnographic research is to look at ". . . cultural phenomena from the perspective of an outsider, and then [seek] to understand the phenomenon from the perspective of an insider" (p. 612). The life history approach or biography is one used in ethnography (Tedlock, 2000). A common approach to ethnographic research is as a participant observer. The investigator enters the social system and lives among those he or she is studying. Another strategy in an ethnographic approach is the use of memoir, or the ethnographic genre. The ethnographic genre has been described as a combination of both memoir and life history approaches (Tedlock, 2000). The researcher, based on his or her experience as a participant observer, writes about the experience as if it were a memoir. Data- collection methods have ranged from the participant observer to the observer participant. Both counseling and education have adopted these approaches to conducting research. They offer an effective new paradigm for understanding major concepts and practices in our fields.

Brown (2006) conducted a study in which she used an ethnographic research approach. The focus of her study was to attempt to understand the culture and perceptions about the quality of mothering by African American women in rural areas. The methods are described as follows: "A holistic ethnographic approach informed the design and data collection method of this study" (p. 22). She further described her methods: "Interview topics included drug use; social networks; values; employment history; childhood experiences; sexual behavior; and HIV/AIDS-related knowledge, beliefs and perceptions" (p. 22). The respondents for this qualitative study were 30 African American women who reported using cocaine at the time of participation. The actual data collection is described in detail: "Multiple data collection strategies (in-depth audiotaped interviews, participant observation, and information interviews) over a prolonged period (four years), monthly peer debriefing between the PI and project director, and member checks were used to enhance the validity/credibility of the data" (p. 23).

Grounded Theory

Grounded theory is a qualitative research approach that was originally developed by two sociologists, Glasser and Strass (Charmaz, 2006). The primary approach to grounded theory is the dynamic interaction of identifying categories, which are analyzed and reconstituted into more complex ones with each continuous level of analysis. Willig (2001) provides the example of identifying initial categories described by participants as anger and anxiety into a broader category of emotions. Each level of analysis may lead to a higher level of abstraction (Willig, 2001). In essence, the more abstract categories are grounded on earlier ones, which are more basic. Theory is built on a systematic analysis and reanalysis of the data. This approach gives the researcher a significant amount of flexibility in adjusting the investigation to the information collected. Isaksson, Lexell, and Skar (2007) used a grounded theory approach in studying how social support affects motivation for those with spinal cord injury. The participants were 13 women with spinal cord injuries, ages 25 to 61. The authors described the data collection as ". . . using repeated in-depth interviews and field notes. The first interview focused on how the women perceived the importance of the current social support from their social network members. The interview consisted of open-ended questions, and field notes were taken after the interview" (p. 24). The researchers went on to describe their procedures using grounded theory: "The interview data were analyzed using a grounded theory approach. . . . Grounded theory was chosen because it uses an interactional approach and contributes to an improved understanding of relationships and interactions between individuals" (p. 24). The interactional approach allows for discovery of the more abstract categories and elements of the situation, or the broader categories of support and motivation.

Phenomenological

A third method of conducting qualitative research is through a phenomenological approach. Willig (2001) noted that the phenomenological approach was developed by Husserl in the early 1900s. The focus of the phenomenological approach is to understand how humans develop a way of knowing the world. What is the human perception of events or things? It is focused on the perceptual phenomena of the world or an event. The intent is to describe phenomena as they occur. In essence, the phenomenological researcher attempts to understand an individual's personal perspective (his or her feelings and reactions) to events under study. A phenomenological method of research is particularly helpful when a researcher wants to identify relevant issues and concepts in the context of a particular event, and possibly conduct quantitative research or other types of qualitative research to further understand the event.

Brunelle, Cousineau, and Brochu (2005) used a phenomenological approach to study youth perceptions of their juvenile drug use. The purpose of the study is described as follows: "Our study has the particularity of focusing on the processes of juvenile deviance, specifically drug use and delinquency, from a phenomenological point of view" (p. 722). The researchers further describe the methods of their study:

> In keeping with the study's phenomenological character, a qualitative approach was used. It has already been established that this type of approach offers a better understanding of the specificity and complexity of the processes at work by providing an insider's point of view. The actual data collection is described as "Data were collected using the autobiographical life account method. . . . Beginning with a very open-ended instruction, this method leaves

room for participants to deliver their accounts spontaneously and allows them to lead the interview." Life accounts are usually incomplete because participants can omit, voluntarily or not, certain aspects of their lives or their interpretations. Phenomenology focuses on the social actors' (conscious) reading of their own realities. (p. 723)

As the researchers noted, the process of the phenomenological approach is to understand the perceptions and realities of the participants from their point of view.

Historical

Historical research is a fourth method of conducting qualitative research, the purpose of which is to systematically understand past events and phenomena to obtain a clearer understanding of current issues. Historical research may involve the use of systematic methods, such as diaries, oral records, and relics (Gall, et al., 1996). Gall, et al. (1996) proposed these steps in historical research: (a) define the problem or develop a hypothesis, (b) identify potential sources of historical data, (c) evaluate the historical sources, and (d) report and summarize results.

Morawski (1992) provided an example of historical research when she studied the place of introductory textbooks in American psychology. She addressed the following questions in her investigation:

Because so little historical appraisal has been done on the topic, it is difficult to assess the function of psychological textbooks. Are they significant artifacts of psychology's place in American culture, or are they the products of ill-conceived educational programs, financial desires, or the discipline's efforts to fit itself into social institutions? Have they made a difference to the discipline or to people's lives, and, if so in what ways? What makes an introductory text, and how has the literary genre evolved over the last century? These questions guided my historical study of introductory textbooks, a study that progressively raised new questions about his ubiquitous yet mysterious literary form. (p. 162)

Her historical study of early psychology textbooks was accomplished through a focus on textual strategies used by the authors. Morawski defined the problems of interest in her research questions. She focused on a specific time period, the late 1800s and early 1900s, and the introductory psychology textbooks written at that time, and described the texts she reviewed (p. 166). Finally, she summarized her findings and attempted to make conclusions. For example, she stated in her summary: ". . . by examining psychologists' work, such as textbooks, we can see more closely the macro- and micropolitics of transforming human welfare" (p. 168). As an aside, it is interesting to note the language used by researchers based on their particular approach. Morawski stated, "My sojourn into this realm of deprecated relics necessarily required a mapping of the literary terrain and compilation of a bibliography" (p. 162). The use of the word *relics* is informative as to the approach used by the researcher.

Summary

Qualitative research provides the researcher with opportunities to study phenomena, events, and experiences in great detail and in a more natural way. Additionally, qualitative methods allow for flexibility in addressing the needs of the situation: The researcher can adjust his or her focus and approach to meet the characteristics of the situation. There has been considerable debate about the validity of conducting research based on qualitative methods, and various attempts have been made to remove some of the identified concerns (Onwuegbuzie & Leech, 2005).

Investigators using qualitative research methods have developed systematic categories for data collection, such as the categories of relationship and groups. Additionally, specific methods or traditions for research procedures have been identified for those conducting qualitative research. There clearly has been an increase in qualitative research reported in the professional literature in counseling and education. In subsequent chapters, there will be examples of qualitative research and the identification of relevant questions to address in analyzing and evaluating such research.

6

Mixed Methods Research

The previous two chapters have addressed quantitative and qualitative research methods. You may have gotten the impression that these two methods are totally exclusive and are never "mixed." However, recently there have been efforts to identify the commonalities and use the strengths of each (Castro & Coe, 2007; Clark & Creswell, 2008; Curlette, 2006; Todd, Nerlich, McKeown, & Clarke, 2004). The integration and mixing of qualitative and quantitative methods have not been easy. In fact, many researchers have noted that discussions of which method is "best" have resulted in philosophical "wars" (Tashakkori & Teddlie, 2008).

In this chapter, I want to give a brief historical overview of the development of mixed methods research. Second, I want to discuss several proposed paradigms for mixed methods. Third, there will be a discussion of the use of triangulation in mixed methods, which is a key component of the mixed methods research paradigm. We will also examine examples of several research studies that employed mixed methods.

History of Mixed Methods Research

The history of mixed methods probably needs to start with a review how both quantitative and qualitative methods developed as paradigms for research. Before I go into the history of mixed methods, I want to discuss the definition of a paradigm, since the traditions of qualitative and quantitative research are founded on paradigms of research. Tashakkori and Teddlie (2008) defined a research paradigm as "the worldviews or belief systems that guide researchers" (p. 7).

In terms of the earlier history of quantitative methods or research paradigms, quantitative research originated out of experimental psychology from the late 1800s (Todd, Nerlich, McKeown, & Clarke, 2004). Such early research was based on data collection at the individual level or single case, and quantitative methods were introduced when more advanced statistical methods were introduced that allowed for aggregating data (Todd, et al., 2004). Quantitative research developed as a positivist paradigm. Lincoln and Guba (1985) identified several characteristics of a positivist research paradigm. One characteristic concerns the nature of reality. A positivist paradigm is based on the view that there is one reality (Lincoln & Guba, 1985). As Lincoln and Guba (1985) stated, "The basic belief system of positivism is rooted in a realist ontology, that is, the belief that there exists a reality out there, driven by immutable natural laws" (p. 19). A second characteristic, according to Lincoln and Guba (1985), is that research and inquiry are not based on any personal values. Another characteristic is that positivism holds that generalizations may be made across situations and contexts rather easily (Lincoln & Guba, 1985). There is a linear relationship between the antecedents to events and the consequences or outcomes, a Newtonian-Cartesian model (Lincoln & Guba, 1985). Todd, Nerlich, McKeown, & Clarke (2004) suggested another characteristic, namely that there is deductive logic, progressing from the general to the specific in focus. During the 1950s and 1960s, the positivist paradigm and tradition became less accepted, and the post-positivist paradigm began to replace it. Post-positivism is a variation of positivism but is based on critical realism (Guba, 1990). The post-positivist position holds that research can be influenced by the personal values of researchers and that reality is constructed, not a unitary reality (Todd, et al., 2004). Objectivity in a post-positivism paradigm is still valued, and it is believed that one may not obtain total objectivity but that one can strive to achieve it by using a critical perspective (Guba, 1990).

The qualitative research paradigm can be traced back to the social constructionists of the early 1900s (Tashakkori & Teddlie, 2008). The characteristics of qualitative research are almost directly the opposite of those from the positivist paradigm. Qualitative researchers hold that there are potentially a number of different constructed realities and that information is value-laden, that is, the researcher interprets data from a personal perspective. Another characteristic of the qualitative research paradigm is that one cannot easily differentiate the cause-and-effect relationship between variables. Last, the qualitative research paradigm uses an inductive logic view, and the intent is to interpret from the specific to the general (Tashakkori & Teddlie, 2008).

One can see from the cited characteristics that these views did not hold promise for bringing together these two different research paradigms. Tashakkori and Teddlie (2008) describe the attempts by different researchers to criticize the other view. This resulted in the paradigm "wars," or debates over which research tradition, quantitative or qualitative, was better. Tashakkori and Teddlie (2008) provide a clear sequence of the evolution of research methodology approaches since the early 1900s. The first period they characterized as the Purist Era because both qualitative and quantitative researchers advanced their view as being the better approach. This initial period lasted from the early 1900s to the 1950s and 1960s. The second period, Period II, according to Tashakkori and Teddlie (2008), started in the 1960s and extended until the 1980s. The focus of this period was a beginning attempt to find commonalities between the research paradigms and to begin to use mixed methods. The research designs were hypothetically viewed as being equal, and the result was models that used parallel methods simultaneously and sequentially—but equally. The 1990s saw a more advanced approach to mixing methods, with the use of different stages of implementing the methods. Based on the purpose of the study, there may be a single research paradigm used, e.g., qualitative, and later, based on a series of studies on the same topic, another method might be used, e.g., quantitative research. Tashakkori and Teddlie (1998) stated that the introduction of mixed methods research models essentially ended the significant debates and "wars" over which research method was superior.

Triangulation

Triangulation in mixed method research is defined in terms of the combined use of methods to investigate and understand the same phenomena (Jick, 2008). Essentially a researcher uses multiple methods to focus on particular phenomena or events. There are several approaches to triangulation, such as scaling, reliability, and convergent validation (Jick, 2008). Scaling is accomplished with the conversion of qualitative data into scaling outcomes or quantitative data. There needs to be some sort of approach for converting qualitative data into quantitative data. The next type of triangulation is reliability. Reliability involves the use of similar methods of data collection, or a within-methods approach, such as multiple reviewers interpreting the same data (Jick, 2008). In this approach, the researcher may use interview methods for both quantitative and qualitative methods. The quantitative approach would employ the use of an interview with well-defined questions and responses, and the qualitative approach may use a more open-ended interview. The last triangulation method is convergent validity (Jick, 2008). This approach involves the use of different but complementary methods of data collection across methods, for example, qualitative and quantitative. For example, a researcher may use a survey to collect data about marital satisfaction and combine the results with an interview.

Mixed Research Models

Six variations of mixed models have been identified: sequential explanatory, sequential exploratory, sequential transformative, concurrent triangulation, concurrent nested, and concurrent transformative (Creswell, Clark, Gutmann, & Hanson, 2008). The first model is the most straightforward and potentially the simplest. Creswell, et al. (2008) described the purpose of the sequential explanatory model as follows: "The purpose of the sequential explanatory design is typically to use qualitative results to assist in explaining and interpreting the findings of a primarily quantitative study" (p. 178). Essentially the researcher conducts a quantitative study and pursues clarification of results, particularly those that are somewhat unusual, by gathering data with qualitative methods. It provides additional explanation of the results in greater depth with the qualitative component.

Creswell, et al. (2008) noted that the purpose of using the sequential exploratory mixed methods design would be "to use quantitative data and results to assist in the interpretation of qualitative findings" (p. 181). The researcher starts with using qualitative methods, followed by quantitative. The results of this study are integrated during interpretation of results. Typically, this mixed model is used in the early stages of theory development (Creswell, et al., 2008).

A third mixed method design is the sequential transformative design (Creswell, et al., 2008). Creswell, et al. (2008) described the purpose of this design this way: "[A] sequential transformative design is to employ the methods that will best serve the theoretical perspective of the researcher" (p. 183). This design also utilizes two phases, but the sequence of the phases is open to the needs of the researcher. The researcher may decide to emphasize the needs of the participants, or the perspective of the participants in the study. The researcher decides which method may best give support to a perspective through his or her choice of sequencing the methods, qualitative or quantitative, for example, the researcher may decide to use the qualitative perspective first followed by the quantitative, or it could be reversed.

A fourth mixed methods model is the concurrent triangulation design (Creswell, et al., 2008). In this model, both methods are given equal emphasis and typically are introduced concurrently. The purpose of this model is to use the strengths of both methods and combine them in the interpretation phase, which promotes the triangulation of the data. Creswell et al. (2008) noted that this particular model is easily understood by most researchers because it has shown solid results.

A fifth mixed model is the concurrent nested design (Creswell, et al., 2008). This mixed method may be used to simultaneously collect data, but in more depth in certain areas. The researcher expects to find certain outcomes and wants to clarify the results through nesting one method within another, which is the predominant method. For example, a researcher wants to explore a particular theory through qualitative methods, but wants to understand a broader perspective about participants through quantitative data.

The last mixed method model is the concurrent transformative design (Creswell et al., 2008). This design allows the researcher to flexibly decide whether to use triangulation or nested approaches depending upon the purpose of the study, e.g., advocacy. Data is collected concurrently with both methods, and the researcher can combine the data for triangulation or decide to emphasize one method over another with the nested method (quantitative or qualitative) depending on the purpose and need of the participants and study. This model gives the researcher the flexibility to make the shift as needed, but the data is collected simultaneously.

Research Study Examples of Mixed Methods

There has been a significant increase in the number of published research articles using mixed methods research over the past 15 years (Castro & Coe, 2007; Kartalova-O'Doherty & Doherty, 2008; Messersmith, Garrett, Davis-Kean, Malanchuk, & Eccles, 2008; Strasser, Binswanger, Cerny, & Kesselring, 2007). Strasser, et al. (2007) conducted a study to understand the effects of eating related distress (ERD) for males with cancer and the effects on their partners. The researchers described their design thus: "Due to the paucity of research relating to concrete elements of ERD, we selected an approach using qualitative methodology supported by related quantitative data" (p. 130). The researchers used a concurrent nested design. Data was collected simultaneously, but the quantitative data were collected to support the qualitative methods.

Castro and Coe (2007) conducted a study with the intent of exploring beliefs and attitudes among rural women in regard to the use of alcohol during pregnancy. They were particularly interested in understanding how traditions, family, and rural lifestyle impacted the use of alcohol during pregnancy. The researchers employed a mixed methods research design. The researchers described their concurrent triangulation design:

> Figure 1 presents a paradigm for an integrative mixed-methods approach to such research. This integrative process begins with conceptualizing information as research evidence, which can take the form of verbal text narrative evidence (qualitative) or numeric data evidence (quantitative). Based on theory, a core construct (e.g. traditionalism) can be featured as a central concept examined under each of six stages within a parallel process that facilitates data conversions (e.g. axial coding) to encode thematic categories into numeric thematic variables.
>
> The greater the qualitative-quantitative parallelism in the study design and its implementation, the easier it is to compare and contrast textual and numeric forms of evidence in an integrative manner. (p. 270)

The researchers give a good example of a concurrent triangulation design with a focus on a parallel process of data collection with equal emphasis given to each method.

Summary

The development of the mixed methods research paradigm has provided a bridge between qualitative and quantitative research methods. The two traditions have had significant differences over the past 100 years. Recent efforts to develop systematic mixed methods designs have led to more integration of the approaches and potentially better research outcomes and utility using the strengths of each paradigm and tradition.

7

Evidence-Based Research Methods

Counseling and education are both practitioner based and involve professional preparation. Key in the preparation of the counseling and educational professional is the exposure to and training in research, as has been discussed in this book. Recently there has been a greater emphasis on linking practice and outcomes. Political and social expectations have changed, and there is pressure for both counseling and educational institutions to show how effective their activities are. In fact, the No Child Left Behind Act (NCLB) requires educational professionals to utilize research-based evidence in their practice (Odom, Brantlinger, Gersten, Horner, Thompson, & Harris, 2005). Evidence-based practice (EBP) is an attempt to address the concern over demonstrating effectiveness. Evidence-based practice originated within medicine and health care (Sackett, Straus, Richardson, Rosenberg, & Haynes, 2000). It has expanded to include counseling, psychology, business, and education (American Psychological Association Presidential Task Force on Evidence-Based Practice, 2006; Rousseau & McCarthy, 2007; Pring & Thomas, 2004). The benefits and arguments of evidence-based practice have been identified (Kettlewell, 2004). Kettlewell (2004) suggested that one benefit is that "evidence-based treatments (EBT) provide guidance to better serve our patients or clients" (p. 190). He points out that most people expect their health care professional to provide the best known treatment. A second argument for using EBT/EBP, according to Kettlewell (2004) is as follows: "Using the scientific approach to evaluate treatment is the best way to advance our knowledge so that we can provide even better care in the future" (p. 190). Developing a fund of information about best practices enhances the status of the field. Another rationale for using EBT/EBP cited by Kettlewell (2004) is that ". . . we need to use wisely the limited resources for mental health services" (p. 190). Currently, society and politicians want evidence about outcomes in making funding decisions. An evidence-based practice approach can provide opportunity to educate these constituencies about the effectiveness of the practices. A fourth argument presented by Kettlewell (2004) for using EBT/EBP is as follows: "We have treatments that work and most practitioners do not use them" (p. 190). Whether in education or counseling, practitioners have a tendency not to use the research literature to guide their practice, but make decisions based upon personal beliefs and values. Providing clarity about the effectiveness of practice can be passed along to improve outcomes. A final argument for using EBT/EBP is founded on the question: "Is there a better alternative than to use science to guide practice?" (p. 191). Our society values science and the benefits that science has provided, and this provides credibility to EBT/EBP. The alternative is shifting the focus to making education and counseling an art, or based upon one's personal experience. This may be similar to thinking about training in trades, where one simply learns a trade through observing and working with a master practitioner. Certainly this had its benefits, but the limitations are that education and counseling are much more complex than learning a trade and therefore require more objectivity.

Definitions of Evidence-Based Practice

Several different definitions of evidence-based practice have been proposed (American Psychological Association Presidential Task Force on Evidence-Based Practice, 2006; Hunsley, 2007; Whaley & David, 2007). As previously mentioned, EBP originated in medicine. One of the earliest definitions of EBP is from medicine. Mayer (2004) defined EBP as ". . . the conscientious, explicit, and judicious use of the best evidence in making decisions about the care of individual patients" (p. 9). The American Psychological Association Presidential Task Force on Evidence-Based Practice (2006) defined EBP and concluded it is ". . . the integration of the best available research with clinical expertise in the context of patient characteristics, culture, and preferences" (p. 273). Common among these definitions are statements about the best available research and thoughtfulness in selecting the practices to be used. The interesting point about the use of EBP is the perspective that, in medicine, previously a physician would consult a senior, more experienced physician for answers to problems. The EBP approach does not exclude the use of this approach but encourages the use of more scientific evidence in decision making.

Steps in Evidence-Based Practice

Mayer (2004) suggested six steps in the EBP approach. Step one is the development of a question that needs to be answered. Part of the issue with this question is the identification of the outcome desired. A second step is the review of the professional literature that is relevant and will give the professional the best information available. The third step is the identification of a study that most closely resembles the issue to be addressed and a review of the outcomes. The fourth step is an analysis and critique of the study to determine how useful it is. Step five is to determine how the study findings can be applied to the current situation. The last step is to evaluate the results of what was used in practice—was it successful?

Principles of Evidence-Based Practice

Rousseau and McCarthy (2007) proposed several principles in the use of EBP. The first principle is this: "Focus on principles where the science is clear" (p. 85). What are the basic principles of the discipline? For example, one set of basic principles in counseling involves findings about human development. A second principle stated by Rousseau and McCarthy (2007) is as follows: "Develop decision awareness in professional practice" (p. 87). The idea here is to focus awareness and be open to critiquing how one practices professionally. It is suggested that there is a sharing among colleagues in evaluating and critiquing practices (Rousseau & McCarthy, 2007). A third principle is the diagnosis of underlying factors, which are related to practice decisions (Rousseau & McCarthy, 2007). The basic premise here is that the practitioner develops questions designed to diagnose the problem or identify the problem to be addressed with EBP. One needs to understand that there is an issue with how students, clients, and others are functioning and determine whether something can be done to improve their functioning in the classroom (education) or in their lives (counseling). The next principle concerns the practitioner's understanding the context of the situation and adapting the knowledge to the setting (Rousseau & McCarthy, 2007). This may include developing an awareness of how to adapt the scientific knowledge to the context or situation based upon cultural or environmental issues. The fifth principle states that there should be EBP decision supports (Rousseau & McCarthy, 2000). For example, in schools it may make sense to discuss practices and EBP among teaching faculty on a regular basis. In counseling settings, it may be beneficial to regularly discuss among colleagues EBPs and how they have been tried in particular settings. The last principle is the ongoing acquisition of new information and ways to stay current in EBP (Rousseau & McCarthy, 2007). This may involve attending conferences on a regular basis and subscribing to professional journals.

Criticisms of Evidence-Based Practice

There has not been total acceptance of EBP, and there have been some critiques of the approach (Wampold, Goodheart, & Levant, 2007). Wampold, et al. (2007) suggested caution in using and interpreting evidence-based practice information. The caution centers on the view that not enough is known to suggest that there is evidence that can be used to guide practice. The authors point out that one may miss the importance of the subjective experience of counseling or therapy. Counseling has been called an art, and losing subjectivity of the experience may interfere with this aspect of the process (Nystul, 1999). Wampold, et al. (2007) pointed out that the evidence in psychology and counseling is not unambiguous: "Evidence is not data, nor is it truth" (p. 616). Several important questions arise with these criticisms. One question is, how much of the subjective aspect of counseling and/or education should be part of the practice? Professions have been identified and defined in terms of having a basis of knowledge (Weikel & Palmo, 1996). Despite the practices of counseling and education having a subjective component, both fields need to substantiate their practices on a basis of knowledge, and specifically a research basis. Another question is, what level or amount of evidence is needed to use evidence-based research in practice? What has been suggested is to select the best available evidence and use it, but most important, evaluate the impact or effect.

Examples of Evidence-Based Practice

There have been a number of writings and summaries of evidence-based practice focusing on specific issues in counseling and education (Gowers, 2006; Kaiser, 2007; Stenhoff & Lignugaris-Kraft, 2007). Gowers (2006) provides evidence-based practice information for counseling adolescents with eating disorders using Cognitive Behavioral Therapy. It is interesting to note that Gowers (2006) states that the research evidence for the treatment of bulimia nervosa using Cognitive Behavioral Therapy is relatively good, and it is considered to be the "gold standard treatment" for this condition. However, he notes that the research evidence for using Cognitive Behavioral Therapy with anorexia nervosa is less clear, and there needs to be further research before this can be considered the gold standard. What this means for practitioners using evidence-based practice is that there needs to be a careful investigation into what methods work in what situations. This does not mean that one cannot use a particular intervention, particularly if there is no other "gold standard" available. It is where there is a commonly accepted and well-documented intervention or approach that the educator or counselor should choose the best available one and use it.

Kaiser (2007) reviewed the evidence-based practice for addressing challenging behaviors in early childhood interventions. For example, Kaiser noted that ". . . training parents to implement systematic behavioral interventions is an important example of a strategy in which there is sufficient research for it to be regarded as an evidence-based practice" (p. 116). Despite there being evidence that training parents is supported through research, the actual training of parents and methods to do so are not well developed. She noted that this area of research and evidence needed further study before conclusions could be made about EBP in training parents.

Stenhoff and Lignugaris-Kraft (2007) provide a review of peer tutoring with students with mild disabilities in secondary schools. They noted that peer tutoring is designed to help students with educational learning through other, more advanced students or peers. Stenhoff and Lignugaris-Kraft (2007) reviewed four different types of peer tutoring for effectiveness based on an EBP approach. These tutoring models included reverse-role, heterogeneous, homogeneous, and cross-age. Of the four tutoring models, only the heterogeneous approach was supported through EBP. The other three did not have sufficient research support to include in EBP at this point. Essentially what this means is that a practitioner should likely use a heterogeneous tutoring approach rather than any of the other three. Additionally, researchers may continue to gather evidence on the efficacy of the other three methods. Stenhoff and Lignugaris-Kraft (2007) provide a good example of how EBP can be used by practitioners, whereby they clearly identify the "gold standard" of practice in a particular area and demonstrate the criteria for their evaluation.

Kamps & Abbott (2007) used evidence-based practice to inform decision making on the use of small-group reading instructions for English language learners in elementary grades. First, these researchers identify the specific reading skills that have been found to be essential for learning to read. They further noted that a systematic approach to teaching students learning to read is important. According to Kamps & Abbott (2007), evidence-based research also has demonstrated that the instructional environment and the instructional intensity and duration affect learning outcomes. So how long learning instruction occurs and the frequency of learning instruction impact outcomes or student learning (reading instruction for English language learners).

Baban and Craciun (2007) provided a comprehensive overview of research and EBP research on changing health-risk behavior. Examples of health-risk behaviors included smoking, sexual behavior, alcohol abuse, eating habits, screening behaviors, and medication adherence. They discussed different approaches to changing health-risk behavior, such as the Health Action Process Approach and the Transtheoretical Model of Change approach. The authors provide a table outlining the approaches with various health-risk behaviors and the effectiveness of each, based upon research outcomes. For example, the Transtheoretical Model of Change approach was cited as being effective with smoking, alcohol abuse, and screening behaviors. However, it is not cited as effective with sexual behavior or with medication adherence. There could be several reasons it was not found to be effective; for example, there may not be enough research to support a conclusion. Baban and Craciun (2007) provided an interesting view of the use of EBP with linking theories and approaches to specific conditions.

Summary

The pressure for education and counseling to be grounded in evidence-based practice has increased with the passage of federal legislation, such as NCLB and societal requirements and expectations for documented effects. This may be considered good news for these professions because it suggests that we are arriving at a point that there is beginning to be adequate research to support the use of certain interventions and strategies. Such an approach encourages more research to build support for particular interventions or activities. Also, the use of EBP provides the practitioner with information about what does not work in certain circumstances or conditions. The use of evidence-based practice in education (Odom, et al., 2005) and counseling (Gowers, 2006) is increasing and provides practitioners with criteria to use when engaging in their professional practices. Increasing high-quality research in education and counseling will continue to give these professionals information needed to be effective and provide the best services possible.

8

Ethics and Research

This chapter involves a discussion of ethics and research. An important question is: Why study ethics and research? A researcher must be aware of how ethical his or her procedures are in conducting research. There are federal laws that protect human subjects against potentially harmful research practices. However, this book is designed to prepare you to be a thoughtful consumer of research. What difference does it make to consider ethical issues in the articles you read in the professional literature? The answers to these questions are the foci of this chapter.

The purpose of this chapter is twofold: first, to introduce you to ethical guidelines helpful in understanding ethics and research; second, and more important for you as a practitioner, to provide a method of evaluating the ethics of a research design as ethics apply to your use in actual practice of the information from the research. Therefore, this chapter includes (a) discussion of basic principles that may be used to consider and understand ethics and research, (b) a foundation and set of criteria for evaluating research reported in the literature, with a particular focus on the ethics of the research design as the results apply to using the information in actual practice, and (c) a discussion of examples from the current literature, which will illustrate how to use the criteria presented earlier in evaluating research for violations and problems from an ethical perspective for the practitioner in counseling and education.

Ethical Principles and Guidelines

When one considers ethical issues in research, it is helpful to conceptualize the guidelines available in the form of an inverted triangle (see Figure 8.1). At the top of the inverted triangle are general theories of ethics, and the space represents the number of situations that can be addressed with the theories. Conversely, the space may also represent the amount of ambiguity in decision making because there is not the specific clarity that some of the other guides provide. Next are general principles such as autonomy, nonmaleficence, and so on. These general principles allow for a somewhat clearer interpretation than the general theories but do not allow the same number of situations to be addressed. The third type of guide is the professional ethical code, such as that of the American Psychological Association (APA) or the American Counseling Association (ACA). As we move down the triangle with the codes of ethics there is an increased clarity in how and when to use the guidelines and a decrease in the number of situations to which they can be applied. Finally, at the bottom of the triangle are laws and federal or state statutes and regulations. These are the most specific and clear-cut guides for ethical decision making, but they apply to (generally) the fewest situations and circumstances.

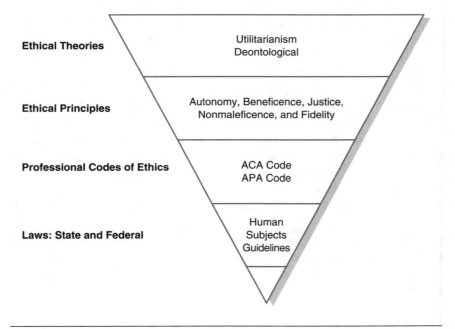

Figure 8.1 Ethical Guidelines for Research

Starting at the top of the triangle, you can see that two major types of theories have been proposed in ethical decision making: utilitarian and deontological approaches (Beauchamp & Childress, 2001). There are a number of other ethical theories that could be included in ethical decision making (Houser, Wilcenski, & Ham, 2006). However, this book is not solely focused on ethics, so I will just cover these two broad theories (utilitarian and deontological). Beauchamp and Childress (2001) defined utilitarian theories in terms of the end justifying or legitimizing the means and the promotion of the greatest good for the greatest number of people. Certainly, ethical decision making can be applied to a great number of situations, but how to proceed is not that clear. Beauchamp and Childress (2001) defined the deontological approach in terms of decisions about right and wrong. There are rules or principles of right and wrong. For example, one rule within this theory is the Golden Rule (treat others as you would like to be treated) that guides actions (Beauchamp & Childress, 2001). In this theory, the outcome is less important than following the rule or principle.

The next level of ethical guidelines is that of general principles. These include autonomy, beneficence, nonmaleficence, justice, and fidelity (Beauchamp & Childress, 2001). Autonomy, according to Beauchamp and Childress, involves the concept of self-rule and self-choice. Self-choice includes full disclosure of information, which makes it possible to make an informed choice. Beneficence refers to doing what is best for another or looking out for another, whereas nonmaleficence is the complementary to beneficence and concerns doing no intentional harm. Justice involves the fair distribution of resources. Finally, fidelity refers to keeping one's promise or commitment (Beauchamp & Childress, 2001).

The next level of ethical guidelines is that of professional codes of ethics (American Counseling Association, 2005; American Psychological Association, 2003). The ethical codes for the ACA address the following areas, under research: (a) research responsibilities of the counselor, (b) the importance of informed consent, (c) reporting of results, and (d) issues of publication. For example, in obtaining informed consent for research purposes, counselors must use language that is clear and understandable to participants. There are exceptions, when deception is required in a study, but deception is used only when no other methods are available. The APA ethical codes address (a) informed consent, (b) communication of risks possible when participating in research, (c) research with special populations, (d) providing participants with results of a study, (e) use of deception, (f) minimizing the invasiveness of data gathering methods, (g) socially sensitive research, and (h) protection for withdrawing from research.

Finally, there are ethical guides that address specific procedures for the protection of human subjects (Office of Protection from Research Risks [OPRR], 1993). Federal legislation (OPRR, 1993) requires that investigators who are associated with institutions that receive federal funds must submit their studies to an extensive review by peers before the studies can be conducted. The primary focus is on ensuring that adequate protections for research subjects are in place. The peer review is done through a formally established institutional body, the Human Subjects Institutional Review Board (IRB). Guidelines for reviewing research proposals include requirements for informed consent, an evaluation of risks and benefits, and confidentiality. The IRB must evaluate the risks as being reasonable in relation to anticipated benefits.

Guidelines for Evaluating the Research Literature

As has been shown, there are several approaches and guides for interpreting ethical issues in counseling research, but which methods are most useful for you as a consumer of research? The answer must be based on the focus and purpose you have. Researchers are most concerned with the protection of the human subjects used in their studies; therefore, the federal guidelines and professional codes addressing the protection of human subjects are most relevant. However, consumers of research are interested in the ethics of research that focuses on interpreting results, and the implications for those for whom they provide services in the practice of their professions.

Gostin (1991) suggested guidelines to consider when conducting and applying research to populations ("population research"). He defined population research as ". . . all research and practice, performed on, or which affects groups of people or populations" (p. 192). Gostin linked the application of ethical principles to populations and stated:

> Ethical principles applied to larger groups of people or populations are designed to protect the human dignity, integrity, self determination, confidentiality, rights, and health of populations and the people comprising them. The kinds of social groupings encompassed in this definition include communities, cultures, social orders, and other minorities. (p. 191)

The concern for practitioners providing counseling and educational services is that research results must be interpreted and implemented based on ethical guides that protect the populations we serve. Several of the previous ethical guides are pertinent to understanding and interpreting counseling research. The ethical principle of nonmaleficence states, "Do no harm." Do no harm can be interpreted in regard to population research based on the results and conclusions from research studies as to whether the outcomes harm the welfare of the populations studied. As Gostin (1991) stated, this means protecting the dignity, integrity, and health of the populations. Neither the APA nor the ACA includes ethical codes that specifically address population research ethics. The focus of professional codes has been on the ethical treatment of research participants, and not so much on the ethics of population research. A question that consumers of research want to ask in reviewing research is this: What negative implications or harm is possible, based on the results from a particular study on the population of interest? Harm may include, as Gostin noted, an effect on the population's dignity, rights, integrity, and/or self-esteem.

A second ethical consideration in regard to population research can be found in the general ethical principle of beneficence. The question here is, What are the possible benefits of the research results for the population? Certainly in our professional capacity we are most concerned with research results that will be useful to those receiving counseling and educational services.

A third ethical guide that is applicable to population research is justice and the fair distribution of research outcomes. A question based on this ethical principle is, Is the sample and population studied fairly representative of the general population that could benefit from the research results? More specifically, did the researcher or researchers present a reasonably clear argument for studying the population if the research was restricted to a particular group? Certainly we cannot expect that a researcher will be able to study every possible group because of cost and time, but the exclusion of certain groups from the benefit of research results may bring the ethics of a study into question. For example, the National Institutes of Health (NIH), which in part funds medical research, has historically approved mostly studies involving White males, to the general exclusion of women. Fortunately, this issue of justice and fairness in funding medical research has changed over the past several years, and NIH now requires researchers to justify the sole use of males in a study (National Institutes of Health, 1994).

A restatement of the questions that consumers of counseling and education research might ask to determine the ethical quality of research published in professional journals could include:

1. What possible negative implications can be applied or harm can come to a population due to the results of a particular study?

2. What are the possible benefits of the research results for the population?

3. Are the sample and population studied fairly representative of the general population that could benefit from the research results? More specifically, did the researcher or researchers present a reasonably clear argument for studying the population, if the study was restricted to a particular group?

Evaluation of Research Presented in the Professional Literature

To illustrate the practical application of ethics and counseling research literature, there will be application of several studies to these three questions, some of which are well known to health and the social sciences.

Tuskegee Syphilis Study

The Tuskegee Syphilis Study was intended to follow the natural course of syphilis, specifically in African American males. The study spanned 40 years, beginning in 1932 and ending in 1972. It was originally hypothesized that there were differences by race in the natural progression of syphilis (Thomas & Quinn, 1991). The study was designed to last for 6 to 9 months and was conducted in Macon, Alabama. The Alabama state health officer solicited assurance from the United States Public Health Service (USPHS) that participants would eventually receive treatment (Thomas & Quinn, 1991). However, the participants in this study never received treatment, even though treatment was available as early as 1943, when the USPHS began administering penicillin as a treatment for syphilis across the country. One reason given for not providing treatment was that of the attitudes of the officials who were overseeing the study. For example, Dr. John Heller, Director of the Division of Venereal Diseases, stated that: "the men's status did not warrant ethical debate, they were subjects not patients, clinical material, not sick people" (Jones, 1981, p. 179).

The Tuskegee study was ended in 1972 when it became public that these men had had standard, effective medical treatment withheld. Numerous other reasons were cited for the treatment these men received, and many centered on the attitudes of the medical community toward those of different races, particularly African Americans (Gamble, 1993; Thomas & Quinn, 1991). For example, Gamble (1993) stated that certain assumptions about African Americans led to the unethical treatment of subjects in this study, such as beliefs that African Americans are promiscuous, lustful, and generally do not seek out medical treatment. Consequently, not providing medical treatment was justified in the minds of the study officials. It has been estimated that 28 to 100 of the participants died as a consequence of their untreated syphilis (Gamble, 1993).

The first question to address concerns whether there are any negative implications based on the way the study was conducted and the results obtained for the population. Gamble (1993) described a legacy of mistrust among African Americans toward medical research. She stated: "The Tuskegee Syphilis Study symbolizes for many African Americans the racism that pervades American institutions including the medical profession" (p. 37). Thomas and Quinn (1991) suggested that the Tuskegee Syphilis Study has resulted in such distrust of the medical profession that it hampers acquired immunodeficiency syndrome (AIDS) education and acceptance of treatment among African Americans. Mason (2005) stated: "Historically, African Americans have resisted participation in clinical trials and other research projects because of distrust of the mostly white research establishment" (p. 296). It would not be a stretch to conclude that the effects of this study have had an negative impact on the population of the study, African American males, and their attitudes toward seeking medical treatment.

Are there any potential benefits from this study for the population? It is difficult to identify any. I am not aware of any special knowledge gained from the results that has benefited the treatment practices for syphilis in African American males. One of the few benefits may be broader, in that the exposure of Tuskegee Syphilis Study to Congress resulted in improved oversight of human subject research by the federal government.

The third question we are interested in addressing is, Is there a clear argument for using this particular population for the study? Initially there was speculation in the medical literature on racial differences in the natural course of syphilis (Thomas & Quinn, 1991), but there was no attempt to compare the target group with other racial groups, such as Caucasian males. Gamble (1993) has noted that African Americans historically have been considered by the medical and scientific community to be inferior and, consequently, good sources for medical experimentation. Gamble (1993) cited physicians' use of Black women for medical experimentation during the late 1800s, prior to the use of treatments for White women.

In summary, it appears that the Tuskegee Syphilis Study is of questionable ethical quality when population research is considered. There appear to be no benefits to the population from the study, and in fact, the study appears to have harmed the population, in this case African American males, for example, the distrust of the medical profession and seeking necessary medical treatment.

Milgram Study

A classic study in psychology that has received significant criticism over violations of ethics is the Milgram study on obedience (Baumrind, 1964; Kelman 1967; Milgram, 1963). Milgram (1974) described the aim of the study as ". . . to find when and how people would defy authority in the face of a clear moral imperative" (pp. 3–4). The methods involved the use of deception with the subject involved. Subjects were led to believe by the experiment that they were participating in a learning study. Subjects were requested to train or teach another through the systematic use of electrical shock. In reality, the learner was an actor, who did not actually receive a shock. The "teacher" in this experiment (the actual subject) was instructed to administer an electrical shock whenever the learner responded with an incorrect answer. With each incorrect answer, the teacher was informed that he should increase the intensity of the shock. The electrical shocks were presented on a board to the teacher, starting at 15 volts and rising to 450 volts at 14-volt intervals. Also, there were designations on the shock board indicating slight shock to "danger: severe shock" (Milgram, 1963). Milgram described his experiments with obedience in the following way:

> The man receiving the shock, begins to indicate he is experiencing discomfort. At 75 volts, the "learner" grunts. At 120 volts he complains verbally; at 150 he demands to be released from the experiment. His protests continue as the shock escalate, growing increasingly vehement and emotional. At 285 volts his response can only be described as an agonized scream. (p. 4)

When the teacher (subject) expressed reluctance at continuing with the experiment, the investigator urged him to complete the study and administer up to the maximum shock in the severe range (Milgram, 1963).

Milgram (1963) noted subjects' (teachers') behaviors; several of the initial study's participants exhibited unusual reactions: ". . . nervous laughter and smiling. . . . Full-blown, uncontrollable seizures were observed in 3 subjects" (p. 375). Additionally, Milgram described in detail one subject's reaction: ". . . initially [this subject was a] poised businessman . . . smiling and confident. Within 20 minutes he was reduced to a twitching, stuttering wreck, who was rapidly approaching a point of nervous collapse" (p. 377).

A key consideration in evaluating this study from a consumer's perspective is the use of deception. To answer the first question of harm to the population, I want to cite studies on the use of deception. Sharpe, Adair, and Roese (1992) found that subjects participating in psychological research expressed more negative views of psychological research after participation. Studies like Milgram's may contribute to mistrust in participating in psychological research, or may influence participation in future research. Conversely, it is difficult to find more concrete negative effects on the population as a consequence of these results and research methods being published. The American Psychological Association Code of Ethics (2003) states:

> Deception in Research (a) Psychologists do not conduct a study involving deception unless they have determined that the use of deceptive techniques is justified by the study's significant prospective scientific, educational, or applied value and that effective nondeceptive alternative procedures are not feasible. (APA Code 8.07a)

A possible benefit to the population is an understanding and realization of the vulnerability of humans in reacting to and complying with authority. Milgram's initial interest in studying obedience centered on compliance with authority and participation in aggressive acts, like those conducted by some Germans during World War II. These results may provide insights into why humans may engage in horrendous acts against others, and, consequently, prevention measures may be developed.

The population studied was obtained from several universities and generally involved males. The use of the specific subjects in the study was not clearly defended in the introduction. What effect would it have had on the results to have included subjects not affiliated with a university? However, there does not seem to have been bias toward a particular group.

Overall, the Milgram study provides somewhat mixed results for ethical violations affecting the population. The study may more likely have violated the rights of participants than affected the intended population of the study.

Other Studies

Pandiani, Banks, and Schacht (2001) conducted a study addressing the effects of various children's services on outcomes like incarceration, hospitalization, and pregnancy among young adults. Participants were those over 17 who were receiving one of three services: special education, child protection and juvenile justice, and mental health services. The researchers found that those young males who received either child protection and juvenile justice and special education services had higher incarceration rates than those receiving mental health services and those not having involvement with any of the identified services. Also, those females who received state child protection and juvenile justice services had higher rates of pregnancy than those receiving mental health services or special education. This was a longitudinal study and thus had information on the long-term effects of services on the outcomes of young adults. These findings allow for an interpretation of the impact on the population, or a review of ethics for population research.

The first question is whether there is any possible harm to the population. In the study presented here, the population is those receiving state child services such as special education, mental health services, or child protection or juvenile justice. What potential impact do the study results have on the reputation or dignity of the population? The results suggest that those males receiving special education and child protection and juvenile justice are more likely to be involved with the criminal justice system. One might interpret that someone going through these systems is more inclined to engage in criminal activities.

The benefit of the results from this study for the population is that such an at-risk group can be systematically addressed. Interventions can be focused on this population in an effort to change the outcomes of incarceration or pregnancy. Participants were primarily White and from a specific region, the New England area, and the results do not provide information on other populations, such as those from racial groups other than Caucasian.

In another study, Blanton and Dagenais (2007) investigated whether those with language skills deficits had more incidents of criminal behavior and court involvement compared to those who did not have language skills deficits. They included males and females who were either court involved or not court involved. Also, they categorized them as having language impairments or not. The authors provide a review of the literature, which noted that language acquisition is a critical issue during preschool years and the development of language. The authors found that language problems in children predicted later male criminal activity. The first question to address ethically is whether these results have a negative impact on or harm the population, young males with language problems. Certainly if an educator working with young males read these article results, he or she would need to carefully understand the implications and that not every male with a language disorder is going to engage in criminal activity as he gets older. The ethical use and interpretation of these results is that young males with language disorders are more likely to engage in criminal activities in later life, but it is not an absolute, and these students should not be treated differently, e.g., not be trusted, because they may engage in criminal behavior in the future. The potential positive use of the outcomes from this study is that educators and school personnel could target interventions to help young males, first with their language disorders and secondly to develop interventions to address possible future criminal behavior and encourage prosocial behavior. The study was conducted in Alabama, and only Caucasian and African American youth were included. Latino, Asian, Native American, and other racial groups could potentially benefit from being studied in this area.

Summary

As a consumer of research, it is important to consider ethical principles in interpreting and applying study results from population research. Three ethical principles seem particularly relevant: nonmaleficence, beneficence, and justice. Nonmaleficence concerns determining whether the results of a study, when interpreted and implemented, may harm the population. This includes how those interpreting the results use the results.

Beneficence is almost diametrically opposed to nonmaleficence and concerns whether study results benefit a population when implemented and made public. Researchers have the intention of finding results that benefit others, particularly in counseling and education. However, those using research results need to consider the benefits and how they can best be applied in practice. Finally, justice concerns the extent to which study results may be applied to all those in the population of interest, and not just a select group.

Exercises

Directions: Locate an article in the professional literature addressing a topic you are interested in exploring. Evaluate ethics and population research based on the questions addressed in this chapter. Try to explain and justify your answers based on specific examples from the article.

1. What are some possible negative implications that could be applied to the population, or harm that could come to it from the results of your chosen study?

2. What are the possible benefits of the research results for the population?

3. Are the sample and population studied fairly representative of the general population that could benefit from the research results? More specially, did the researcher or researchers present a reasonably clear argument for studying the population, if the study was restricted to a particular group?

II

Evaluating Articles in the Professional Literature

9

Evaluating the Literature Review

The previous chapters have provided you with basic concepts you need to begin to be an effective consumer of counseling and educational research. Chapters 9 through 15 are focused on ways to evaluate research published in professional journals. Students have frequently commented to me, after receiving instruction in evaluating research, how surprised they are at the limitations of studies reported in the professional literature. Generally they have accepted what was present in the professional literature as basic truths.

The methods and guidelines for evaluating professional journal articles are fairly detailed. At first the guidelines may seem tedious to use, but as with learning any new task, it becomes easier with practice. Certainly once you have acquired the knowledge and skills to be an effective consumer of counseling and educational research, you will not need to evaluate each article you read in such detail. The intention is that after in-depth practice you will be able to note areas of potential problems and focus on these more specifically, rather than on every single detail of the research article. It is important to remember that research with humans is complex, and *every* study will have some (or many) limitations. The purpose of developing a "critical eye" in reading and using research is to become a more effective consumer and user of research. Generally, no one error or limitation of a study should cause you to totally reject the findings. The evaluation approach suggested in this text is a guide for consumers and users of research. It may be used to systematically determine which components of a study are more valid and what needs to be accepted with caution.

A beginning point for evaluating a research article is the characteristics of a literature review. Guidelines and questions for evaluating counseling and educational research are discussed. Finally, examples are provided from the literature to illustrate how to use the guidelines to evaluate research.

The general purpose of the literature section is to provide an argument for conducting the study. Consequently, researchers attempt to systematically cite previous, related research to frame the problem dealt with in their own study. In addition, they attempt to identify any gaps in the current literature. Typically, primary sources (other research conducted on the topic and reported in the professional literature) are used to develop the argument. The researchers should present a rationale or identify the significance of their own research in light of how it will add to current knowledge. The literature review should be thorough and comprehensive enough to develop the argument for conducting the study. You may find that a literature review varies in length depending on the intent and purpose of the particular journal in which the study is published. The majority of journals encourage researchers to present a thorough and comprehensive argument for conducting a study. A few journals, particularly journals where brief reports are published, may not require, or even allow, a longer literature review. It is important to first identify whether an article is intended to be a "brief report" before engaging in your detailed analysis of the literature review.

Researchers typically conduct a study because they are interested in the topic. Also, how they frame the study is influenced by their personal views and expectations about the possible results. This seems a contradiction to the idea of objectivity in research, but a researcher typically does not conduct a study unless he or she has a particular interest, and potentially a particular hypothesis, in mind. Many researchers have commented that they conduct studies because of the interest the subjects hold for them. A researcher's interest could be influenced by some personal events that could slant the way the study is presented. Additionally, the study could be a follow-up to a previous study, and thus certain outcomes might be expected. Because of researcher expectations and personal experiences, it is important to note any biases in the literature review.

Even though anyone reading a study reported in a professional journal is generally familiar with the field, the researcher needs to define any new or relatively unknown concepts in the literature review. Another intent of those writing the literature review may be to describe new or common research methods in a particular area of study that may be of interest in the current reported study.

Guidelines and Questions for Evaluating Research

As mentioned earlier, the major purpose of the literature review is to develop an argument for conducting the study. Several related questions may be asked concerning this argument: (a) Do the researchers present *an adequate* rationale for conducting the study? (b) So what? Or a related question is, What difference will the study make to the fields of counseling or education?

As has been noted, science and research have an intent of pursuing objectivity, but researchers may potentially include personal biases in the construction of a study. A relevant question then is, Do the researchers present any potential biases in the literature review? For example, does the researcher cite only his or her own prior research? A related question is whether the researcher presents only one side of a theory or view. Generally an issue or research topic has more than one viewpoint.

Previously, it was suggested that the literature review should include relevant definitions and descriptions of unknown concepts. A question to address here may be, Are all important concepts clearly defined by the researchers?

Another area of concern is whether the literature is thorough and comprehensive enough to develop the argument for conducting the study. It is relevant to note whether important researchers and theorists are cited in the review. For example, if a researcher was addressing self-efficacy, he or she would want to acknowledge the works of Bandura (1977), who developed the concept. So the question to address may be, Is the literature review thorough and comprehensive?

Finally, the literature review should include a description of any new methods in a particular area of study that relate to the current study. The question to ask is, Do the researchers clearly describe previous methods that are relevant to understanding the purpose for conducting this study?

To review:

1. Do the researchers present *an adequate* rationale for conducting the study?

2. So what? or, What difference will the study make to the fields of counseling or education?

3. Is the literature review thorough and comprehensive?

4. Do the researchers demonstrate any potential biases in the literature review?

5. Are all important concepts clearly defined by the researchers?

6. Do the researchers clearly describe previous methods that are relevant to understanding the purpose for conducting this study?

Evaluation of Examples From the Research Literature

Study 1 Quantitative Research

Henderson, Rosen, and Mascaro (2007) studied the effectiveness of using mandalas in working with those with post-traumatic stress. The literature review is cited below:

The expression and disclosure of previously experienced traumatic events is associated with better subsequent physical and mental health (Esterling, L'Abate, Murray, & Pennebaker, 1999; Smyth & Helm, 2003).

Extensive attention has been given to the efficacy of written expression of traumatic events in promoting physical and psychological well-being and various studies have resulted in a body of research supporting a written disclosure paradigm (see Pennebaker, 1997a, 1997b for a review). According to this paradigm set forth by James Pennebaker, writing about traumatic or stressful events in an emotional way for as little as 15 minutes over 3 to 4 consecutive days brings about improvements in physical and mental health (Pennebaker & Seagal, 1999).

The principle of therapeutic exposure posits that repeated exposure to aversive conditioned stimuli leads to the extinguishment of negative emotions associated with such stimuli, resulting in beneficial outcomes (Foa & Rothbaum, 1998). Some researchers contend that written disclosure serves as a context in which individuals are repeatedly exposed to traumatic memories (i.e. exposure to aversive stimuli and the negative emotions associated with it), which allows for the gradual extinction of negative emotional associations across sessions (Kloss & Lisman, 20020; Pennebaker, 1997b; Sloan & Marx, 2004a, 2004b). This is theorized to be one of the mechanisms underlying the overall effectiveness of the written disclosure paradigm.

Another theory regarding the effectiveness of written disclosure on physical and mental health has to do with the cognitive changes associated with this type of writing. Once a meaningful and integrated narrative is formed, it is hypothesized that the traumatic event can then be summarized, stored, and allowed to become a nonthreatening memory rather than a ghost that chronically haunts consciousness, subsequently leading to a decrease in psychological distress (Msyth, True & Souto, 2001).

Although the innovative work of Pennebaker and other researchers has supported the utility of the written disclosure paradigm and the numerous benefits associated with the disclosure of trauma, the written disclosure paradigm has been found to be ineffective among individuals with disordered cognitive processes of relatively severe depression (Gidron, Peri, Onnonly, & Shaley, 1996; Stroebe, Stroebe, Schut, Zech, & van den Bout, 2002).

The vast majority of written disclosure studies involve only written expression; however, Judith Pizarro (2004) performed a recent study that examined whether art therapy was as effective as writing therapy in improving the outcomes of psychological and health measures.

Pizzarro sampled 41 participants using two experimental groups (expressive art therapy or writing therapy) and a control art condition.

Consistent with Pennebaker's findings, there was a significant decrease in social dysfunction within the writing group, however, the participants in the art groups did not have similar health benefits. Although the art groups did show a greater enjoyment of the experience, the researcher surmised "generating art" may not provide sufficient cognitive organization and therefore may not be able to provide the same positive health benefits as writing therapy (Pizarro, p. 10). A combination of the two was suggested in which writing could heal while art could make the process more enjoyable, thus increasing therapy compliance.

Rather than completely dismissing art therapy as an effective means of processing trauma, an artistic task that lends itself particularly well to the symbolic expression and disclosure of a traumatic event is mandala drawing.

A mandala, used as a meditative tool in various religions but most famously in Tibetan Buddhist [sic], is a circular design that is thought to promote psychological healing and integration when created by an individual. The use of the mandala as a therapeutic tool was first espoused by Carl Jung, who suggested that the act of drawing mandalas had a calming and healing effect on its creator while at the same time facilitating psychic integration and personal meaning in life (Jung, 1973), which serves as the rationale for using them for traumatic disclosure tasks. The mandala functions as a symbolic representation of emotionally laden and conflicting material, yet at the same time provides a sense of order and integration to this material.

In this manner, drawing a mandala is similar to a written disclosure in that it provides cognitive organization to complex emotional experiences. Art psychotherapists use the mandala as a basic tool for self-awareness, self-expression, conflict resolution, and healing (Siegelis, 1987). Within the realm of art therapy, the mandala generally refers to any art form that is executed within a circular context. Although most research into the healing aspects of mandala drawing has been limited to case studies argue [sic] for using mandalas therapeutically within numerous populations and settings, including schizophrenia and psychotic disorders, dissociative disorders (Cox & Cohen, 2000), attention-deficit/hyperactivity disorder (Smitherman-Brown & Church, 1996), and dementia patients (Couch, 1997). Cox and Cohen note that, particularly for individuals regarding abuse, illustrative coding of traumatic events in drawings allows clients the ability to maintain secrecy (both from their therapists and from themselves), while at the same time symbolically communicating and resolving material (Cohen & Cox, 1989, 1995).

To date, empirical research on the use of mandalas as a therapeutic tool is limited. In one of the first attempts undertaken to examine scientifically Jung's theory that mandala creation promotes psychological health Siegelis (1987) found that those who drew inside a circle experienced more positive affect than those who drew within a square. Although the results of the Siegelis study lend support to the argument that mandalas have calming and healing properties, the experimental design and data were limited and inhibit the inferences that can be drawn from the results.

A recent study by Curry and Kasser (2005) evaluated the effectiveness of mandala drawing in the reduction of anxiety. Anxiety levels were measured before and after an anxiety induction exercise, and after one of the three coloring conditions (free-form, mandala-drawing, or plaid-form). Decreases in anxiety were experienced for those in the mandala and plaid-form conditions.

Although these results show potential, the design of the research used predrawn mandala forms and predrawn plaid patterns, so the results could be interpreted in various ways, such as the calming effects of art therapy in general versus the effects of actually creating a mandala.

Our study sought to test in a controlled manner, the psychological and physical health benefits of mandala drawing within a trauma population. In choosing a research design and methodology that would adequately achieve this goal, we drew upon the techniques and methodology used in a body of research by James Pennebaker and colleagues that examines the physical and psychological health benefits of disclosure of traumatic events through writing (Pennebaker, 1997a, 1997b; Pennebaker & Seagal, 1999; Pennebaker & Susman, 1988). Our study design is modeled closely after the recent study conducted by Sloan and Marx (2004a). It applies a creative variation of the disclosure paradigm and this sort of creative extension has been encouraged (King, 2004, pgs. 148–149).

The first question to address is whether the researchers provided an adequate rationale for conducting the study. Henderson, et al. (2007) introduced research that supports the view that writing about trauma reduces stress and is beneficial. The answer to this first question is that the researchers do present an adequate rationale and cite relevant research. The citation of Pennebaker's work on using writing to reduce stress provides support for their view. Specifically, they suggested that writings allow for cognitive integration of the experience. They then introduced the idea of using art to improve psychological functioning and reduce stress and argued that it is similar to writing in expressing connections to the traumatic experience. Next they introduced the idea of using art and specifically mandalas to achieve similar results to writing, e.g., reduced stress and better physical and mental health. The authors noted the limitations of the research to support improving psychological functioning. However, they noted that there is preliminary research to support the use of art in reducing stress and anxiety. Their ultimate argument is that there is not enough research on using art to reduce the effects of post-traumatic stress disorder (PTSD) and more research needs to be conducted, the rationale for conducting their study.

The next question to address is, So what? or, what difference does conducting the study make to the field? The researchers do not explicitly state the effect of the study results on the field, but they provide an adequate rationale and a method for meeting the needs of the community. Counselors and therapists can use art therapy, specifically the drawing of mandalas, to promote psychological functioning and well-being. So the authors are proposing a technique to use in counseling to assist those individuals with PTSD to improve their quality of life, reduce stress, and improve mental health functioning.

In regard to the third question, whether the literature review is thorough and comprehensive, it appears that the researchers do accomplish this goal. They cite research supporting their proposition that writing about PTSD affects stress levels and improves mental health functioning. Additionally, they provide research support for their proposal that art may be similar to writing about PTSD experiences and therefore is worthy of additional research coverage. Specifically, they cite research and theoretical views presented by Pennebaker to give a thorough review of the appropriate and relevant literature. Citations are generally 10 years old or newer, with the majority being published after 2000.

The fourth question when evaluating the research literature section of an article is, Do the researchers present any potential biases in the literature review? The researchers do provide several different theoretical views on the use of writing and art in treating those with PTSD. Also, the researchers cite research that shows the limitations of using writing to treat those with PTSD, e.g., it is not effective with those with schizophrenia, mental retardation, and other disorders. It appears that the researchers do not show any significant bias in presenting the literature review.

The next question that is important to address is, Are all important concepts clearly defined by the researchers? Post-traumatic stress disorder is not defined, nor is traumatic event. It would be helpful for the reader to know explicitly how the researchers define these terms. Also, written disclosures are not well defined or clearly identified. Finally, mandalas are not clearly identified or defined. The study focuses on the use of mandalas as the treatment to be evaluated, the researchers but do not adequately define and identify the concept.

The final question to address is, Do the researchers clearly describe previous methods that are relevant to understanding the purpose for conducting this study? The researchers do not describe in much detail any previous methods. They do cite previous researchers who have used mandalas (by naming "Siegelis, 1987"), but they do not go into any detail about the methods used.

In summary, the researchers, Henderson, et al. (2007) do give an adequate rationale for conducting the study and how the study potentially can have important implications in the treatment of those with PTSD. Also, the literature review appears to be thorough and does not present any particular bias. Several important concepts are not clearly defined, and no description of previous methods is provided.

The questions to address with qualitative research in evaluating the literature review are similar to those asked with quantitative research. So the same six questions will be used in the following example of a qualitative study.

Study 2 Qualitative Research

Fry (2007) investigated first-year teachers' experiences in entering schools and their induction support, or support for entrance into the teaching profession. She used a qualitative method; specifically, she employed a case study method. The literature review is described below.

Many new teachers adopt traditional teaching methods during their student teaching and early in-service years instead of utilizing the innovative ones they were exposed to in teacher preparation (Feiman-Nemser, 2001; Veenman, 1984). This tendency can result from interactions with experienced colleagues who deride innovative research-supported teaching methods (Clark, 1999). Survival plays a role as well; faced with seemingly insurmountable classroom management issues, beginners often adopt traditional teaching methods that keep the students working quietly in their seats, and thus are easier to control (Veenman, 1984). These factors led Feiman-Nemser to conclude, "sink or swim" induction encourages novices to stick to whatever practices enable them to survive whether or not they represent "best" practice in that situation" (p. 1014).

In contrast, well-designed induction programs can provide beginning teachers with support that helps them survive the classroom management challenges, seemingly endless curriculum and instruction questions, and feelings of isolation that contribute to retained high percentages of beginning teachers. For example, studies of induction programs at Santa Clara, California; Walla Walla, Washington; and southern Illinois.

Reported retention rates that were greater than 90% over 6, 5, and 3 year time periods, respectively (Boss, 2001; Chubbuck, Clift, Allard, & Quinlan, 2001; Linik, 2001). Although these studies reported the successes of individual induction programs, the collective impact of induction programs may not be as significant. Smith and Ingersoll (2004) reported that nearly 80% of 1st-year teachers nationwide participated in some form of induction an increase of approximately 40% from 10 years earlier. This increase in induction program participation does not seem to have correlated in reduction of attrition rates, which remain near 29% for the first 3 years of teaching (Ingersoll, 2001, 2002).

Attrition rates may have remained stable despite increased participation in induction programs because of variability in the type of support offered. Smith and Ingersoll (2004) analyzed the impact different forms and combinations of induction had on attrition using results from the 1999–2000 Schools and Staffing Survey (SASS), a national study that includes data from approximately 52,000 elementary and secondary teachers. After controlling for differences in teacher and school characteristics, Smith and Ingersoll found that predicted attrition rate for beginning teachers receiving no form of induction support; mentoring, supportive communication from an administrator or department chair, common planning time with other teachers in the grade or content area, or seminars for beginning teachers. Receiving only one of these forms of induction support did not have a significant impact on the predicted attrition rate. A combination of mentoring and supportive communication from an administrator, which Smith and Ingersoll refer to as "basic induction," produced a predicted attrition rate of 39%. The predicted attrition was reduced to 27% when beginning teachers had basic induction plus common planning time with other teachers in the grade or content area, and participated in seminars for beginning teachers. The lowest predicted attrition rate was 18%; this was achieved when beginners received the combinations described above plus one of the following: a teacher's aide, reduced number of preparations, or participation in an external network of teachers. Smith and Ingersoll's analysis suggests that the mere presence of induction programs is not enough to reduce attrition rates among beginning teachers; the form and quality of induction that schools provide is important.

Smith and Ingersoll's (2004) research was based on a quantitative data set (SASS) that determines whether or not beginning teachers received specific forms of induction. SASS does not measure how useful teachers found their induction experiences. Since the presence of induction may not be enough to reduce attrition rates, research needs to move beyond determining the prevalence of induction and begin to assess form and quality. Interviewing beginning teachers about their experiences and the support they receive is a valuable way to assess the form and quality of induction in the schools. Interviews provide evaluative data immediately so schools do not need to wait until the 3-year induction period is over to see whether or not beginning teachers become attrition statistics.

The same six questions that were used to evaluate quantitative research can be used to evaluate the study by Fry (2007), which is a qualitative study. The first question is whether the researcher presents an adequate rationale for conducting the study. Fry notes the problems with school systems not providing adequate teacher induction programs and the use of traditional methods by new teachers that keep students docile and sitting in their seats. Fry describes these efforts as "survival" practices by the new teachers. Another major problem with not having helpful teacher induction programs is that there is a high attrition rate; new teachers leave shortly after beginning their careers in education. The author noted that a significant issue may not be simply the attrition rates of new teachers leaving the job but the quality of any induction methods used by school districts to keep and support new teachers. The rationale provided is clear and is based upon previous research, and the problem of attrition is a good rationale for conducting a study in this area. Also, finding specific factors that contribute to quality teacher induction appears to be reasonable.

The next question is to ask, So what? or, what difference will the study results make for those in counseling and education? The benefit of understanding the quality of teacher induction is noted with the author stating, "Interviewing beginning teachers about their experiences and the support they receive is a valuable way to assess the form and quality of induction in schools. Interviews provide evaluative data immediately so schools do not need to wait until the 3-year induction period is over." The point here is that schools can benefit from the study information and can potentially provide improved quality of teacher induction methods.

The third question concerns whether the literature review is thorough and comprehensive. Fry (2007) discusses various induction programs for new teachers and cites numerous studies and writings on the topic. She cites seven different studies and describes two different programs that have used new teacher induction methods. The citations ranged from 1984 to 2004, with most citations being recent, within the previous seven years. A related question is whether the author presents any potential biases in the literature review. The author does not cite her own research. However, she does not note any limitations or problems with other studies or research. She does cite research that found lower levels of successful induction procedures (Smith & Ingersoll, 2004). It is not clear whether she demonstrates much bias in her literature review. It would have been helpful to see research outcomes showing a potential difference from the positive research she cites on new teacher induction.

The next question to address in evaluating the literature review is whether the author has defined important terms. The most important term in Fry's study is induction (new teacher induction). Fry (2007) does not define induction for the reader, so it is difficult to know exactly what she means by this term. She does describe induction support as referring to supportive communication from an administrator, common planning time with other teachers, and other efforts. Despite these descriptions, it is difficult to know what induction or induction support actually is.

The last question is whether the researchers describe previous methods. Fry (2007) does cite two other new teacher induction programs in Washington and California, but does not describe the methods used. More detail about the actual induction procedures would have been helpful to the reader.

Summary

The literature review is the initial introduction to the reader and consumer, outlining the argument or rationale for conducting a particular study. Generally, there should be a strong and clear argument developed by the researchers for conducting the study based on previous research, theory, or personal experience. Several criteria have been proposed for evaluation of the literature review. One of the most important guidelines or questions for me is the answer to the "so what?" question. Why is it important to conduct this study? What difference will it make to counseling and education? If this question cannot be adequately addressed, I do not see the need to continue reading or using a particular article or study. Both quantitative and qualitative research studies can be evaluated using the same set of questions.

Exercises

Directions: Locate an article in the professional literature addressing a topic you are interested in exploring. Evaluation the literature review based on the questions addressed in this chapter. Try to explain and justify your answers based on specific examples from the article.

1. Do the researchers present *an adequate* rationale for conducting the study?

2. So what? or, What difference will the study make to the fields of counseling and education?

3. Is the literature review thorough and comprehensive?

4. Do the researchers demonstrate any potential biases in the literature review?

5. Are all important concepts clearly defined by the researchers?

6. Do the researchers clearly describe previous methods that are relevant to understanding the purpose for conducting this study?

10

Evaluating the Purpose Statement and Hypotheses

The purpose statement or aim of a study is an attempt by the researchers to identify, in a sentence or two, the intent of the study. Sometimes the purpose is thought of as a research problem (McMillan, 2004). The purpose statement is generally devoid of technical terms and should be based on the argument developed in the literature review. Moore (1983) suggested that the purpose statement may be expressed in either a declarative statement or in the form of a question or questions. The purpose is typically found in the literature review section of an article, toward the end of the review and most frequently in the last paragraph before the methods section. Many, but not all researchers provide a purpose statement in the study, but instead only use a hypothesis.

The purpose statement or research questions provide important information to the reader. First, the purpose statement should identify whether the study is a comparison among the groups of interest, an attempt to determine relationships between variables, or an attempt to clarify phenomena through descriptive or qualitative research. Identifying whether a study involves a comparison or a relationship directs the researchers in choosing a statistical method. It also gives the reader information about what type of study was conducted.

A comparison study may be identified when the researcher, in the purpose statement, affirms that there will be an attempt to determine differences between two or more groups. Greenberg, Evans, Harris, Loyo,

113

Ray, Spaulding, and Gottlieb (2007) provide an example of a purpose statement, which describes a comparison study. They described their purpose this way: "[T]his study examined WIC participants' preschooler feeding practices and beliefs and compared differences in preschooler feeding practices among Spanish-speaking Hispanic, English-speaking Hispanic, and non-Hispanic WIC participants" (p. 259).

Researchers using the type of study that focuses on a relationship are interested in determining how two or more specific variables correlate. Baldwin, Wampold, and Imel (2007) conducted a study that focused on using correlational methods. They described their purpose as follows: "The primary aim of the present study was to explore the relative importance of patient and therapist variability in the alliance as they relate to outcomes. In addition, our analyses also have implications for the hypothesis that the alliance is a consequence of early symptom change" (p. 843). Essentially they were interested in the correlation or relationship between therapist and client variables involving the therapeutic alliance between them and the outcomes of the treatment.

In addition to comparisons and relationships, investigators may be interested in clarifying phenomena or events. This may be achieved, as discussed, through descriptive or some qualitative research methods. Therefore, the purpose statement will be expressed as an attempt to clarify or describe identified phenomena, characteristics, or events. Isaksson, Lexell, and Skar (2007) conducted a qualitative study with the following purpose statement: "The aim of the current study was to describe how women with spinal cord injuries perceive the importance of social support for participation in occupation" (p. 24). The key term in this purpose statement is "describe," which denotes an attempt to identify phenomena, events, or experiences.

Moore (1983) stated that the purpose statement should include delineation of the variables studied. Generally, in quantitative research methods involving the use of true experimental and quasi-experimental designs, the researcher identifies independent and dependent variables. An independent variable is defined as an event, condition, or measured attribute or characteristic that the researcher, for the most part, controls. (There is no manipulation or control of an independent variable that is measured.) Additionally, an independent variable must have at least two levels or groups to compare. The dependent variable is defined in terms of changes in the subject as a consequence of the independent variable. For example, Hatinen, Kinnunen, Pekkonen, and Kalimo (2007) described the independent and dependent variables in their purpose statement this way:

The primary purpose of the present study was to test a new strategy for treating burnout and to compare it to the traditional strategy normally used in rehabilitation for burnout in Finland. We analyzed the short-term and long-term effects of both interventions on the outcome variables (burnout symptoms and perceived job conditions) over an intervention lasting one year. (p. 229)

The dependent variables were burnout symptoms and perceived job conditions, and the independent variable was the type of burnout intervention program, new intervention versus traditional. The independent and dependent variables should be clearly and concisely identified in the purpose statement when the researchers decide to use quantitative methods. Moore (1983) suggested that the identification of these two variables, independent and dependent, in the purpose statement should not be too detailed; specific, detailed descriptions should be provided in the methods section. In qualitative research and in quantitative descriptive studies, researchers typically do not have independent and dependent variables, but there are variables of interest that should be clearly and concisely identified.

A third component that should be included in a purpose statement is the identification of the population studied. Citation of the population should be clear but not too specific. When interpreting a study, readers of research articles need to know what specific population the results may be applied to. If the researchers identify the population too specifically, it may violate the subjects' confidentiality. The study (qualitative) by Isaksson, et al. (2007) provides an example of identifying the population without being too specific. They stated that: ". . . the current study was to describe how women with spinal cord injuries . . ." (p. 24). The identification of the population is women with spinal cord injuries, and no specific information is provided that would identify them or give too specific information.

Another issue to address in understanding and evaluating the purpose statement is ensuring that the purpose and the problem are researchable (Moore, 1983). A study may be considered researchable if the independent variables, dependent variables, and/or variables of interest can be operationalized (i.e., converted into measurable and, preferably, objective operations). Moore described research focusing on philosophical or vague ideas as unresearchable. Examples of unresearchable problems are whether there are ghosts or whether there are unidentified flying objects (UFOs). With advances in science and technology, some "unresearchable" problems may become researchable, but we are concerned only with whether the study was researchable at the time it was done, given the available methods. King, Burton, Hicks, and Drigotas (2007) studied positive affect and superstitious beliefs such as whether there are ghosts. They were able to collect data on participants' mood and perceptions, which can be converted to measurable variables. The difference here is the opportunity to operationalize the dependent variable so it can be measured.

Guidelines and Questions for Evaluating the Purpose Statement

I suggest using the following five questions and guidelines to evaluate the purpose statement:

1. Is the purpose statement clearly based on the argument developed in the literature review? Is there a clear connection?

2. Can the type of study that was conducted be identified based on the purpose statement? Does the researcher use words such as *comparisons, relationships, illuminate,* or *describe?*

3. Are the variables of interest clearly identified in the purpose statement? If the study is a true experimental design, do the researchers clearly identify the independent and dependent variables? What are they? In qualitative or descriptive studies, is there at least one variable of interest that is clearly identified? What is it?

4. Is the population of interest clearly identified in the purpose statement?

5. Do the study and the purpose statement focus on problems that are researchable?

Evaluation of Examples From the Research Literature

Study 1 Quantitative Research

Henderson, et al. (2007) use the following purpose statement in their study focusing on the healing effects of mandalas:

The primary purpose of our study was to examine the healing aspects of drawing mandalas. Specifically, the psychological and physical health benefits of mandala drawing were viewed as a creative means of traumatic disclosure that would symbolically organize and integrate emotions and experiences, while serving the same function as writing a narrative. (p. 149)

The first question in our evaluation is whether the purpose statement is clearly based on the argument developed in the literature review. Is there a clear connection? We can refer back to Chapter 8 to determine whether the literature review provides a good argument for this purpose statement. The authors cite research that illustrates the benefits of using written expression in coping with traumatic events. They suggest that exposure to reviewing the experience through writing and other methods leads to reduction in psychological and physical problems. They attempt to bridge the connection between written forms of expression and other forms like art to achieve the benefits of reducing psychological and physical health problems. Other research that is cited, which is limited, focuses on the use of art therapy, but with limited results in improving health benefits and psychological functioning. The argument for then using mandalas, which is presented as similar to art therapy, is less clear. However, the authors do cite some research into the effects of using art and mandalas in reducing anxiety.

The second question or guideline to address is this: Can the type of study conducted be identified, based on the purpose statement? The researchers use the term *examine* in the purpose statement, which does not give the reader a clear understanding of what type of study was conducted. *Examine* could refer to a descriptive or comparative study. The researchers did not provide information in the purpose statement that they were comparing a control and experimental group.

The third question concerns the identification of variables of interest and whether they are clearly identified in the purpose statement. The researchers do identify the variables of interest, the independent variable of drawing mandalas and the dependent variables of psychological and physical health.

A fourth question to address in evaluating the purpose statement concerns whether the population of interest is clearly identified in the purpose statement. The researchers do not give any information on the population of interest in the purpose statement. It is clear in the methods/participants section that the population of interest are those with traumatic stress experiences and who experience post-traumatic stress: The researchers state: "Participants were prescreened for both the experience of trauma and trauma severity" (p. 149).

The final guideline or question I want to address is whether the purpose statement identifies a purpose that is clearly researchable. The researchers identify the purpose as examining the healing aspects of drawing mandalas, and the outcome or effects being psychological and physical health as the dependent variables. Psychological and physical health both provide a researcher with variables that are researchable. One can measure psychological and physical health. There are numerous instruments for measuring psychological health and perceptions of psychological health.

In summary, the article by Henderson, et al. (2007) provides a clear link between the literature review and the purpose statement. They stated that the study would focus on the psychological and physical well-being of those with traumatic stress. The type of study presented in the manuscript does not give the reader a good idea of the purpose of the study. The researchers do not use any particular words or statements that identify the type of study being conducted, nor is the population of interest identified. The dependent variables of physical and psychological health are quantifiable and can be measured.

Study 2 Qualitative Research

Fry (2007), in a study focusing on first-year teacher induction support, describes her purpose as:

The current investigation contributes to the induction literature by using qualitative research methods to determine how four 1st-year teachers were supported during induction and how they responded to this support. (p. 218)

This study is a qualitative study, but the same questions can be used to evaluate such methods. The first question is whether the purpose is based on the literature review. The researcher systematically discusses several specific examples of teacher induction programs like those in Santa Cruz, California, and Walla Walla, Washington. The researcher cites teacher attrition rates problems and states that these can be addressed with induction programs, but the author notes the lack of research that supports the use of induction methods.

Our second question concerns whether the purpose statement identifies the type of research methods employed in the study. The researcher states: "The current investigation contributes to the induction literature by using qualitative research methods" (p. 218). It is clear from the purpose statement that this is a qualitative study.

A third question to address is whether the variables of interest are clearly defined. The variables of interest in a qualitative study are not always as clearly defined as those in a quantitative study. The researcher identifies teacher induction or induction support as one variable of interest in the study. It is clear from the purpose statement that the target population is first-year teachers. Finally, we are interested in whether this study is clearly researchable. The study appears to be researchable because one can identify and observe induction procedures for first-year teachers.

In summary, the study conducted by Fry (2007) shows the purpose statement as partly connected and clear from the literature review. At times, the citations used are not consistent with the purpose of the study, e.g., attrition rates are stable despite increases in the use of induction methods. The type of study conducted is clearly identified in the purpose statement. The variable of interest in the study is teacher induction methods, and this is clearly identified in the purpose statement. Also, the population of interest is clearly identified as first-year teachers. Finally, the study and the variable of interest, teacher induction procedures, are researchable and can be operationalized.

Summary

The purpose statement should provide the reader with a clear description of the intent of the study. It may be presented as a declarative statement or in the form of one or more questions. Even though the purpose statement may be only a sentence or two, it can provide the reader with significant information and clues about the type of study conducted, the population of interest, and the variables of interest. I want to reiterate the intent of careful evaluation of different sections of a journal article, which is to provide a guide for consumers and users of research to systematically determine which components of a study are valid and which need to be accepted with caution. In evaluating the purpose, a poorly written intent or goal of a study is a problem because the reader may not know whether the researchers have accomplished an identified purpose.

Exercises

Directions: Locate an article in the professional literature addressing a topic that you are interested in exploring. Evaluate the purpose statement based on the questions addressed in this chapter. Try to explain and justify your answers by using specific examples from the article.

1. Is the purpose statement clearly based on the argument developed in the literature review? Is there a clear connection? Explain your response.

2. Can you identify the type of study conducted based on the purpose statement? Does the researcher use words such as *comparisons, relationships, illuminate,* or *describe?* Explain.

3. Are the variables of interest clearly identified in the purpose statement? If the study is a true experimental design, does the researcher clearly identify the independent and dependent variables? In qualitative or

(Continued)

(Continued)

descriptive studies, is there at least one variable of interest that is clearly identified? Explain.

4. Is the population of interest clearly identified in the purpose statement? Explain.

5. Do the study and the purpose statement focus on problems that are clearly researchable? Explain.

Quantitative Research Hypotheses

A hypothesis is a formally stated expectation of outcomes; the researchers develop it based on theory, previous research, or personal experience. We make predictions and "educated guesses" about outcomes on a regular basis in our everyday lives. George Kelly (1955), a personality theorist, suggested that we are all scientists and that we all engage in hypothesis testing on a regular basis. What is the difference between this type of thinking and the scientific approach to hypothesis testing? The difference lies in the degree to which a formal argument is developed for the hypothesis in the literature review. As stated, the hypothesis may be based on theory, previous research, or personal experience. In our everyday lives, we generally do not make predictions based on theory or previous research results. Most of our hypothesizing in everyday life is based on personal experiences. A research hypothesis is developed from a clear argument based on the literature review. Obviously, in everyday life we do not develop or formulate a formal written hypothesis about our expectations. A hypothesis may be used in research methods of true experimental, quasi-experimental, and descriptive comparative designs. Hypotheses are not typically used in most descriptive and qualitative designs. A different approach to hypothesis testing that can be used in qualitative methods will be described later in this chapter.

Indirect Proof: An Orientation to the Scientific Approach

To further understand the scientific approach to developing and evaluating a research hypothesis, I want to discuss the idea behind "indirect proof." Moore (1983) stated that researchers should initially assume that there is no effect from the variables of interest to any outcome. Additionally, he stated that we can never prove a hypothesis. This is based on the notion that we conduct research on samples of the population, and they *represent* possible responses, but this is only a representation and *not a fact*. Instead of proving hypotheses, researchers gather evidence to support their hypotheses. Leary (2001) proposed the following: "Theories cannot be proved because obtaining empirical support for a hypothesis does not necessarily mean that the theory from which the hypothesis was derived is true" (p. 19). What it means is that there can be evidence that supports a theory, but it does not prove the theory. In fact, there can be research support from competing theories, but this does not prove that one theory is better than another (Leary, 2001). Leary (2001) further stated that ". . . merit of theories is judged, not on the basis of a single research study, but on the accumulated evidence from several studies" (p. 20). In essence support for a particular theory or hypothesis is accomplished through a number of research studies, and the quality of these studies impacts the support provided.

Types of Hypotheses

Three different types of hypotheses have been identified: null, alternative nondirectional, and alternative directional (Minium & King, 2003; Moore, 1983). The null hypothesis is where an investigator starts in the research process. I say this because the initial assumption the researcher should make is that there is no relationship or cause-and-effect outcome between the variables of interest. An assumption that there is no relationship or difference between groups is the key foundation of the scientific method, maintaining an objective view. Leary (2001) described the null hypothesis as ". . . the independent variable did not have an effect on the dependent variable" (p. 246). Researchers have developed a method to represent the null hypothesis with symbols:

$$H_O \; \mu_1 \neq \mu_2$$

Ho denotes the null hypothesis. The Greek letter mu (μ) indicates the population average or mean. μ_1 and μ_2 refer to two different groups of interest. Essentially, this may be interpreted as the means for Group 1 being no different than the means for Group 2, determined by the variables of interest (the dependent variables). The null hypothesis is grounded in statistical methods, and essentially the researcher begins his or her investigation with the notion that there is no significant statistical difference between two or more groups of interests, based on comparison of results on the means of the dependent veriable or variables. It is not typical that researchers state the null hypothesis. However, there is a journal, *Journal of Articles in*

Support of the Null Hypothesis, that publishes articles that do not find significant differences. However, in most published research, the reader is meant to infer that every researcher has started with the null hypothesis, even though this is not stated.

Researchers typically identify alternative types of research hypotheses in the literature when there is enough evidence to predict a difference or a given direction. One type of research hypothesis, the alternative nondirectional hypothesis, implies that the researcher has enough evidence from previous research to suggest that there is likely to be a difference in groups, but there is not enough evidence to predict the exact direction. Essentially, the researcher is stating that a significant difference is based on the variables of interests (in this case, the independent variable). An alternative nondirectional hypothesis is based on the statistical premise that the results will be that one group mean is significantly higher or lower than another or others, but does not predict which direction. The researcher cannot predict the direction, but is hypothesizing a difference. An alternative nondirectional hypothesis is symbolically denoted as

$$H_A \; \mu_1 \neq \mu_2$$

H_A refers to the alternative nondirectional hypothesis. μ_1 and μ_2 denotes the population means for the two groups.

The third type of hypothesis, the alternative directional hypothesis, is used when the researcher has enough evidence from previous research to support the prediction of a direction of outcome. This means that if a researcher is comparing two groups, using an independent variable, one group is expected to score higher on the dependent variable, as predicted by the researcher. Statistically, the researcher is indicating that the outcome of the research data will be either significantly above or below the mean and predicts the direction. The alternative directional hypothesis is denoted symbolically as:

$$H_A \; \mu_1 \overset{>}{_{<}} \mu_2$$

H_A indicates an alternative hypothesis, and μ_1 and μ_2 represent the population means for the two groups of interest. There could be more than two group comparisons.

A hypothesis should be based on the argument developed in the literature review. In addition, the hypothesis should extend from the purpose statement. The purpose statement and hypothesis serve the researcher and consumer of research differently. First, the purpose statement provides the general intent of the study, whereas hypotheses are designed to provide insight into the researcher's anticipation and expectations about outcomes based on critical thinking: specifically, as presented as a foundation or argument in the literature review. This means that, in the literature review, the researcher should provide an argument for why he or she chose a particular alternative hypothesis (i.e., alternative directional or alternative nondirectional).

Researchers have proposed that hypotheses should be testable and falsifiable (Heiman, 1995). The issue of whether a hypothesis is testable is similar to the question used when evaluating the purpose statement: Is the purpose statement researchable? Heiman (1995) stated that under this criterion, the researcher must be able to develop a method of testing and implementing a hypothesis. Gliner and Morgan (2000) described a hypothesis that should be: ". . . testable, by empirical methods; it should not be just a statement of your moral, ethical, or political position" (p. 47). An example of a hypothesis that is not testable is the statement that there is life in other solar systems. Currently this is not testable because we do not have the technology to send spacecraft to the distances necessary to test this hypothesis.

A hypothesis must also be falsifiable, which means that one can gather evidence to show that it is incorrect. An example of a hypothesis that is not falsifiable may involve, for example, supernatural phenomena, such as those said to occur in the "Bermuda Triangle." We can establish methods for testing a hypothesis about unusual events happening in a particular region—we can go to Bermuda to collect information—but we do not have the instruments to measure supernatural events, such as unexplained reasons for loss of power in boat or airplane engines. Therefore, we cannot gather evidence that such a hypothesis is incorrect.

Another important issue to consider when evaluating a hypothesis is whether it is rational and parsimonious (Heiman, 1995). Heiman stated that a hypothesis should be rational, and this refers to whether it is even possible for the hypothesis to be true. For example, is it rational to hypothesize that IQ is related to bumps on someone's head? There is certainly no evidence that this is true, and there is no rationale that might support this view.

Parsimony concerns how well a hypothesis fits into current views of a particular theory or field of study. Parsimony, then, is concerned about whether the hypothesis is consistent with current theories (Heiman, 1995). An example of a violation of this issue might be a hypothesis addressing, in behavioral theory, intrapsychic processes such as dreaming. Studying dreams creates a basic conflict with this approach: In behavioral theory, phenomena must be observable and measurable, not intrapsychic.

Moore (1983) proposed that brevity and clarity also be considered important when evaluating the efficacy of a hypothesis. Brevity concerns stating the hypothesis as concisely as possible. A hypothesis should not be several paragraphs long unless the researcher is proposing numerous hypotheses. Clarity refers to how easy it is for others to understand the hypothesis. As Heiman (1995) pointed out, the hypothesis should not be overly complex just for the sake of complexity. This creates something of a dilemma for researchers because they must identify the relevant variables of interest but not be too specific; at the same time, they must be clear enough so the reader understands the hypothesis. A related perspective is broad versus narrow focus of the research hypothesis (Gliner & Morgan, 2000). They noted that science advances in small steps, and thus one needs to limit studies that are too broad and cannot be conducted because of their complexity. Moore noted that it is not necessary to restate the population in the hypothesis once it is indicated in the purpose statement.

A hypothesis provides a guide for the researcher to use when determining which statistical tests are best suited to his or her research. The tests chosen will then be reported in the results section. There should be consistency between the hypothesis identified and the type of statistics employed. More specifically, if a researcher states that he or she expects one group to score higher than another group on a measure of stress, there should be a statistical test reported in the results section that addresses this hypothesis. Again, we are looking for consistency throughout a study. We will come back to answering this question in the results section: Does the researcher employ statistical methods reported in the results section that address each hypothesis identified?

Guidelines and Questions for Evaluating Hypotheses

The following questions may be used to evaluate the hypothesis proposed in a journal research article:

1. What type of hypothesis is presented? Is it an alternative nondirectional, alternative directional, or null hypothesis?

2. Do the investigators provide a clear rationale for the direction of their hypothesis, based on the literature review?

3. Is the hypothesis testable and falsifiable?

4. Is the hypothesis rational, or is it reasonable to expect that it could be true, based on theory or previous research?

5. Is the hypothesis parsimonious with current theories or research?

6. Is the hypothesis stated with brevity and clarity?

Evaluation of Examples From the Research Literature

Study 1 Quantitative Research

Henderson, Rosen, and Mascaro (2007) conducted a study focusing on the healing aspects of the use of mandalas. Mandalas are considered to be graphic or artistic representations, most often of the universe. The researchers stated that:

It was hypothesized that individuals assigned to a mandala-drawing condition would show a significant increase in psychological and physical health relative to control group participants both immediately after the intervention and at a 1-month follow up. Improvements in psychological health would be evidenced by decreases in self-reported depression, anxiety, post traumatic stress disorder (PTSD) symptom severity, and an increase in spiritual meaning. Improvements in physical health were determined through decreases in the self-reported frequency of occurrence of physical health problems. (149)

The researchers have chosen an alternative directional hypothesis for this study. They have clearly identified the direction of the hypothesis: ". . . those assigned to a mandala-drawing condition would show significant increase in psychological and physical health" compared to a control group. The researchers do present a clear argument for the direction of their hypothesis when they cite studies supporting the effectiveness of mandala drawing, they cited Curry and Kasser (2005). (See the Chapter 8 citation of the literature review). The study by Slegelis (1987) also provided support, but as the authors noted, the research design was not necessarily strong.

The next question concerns whether the hypothesis is testable and falsifiable. Both physical and psychological health can be measured and tested, so the researchers do meet the requirement for the study being testable. In regard to whether the study is falsifiable, the researchers can have participants construct mandalas and collect data on the effects of the mandalas on their psychological and physical health. Consequently, the researchers can refute a hypothesis that the construction of mandalas has an impact on psychological and/or physical health.

The fourth issue in addressing the hypothesis focuses on whether it is rational or reasonable to expect that the hypothesis could be true, based on theory or previous research. The researchers present an argument based on written disclosure paradigm and theory. For example, the theory states that ". . . repeated exposure to aversive conditioned stimuli leads to the extinguishment of negative emotions . . ." (p. 148). A second theory included as part of the researcher's rationale is cognitive change theory. The hypothesis does present a rational link to the theories presented.

Related to whether the hypothesis is rational is whether it is parsimonious with current theories or research. The researchers state in the literature review, discussing cognitive change theory, that ". . . cognitive restructuring serves to resolve the traumatic experience, as well as bring a sense of meaning to the event as insights are gained through the process of writing" (p. 148). This description of the theory is parsimonious with the hypothesis that proposes to increase psychological and physical health.

Finally, we want to know if the hypothesis is stated with brevity and clarity. Henderson, et al. (2007) present a hypothesis that is relatively brief and gives clarity to the expectations of the researcher. The variables of interest are clear, and they are concisely stated.

In summary, the hypothesis presented by Henderson, et al. (2007) gives a clear alternative directional hypothesis. They provide a rationale based on the literature for the direction of their hypothesis; they cite studies that have found positive effects of mandalas and the use of art with anxiety disorders. The study is testable and falsifiable, since the researchers can collect information about psychological and physical functioning, and the use of mandalas can be implemented. Previous research provides a rationale for conducting the study, since there have not been significant amounts of research into this area. The hypothesis is consistent with two theories, written disclosure theory and cognitive change theory. Finally, the hypothesis is stated with brevity and clarity, with the variables of interest identified and concisely stated.

Study 2 Qualitative Research

Fry (2007) conducted a study that focused on induction support for new teachers. She used qualitative methods in her study. As has been mentioned earlier, qualitative studies typically do not involve the use of formal hypotheses. However, the researcher does provide insight into how she predicts expected results. For example, she stated: "Since the presence of induction may not be enough to reduce attrition rates, research needs to move beyond determining the prevalence of induction and begin to assess form and quality" (p. 218).

Evaluating a Hypothesis in Qualitative Research Methods

A formally stated hypothesis is generally not made in qualitative research. Qualitative research has been descried as theory building (Brannen, 1992) and involves formulating an area of interest and collecting information to develop, support, or refute a theory. Brannen suggested that qualitative, ethnographic methods may be defined in terms of a "working hypothesis": a hypothetical explanation of phenomena in which information is gathered to determine whether the facts fit the working hypothesis or explanation. Typically, researchers present their working hypothesis in qualitative research in terms of theories to be tested, rather than as formal hypotheses such as directional and nondirectional hypotheses, which would be found in quantitative research methods. Different questions are relevant in determining the quality of the "working hypothesis." One question is, Do the researchers identify a working hypothesis or a theory they are testing? When evaluating qualitative research, not all qualitative studies identify a working hypothesis, in part because so little is known about a particular topic and also because of the nature of qualitative research, an intent to explore the topic or issue without an expected outcome. The literature will typically provide some insight into whether enough information is available to generate working hypotheses. A second question to consider with qualitative research and a hypothesis is, Is the hypothesis parsimonious with current theories or research? As with quantitative research, qualitative research does consider theoretical perspectives (Best & Kahn, 1998).

Admi (1996) completed a descriptive exploratory study focusing on growing up with a chronic health condition, cystic fibrosis. Admi stated:

> A different theoretical perspective, which challenges some of Goffman's (1963) assertions, is offered by current social-psychological view on disability and chronic health conditions (e.g., Fine & Asch, 1988; Frank 1988; Gliedman & Roth, 1980; Hahn, 1988; Mest, 1988; Schneider & Conrad, 1980). These theories are based on the minority group model, in which the problems of people with disabilities are assumed to stem primarily from society's discriminating attitudes and restricting physical environment . . . the minority group model shifts the focus from the individual with the disability to the physical and attitudinal environment. (p. 167)

No working hypothesis is identified by Admi. In this statement, the researcher (Admi, 1996) makes clear that she is testing a theory, the minority group model. In answer to our second question (about parsimony), the researcher notes that there is disagreement in the literature on the processes of growing up with a disability. However, she provides support for her working hypothesis when she cites research and writings from the minority group model.

Summary

In quantitative research methods, a hypothesis is a guess about expected outcomes. Different types of hypotheses have been identified: directional hypotheses and nondirectional hypotheses. As with the purpose statement, we are interested in a clear explanation of how the hypothesis was developed (from the literature review), consistency, and clarity for the reader. It is important to remember that not all quantitative research will involve a hypothesis. Descriptive research generally does not present a hypothesis because the intent is to clarify the characteristics of phenomena. Traditional methods of presenting a hypothesis also are not employed in qualitative research. In qualitative research, there may be statements that describe efforts at theory building or working hypotheses.

Exercises

Directions: Locate an article in the professional literature addressing a topic you are interested in exploring. Evaluate the literature review based on the questions addressed in this chapter. Try to explain and justify your answers based on specific examples from the article you choose.

Quantitative Research

1. What type of hypothesis is presented (alternative nondirectional, alternative directional, or null hypothesis)?

2. Do the investigators provide a clear rationale for the direction of their hypothesis, based on the literature review?

3. Is the hypothesis testable and falsifiable?

4. Is the hypothesis rational, or is it reasonable to expect that it could be true based on theory or previous research?

5. Is the hypothesis parsimonious with current theories or research?

6. Is the hypothesis stated with brevity and clarity?

Qualitative Research

1. Do the researchers identify a working hypothesis or a theory they are testing?

2. Is the hypothesis parsimonious with current theories or research?

11

Evaluating the Methods Section—Sampling Methods

The methods section, which will be the focus for Chapters 11, 12, and 13, consists of the sample, the procedures, and the instrumentation. These three chapters include detailed descriptions of how the study was conducted. There are several reasons the scientific community requires researchers to provide detailed descriptions of their methods in a journal article. The first reason is to allow those reading the results to determine the efficacy of the study. The second reason concerns the potential for replication of the study; detailed information would be needed if a researcher was interested in reproducing the results. As consumers of research, we are most concerned with the first reason: How effective are the methods used in the study in achieving reliable results? In this chapter, I will first review the basic principles of selecting a sample or subjects for a study. Second, I will present information on sample selection procedures. The next section will address sampling bias and sampling errors. Fourth, I will provide a series of questions or guides for evaluating the sample parts of the methods section. Finally, I will provide examples from the professional literature and evaluate several methods sections, focusing on the sample, to illustrate this approach to evaluation.

To understand what a sample is, we must start with concepts defining the population. Researchers are ultimately interested in understanding how research results apply in the natural environment and with a specific group of individuals "the population." Several definitions of a population have been proposed (Best & Kahn, 1998; Gall, Gall, & Borg, 2002; Charles, 1995).

Gall, et al. (2002) differentiated the population and the sample: "Quantitative researchers attempt to discover something about a large group of individuals by studying a smaller group. The larger group that they wish to learn about is called a population, and the smaller group they actually study is called a sample" (p. 167). Best and Kahn (1998) stated that a population is ". . . a group of individuals who has one or more characteristics in common that are of interest to the researcher" (p. 12). For our purposes, I want to define population as the group to which the researcher intends to apply his or her results and that is identified by clearly defined characteristics of interest. If a researcher is interested in understanding how a new drug for depression works, the population of interest may be all those individuals with major depression. The researcher may define the sample by stating that it is composed only of those with certain characteristics, such as those with major depression as defined in the *DSM-IV,* only adults, and so on.

Gall, et al. (2002) differentiated between two types of populations: the *target population* and the *accessible population.* The target population is defined as all individuals or objects the researcher is interested in and to which the study results are applied. However, a researcher is generally not able to access the entire target population, particularly if it is a large population, so for practical reasons an accessible population must be identified. If we return to our example of those with major depression, we can see that a researcher cannot realistically access all those with major depression throughout the world. Therefore, he or she is left with identifying the accessible population, for instance those from the northeastern United States.

Most research involves populations that are quite large, which makes inclusion of all members of a population in a study practically impossible. First, the cost of including all individuals in a population would be prohibitive, e.g., contacting them via mail, e-mail, or phone is time consuming. Second, the time required to conduct such a study would be tremendous. Consequently, researchers have developed methods of selecting representatives of the accessible population (a sample). Charles (1995) defined a sample as ". . . a small group drawn from a population carefully selected to reflect closely the characteristics of the population" (p. 124).

One major step in constructing a sample from the accessible population is the identification of relevant demographic characteristics. Examples of demographic characteristics include socioeconomic status (SES), gender, ethnicity, occupation, level of education, and religious affiliation. The researcher must determine relevant characteristics based on the population of interest. For example, a researcher would not identify occupation in a school-age population. Another example may be religious affiliation; if a characteristic does not concern the population of interest and the purpose of the study, then it would not be considered in constructing the sample and population. Key in deciding which demographic characteristics to identify are (a) the purpose of the study, and (b) whether any relevant demographic characteristics potentially influence the outcome or the dependent variable.

Once a researcher identifies the population of interest, the next step is selecting a sample that is representative of the larger population. Researchers have raised the issues of whether it is truly possible to select sample that mirrors the population of interest (Heppner, Kivlighan, & Wampold, 1992). Gall, et al. (2002) defined population validity as ". . . the extent to which the results of an experiment can be generalized from the sample that participated in it to a larger group of individuals, that is, a population" (p. 164). There are sampling methods that improve the chance of obtaining a fairly representative sample. The extent to which a sample represents a population is critical in determining how easily and validly the researcher can generalize the results back to the entire target population; this is called population validity. Consequently, researchers have proposed several different methods of selecting a sample. These methods vary in their effectiveness in creating a sample that is most representative of the larger accessible population.

Sampling Methods Used in Quantitative Research

More common approaches to sampling in quantitative research include simple random sampling, systematic random sampling, stratified sampling, cluster sampling, and convenience sampling (see Table 11.1).

Simple random sampling generally involves selecting a subset of individuals from the accessible population so that every single individual has an *equal chance* of being chosen and each selection is independent of any other selection (Table 11.1). Several methods may be used to obtain a simple random sample. A random numbers table is one method of ensuring that every individual in the population has an equal chance of being selected for a study. A random numbers table typically consists of rows and columns of computer-generated random numbers. First, each person is assigned a number and a researcher randomly selects where to start on the random numbers table. The researcher selects down the random numbers table until an adequate number of participants are selected. Another method of selecting a sample through random sampling is by simply assigning a number to all possible individuals from a population. Next, the researcher places the numbered slips of paper representing each person in the population in a container and then randomly draws out numbers and names. Those numbers drawn indicate who has been selected for the study. Numbered slips continue to be chosen until an adequate sample has been achieved.

Table 11.1   Types of Sampling: Quantitative Methods

Type of Sampling	Description	Advantages	Limitations
Simple random sampling	Every single individual in the population has an equal chance of being chosen.	If completed adequately, the results can readily be generalized back to the population.	It is difficult to ensure that every individual in the population has an equal chance of being chosen.
Systematic random sampling	A finite list of those in the population where every nth person is selected.	An easy, simple method to use.	Difficult to identify everyone in a population.
Stratified sampling (proportional and nonproportional)	Selection of individuals from the population who represent subgroups.	Ensures adequate representation on relevant variables (e.g., ethnicity).	May focus on variable that is not as important as others.
Cluster sampling	Random selection of intact groups (e.g., whole classrooms).	Allows the researcher to conduct studies with naturally intact groups.	The researcher cannot study differences between individuals in intact groups.
Convenience sampling	Section of a population that is convenient and accessible to the researcher.	Convenient; reduces costs and amount of effort in conducting a study.	Severely limits potential for generalizing the results back to the population; affects population validity.

A similar approach to simple sampling is systematic random sampling. This kind of sampling is more convenient and systematic than simple random sampling (Table 11.1). The researcher can ensure that all in the population will be considered as part of the sample, based on the concrete list of the population. This method of sampling is implemented by the researcher assigning each person in a population a number and subsequently choosing the nth number, depending on the total number projected in the sample. More specifically, if there are 10,000 individuals in a population (it is assumed that the researcher has a list of all those belonging to a particular group) and the researcher has determined that a sample of 100 is adequate, then the researcher would choose every 100th person. He or she may start by choosing a number randomly from a random numbers table, and this will be the first person taken for the sample. Every 100th person after that will be selected for the sample.

A third type of sampling, stratified sampling, consists of selecting individuals from the population who represent subgroups (Table 11.1). Choosing the subgroups is done in such a way as to ensure that there is adequate representation of the subgroups. Two strategies have been employed in stratified sampling. In proportional stratified sampling, the subgroup participants are chosen based on the same proportions found in the accessible population. For example, if a researcher is interested in studying reading achievement and he or she wants to ensure that various socioeconomic groups are represented, he or she would select participants based on the proportion of those in various socioeconomic groups in the population. So if 20 percent of the population was from upper middle class, 20 percent of the sample would be selected from the upper middle class. Furthermore, if 25 percent were from the lowest SES, then, again, 25 percent would be chosen to represent the population from this subgroup.

A nonproportional, or equal-size, approach to stratified sampling involves equal numbers from each subgroup being chosen. For example, if the researcher is interested in obtaining a total of 100 participants and there are five subgroups, then 20 would be chosen from each subgroup, regardless of the proportion in the population. In this method of sampling, the researcher focuses on ensuring that there are equal sample sizes across the comparison groups.

The next approach to sampling, cluster sampling, is used when groups of the target population may not be separated (Table 11.1). For example, if a researcher wanted to investigate the effects of a specific teaching approach to math, he or she would not necessarily be able to separate or assign high school students to a certain algebra class. Thus, if the researcher had access to a population of 30 algebra classes, he or she might randomly select 10 classes for the study, a cluster. As with simple random selection, the researcher might use random methods to choose the clusters such as the use of a random numbers table.

Convenience sampling is a common approach used by researchers because many of the methods previously identified are more difficult to implement (Table 11.1). Gall, et al. (2002) noted that researchers will frequently select a sample because it is easy for the researchers to access, such as a sample from an undergraduate college class (typically a psychology class). Another reason a researcher may choose a particular sample is that an administrator of an agency or school is associated with the researcher, and that administrator gives the researcher permission to use and access to a particular sample. The issue for the researcher and those reading and using the information in this study and article is to determine whether the results can be reasonably generalized to the population of interest, when the sample is one of convenience and possibly not adequate to representing the intended population.

An important issue for researchers, regardless of the type of selection method used, is the use of volunteers (those agreeing to participate) (Gall, et al., 2002). Researchers must respect the right of those they have identified as desirable participants in a study to refuse participation. If a large number of those chosen refuse to participate, the researcher may lose the benefit of having selected participants randomly and objectively and obtain a sample that is not necessarily representative of the larger population of interest. To address the issue of volunteers, researchers sometimes attempt to determine whether those not choosing to participate in a study are significantly different in relevant variables from those participating. This is accomplished by contacting those not participating and asking them to provide relevant demographic characteristics and rule out any significant differences in those choosing to participate and those who choose not to participate.

Almost all current researchers use volunteers in their research. One criterion used to determine whether this volunteer status affects the ability to generalize back to population is the return, or participation rate, of all requested to participate. Babbie (2006) stated that an acceptable response rate for survey research is at least 50 percent. The same criterion could be used to determine the appropriateness of requests to participate in an experimental study or manipulation.

Sample Size

Another relevant issue that researchers consider when constructing a sample is sample size. Several factors influence the sample size used by a researcher. One factor is the design of the study and whether qualitative or quantitative methods are used. Different formulas have been suggested for different quantitative study designs, although it has been noted that the largest sample size feasible is a good rule to follow (Gall, et al., 2002). For example, if researchers planned to use a true experimental design (e.g., a pretest–posttest design) and wanted to compare the effects of two counseling interventions and a control group, they would need a certain number of subjects. More subjects would be needed if they were comparing three treatment groups and a control group. Typically, researchers propose 15 subjects per group in a research design (Gall, et al., 2002; Moore, 1983). Based on this formula, the first study would need at least 45 subjects, and the second study would require 60 subjects. Survey researchers should typically use a minimum of 100 subjects per major subgroup. A minimum of 30 subjects per variable is suggested for correlational research (Gall, et al., 2002).

Researchers have developed a more sophisticated method of determining sample size when certain information is available. It is called statistical power analysis. Gall, et al. (2002) defined statistical power analysis as

". . . the probability that a particular test of statistical significance will lead to rejection of a false null hypothesis" (p. 141). A formula for determining the number of subjects needed to reject the null hypothesis is used. Four factors are considered in calculating statistical power: sample size (the larger the sample, the more likely there will be a rejection of the null hypothesis); level of significance; directionality; and effect size (Gall, et al., 2002). Levels of significance involve the probability of an error's being made in statistical calculations. (Levels of significance will be defined in more detail in Chapter 13.) The stricter the level of significance (the less likely the chance of error), the more statistical power the researcher loses.

A third factor relevant to calculating statistical power analysis is directionality. Directionality involves statistics and concerns prediction by the researchers about the direction of outcomes, such as in a directional hypothesis. If a researcher is not sure whether one particular intervention is better than another and cannot predict the direction of the outcome, he or she loses statistical power.

The fourth factor in determining statistical power analysis is effect size. Effect size concerns researchers' expectations of or predictions about the strength of outcomes; this is typically based upon previous research results. Gall, et al. (2002) noted that tables have been developed for calculating statistical power that consider these four factors and provide researchers with a systematic method of determining sample size.

Sampling Methods in Qualitative Research

Sampling methods in qualitative research share some similarities to those used in quantitative research, and there are some differences. Berg (2004) suggested that the use of simple random sampling, systematic random sampling, stratified random sampling, and convenience sampling may be used in qualitative research. We have discussed the procedures for obtaining a sample with these methods. Other methods of sampling in qualitative research include purposive sampling, snowball sampling, and quota sampling (Berg, 2004). No specific number of subjects or participants has been suggested for conducting qualitative research. In fact, single subjects may be used in qualitative research. Berg (2004) described purposive sampling as researchers using ". . . their special knowledge or expertise about some group to select subjects who represent this population" (36). A potential example of purposive sampling can be found with Abraham Maslow's (1976) study of self-actualization. Maslow stated, "The people I selected for my investigation were older people, people who had lived much of their lives out and were visibly successful" (p. 41). He further stated, "When you select out for careful study very fine and healthy people, strong people, creative people, saintly people, sagacious people—in fact, exactly the kind of people I picked out—then you get a different view of mankind" (p. 41).

Snowball sampling is another approach used in qualitative research. Berg (2004) described the technique of snowball sampling: "The basic strategy of snowballing involves first identifying several people with relevant characteristics and interviewing them or having them answer a questionnaire. These subjects are then asked for the names of other people who possess the same attributes as they do" (p. 36). The intention is to find subjects with similar characteristics; this is particularly helpful with unique populations. Curry, Sporer, and Pugach (2007) investigated tobacco cessation programs for youth. They described their participant sampling techniques as follows: "Our goal was to identify contacts at the local level who were knowledgeable about tobacco cessation programs for youths in their communities or who could lead us to such persons. Snowball sampling progressed through 2 tiers and ended with the identification of a program informant who administered a tobacco cessation program for youths in the community" (p. 173).

Another approach to sampling in qualitative methods is the use of quota samples (Berg, 2004). This sampling method involves establishing characteristics of interest and then determining how many participants the researcher needs in each characteristic, or cell. Multiple cells or characteristics may be identified (Berg, 2004). Barton, Sulaiman, Clarke, and Abramson (2005) provide an example of using quota sampling in qualitative research. They studied the experiences of Australian parents in caring for their children with asthma. The researchers describe their sampling methods as a combination of random sampling, purposeful sampling, and quota sampling, which they say "was used to select a manageable number of care-givers for a home visit. . . ." (p. 304). They describe the specific approach to quota sampling this way: "Quota sampling was then used to obtain a minimum of ten participants each from the intervention and control . . ." (p. 304).

Sampling Errors and Sampling Bias

Sampling error refers to the researchers not obtaining an accurate sample of the population. Wiersma and Jurs (2005) defined sampling error as ". . . variation due to fluctuation when random samples are used to represent populations" (p. 301). Sampling errors occur by accident or chance when those selected do not represent the population. For example, smaller sample sizes may result in more frequent sampling errors because there is a greater chance of not obtaining a representative sample of the population when the sample size is too small. Conversely, larger sample sizes decrease the chance for sampling error.

Sampling bias is different from sampling error, in that the former is under the control of the researcher. As with sampling error, the sample is not representative of the population, but for different reasons. Wiersma and Jurs (2005) defined sampling bias as ". . . a distortion caused by the way the sample was selected or formed, so that the sample is no longer representative of the population" (p. 301). In sampling bias, the researcher has actively chosen to select individuals in such a way that bias occurs in the sample. For example, samples of convenience typically contain sampling bias. An example of sampling bias is a researcher who wants to study different methods of teaching reading and has a friend in an elementary school who will let the researcher into the school to conduct the study. This is a sample of convenience and does not necessarily represent the larger population. The school may be in an affluent suburb. A great deal of psychological research has been conduced with undergraduate psychology students. This sample is one of convenience but is not necessarily representative of the larger population. Generalization of results from a sample of convenience to a larger population creates the potential for sampling bias and affects the validity of generalizing to the target population.

There are several methods a researcher can use to reduce sampling bias. The best solution to the problem of sampling bias is the use of random selection from the accessible population. A second way to reduce sampling bias that is not as reliable is for researchers to compare significant demographic characteristics of their sample to those in the population to ensure similarity.

Guidelines and Questions for Evaluating the Methods Section Sample

The following questions may be used to evaluate the methods section sample proposed in a journal research article:

1. Are relevant demographic characteristics of the sample clearly identified?

2. Do the methods of sample selection used by the researchers provide a good representative sample based on the population?

3. Are there any apparent biases in selection of the sample?

4. Is the sample size large enough for the study proposed?

5. Does the researcher use the appropriate sampling technique for the purpose and type of research design employed?

6. Are volunteers used? If so, what is the response rate? If the response rate is low, has the researcher attempted to determine if those who volunteer are significantly different from those who do not participate?

Evaluating Examples From the Research Literature

Study 1 Quantitative Research

As in preceding chapters, I want to provide examples by evaluating two studies published in the professional literature, using the questions and guidelines proposed here (Fry, 2007; Henderson, et al., 2007). I want to start, as in other chapters, with the quantitative study. Henderson, et al. (2007) described the participants as follows:

Participants were prescreened for both the experience of trauma and trauma symptom severity using the Posttraumatic Stress Disorder Scale (PDS; Foa, 1995). Those who reported experiencing one or more traumatic stressors (determined by responses drawn from a checklist contained in the PDS) and who showed at least moderate levels of PTSD symptom severity (i.e. greater than 10 on the PDS) were regarded as potential participants for the study. Potential participants were excluded from the study if they reported being currently in psychotherapy or currently taking psychotropic medication. This exclusion criterion was included to ensure that changes in outcome measures were due to experimental manipulation and not the effects of therapy or medication. These criteria were modeled after the Sloan and Marx study on written disclosure (see Sloan & Marx, 2004a).

The first question concerns whether the researchers have clearly identified relevant demographic characteristics of the sample. In this study, several major demographic characteristics are described: gender (37 females, 11 males); occupation (students at a public university); age (18 to 21 years); and years in college. In addition, the sample was identified to have experienced significant parental nurturance deprivation during childhood. It appears that several major demographic characteristics were well documented. One major demographic characteristic was missing from the description: the ethnicity of the sample. Additionally, it might have been helpful to know the status of intimate relationships of the sample. One could argue that individuals who have intimate relationships may have nurturing needs met.

Our second question in evaluating the sample given in the methods section is whether the sample is a good representation of the target population. Recall that in this study, the target population was older adolescents who had been determined by the researchers to have experienced significant nurturance deprivation during childhood. It does not appear that a sample of college students from a public university is a good representation of the target population. Fewer than half of the citizens of the United States attend college, and, consequently, the researchers were ignoring a large portion of their target group.

The third question is whether the researchers showed any biases in the selection of their subjects or sample. This appears to be a sample of convenience, one that is available to the researchers (it is likely that the sample was taken from students where the researchers were employed). Also, the sample was composed of volunteers. There appears to be sampling bias present in this study, basically because it was a sample of convenience and not necessarily representative of the larger target population. If the researchers had intended the target group to be college students, for whatever reason, then this might have been a better representation of the population.

The researchers used a true experimental design for the study and randomly assigned subjects to either an experimental or control group. The experimental group received the forgiveness education program and training focusing on forgiving their parents for not providing adequate nurturing and love. The control group did not receive any training. According to the basic formula presented earlier for determining sample size, the researchers needed at minimum 30 subjects, 15 for each group. Thus the sample size for this study appears to be adequate, as 48 participated.

The next questions are, What are the sampling techniques used? Are they appropriate for the research design used? It appears from the description that simple random sampling from a larger pool of individuals was used. Initially, 78 students who had been identified as meeting the desired criteria (scoring significantly on a parental love-deprivation scale) were used as the pool for selecting subjects randomly. However, this was not truly random sampling because each person in the larger accessible population did not have an equal chance to be selected to participate in the study. The researchers might more effectively have used stratified sampling and selected individuals from other groups of older adolescents, such as those attending a community college or technical school.

The final questions are whether volunteers were used and what the participation rate was. Based on the information provided, the researchers did use volunteers. No participants were reported to have refused participation from the larger group identified as possible subjects, the 78 individuals identified as having experienced nurturance deprivation as children. However, if the researchers had used a more representative sample of the population it might not have resulted in such a high response rate (it appears to have been 100 percent). College students are typically agreeable to research participation.

In summary, most relevant demographic characteristics were adequately identified, with the major exception of ethnicity. It does not appear that this sample was a good representation of the target or the accessible population. The sample was taken solely from a 4-year college population that did not include individuals from other settings where there are young adults. There appears to be sampling bias present in this study, basically because the researchers used a sample of convenience that did not necessarily represent the larger target or accessible population. The sample size used appeared to be adequate based on the research design. Simple random sampling was used, but this was not truly random sampling because each person in the larger accessible population did not have an equal chance to be selected to participate in the study. Based on the information provided, the researchers did use volunteers, and no participants from the larger group identified as possible subjects were reported as having refused to participate. The selection methods used in this study were inadequate, and any attempt at generalizing the results back to the larger population should be made with caution.

Study 2 Qualitative Research

Fry (2007) provides an example of a qualitative study and describes her participants in the following way:

> Four 1st-year teachers participated in this study: Stella, Shari, Becca, and Laura (pseudonyms). The participants, all women, graduated with elementary education degrees from the same land-grant university located in the Rocky Mountain West. The university has approximately 10,000 undergraduate and graduate students, and approximately 120 elementary education majors graduate from the teacher preparation program each year. The participants were part of the same student teaching cohort, and were between 22 and 24 years old at the time of the study. Stella spent her first in-service year teaching 5th grade in a town of approximately 7,000 people that was located less than 20 miles away from a large city. Shari taught 3rd grade in a community of fewer than 1,200 people, located approximately 2½ hours away from the nearest major city. Becca and Laura taught kindergarden and 1st grade respectively. Becca's school was in a suburban area of a large city. Laura taught in a town of fewer than 30,000 people, located 90 minutes from the nearest city (All population data was obtained from the U.S. Census, 2000).

Participant involvement was requested based on involvement in an earlier, related study about the impact of an induction network they used during their student teaching experiences (Fry, 2006). Purposive sampling, a procedure that involves choosing participants with the qualities the researcher wants to investigate (Bogdan & Biklan, 2003), was used to identify appropriate participants for the original study. During the original study, Stella, Becca, Shari, and Laura demonstrated writing and speaking strengths as well as strong reflective abilities that may have developed as a result of their teacher preparation program's emphasis on educators being reflective practitioners. Each was able to clearly explain the rationale for her teaching decisions, thoughtfully ask questions to help improve her practice, and explain her students' behavior and learning in detail. Because these skills contribute to rich qualitative data, Stella, Becca, Shari, and Laura were invited to participate in the present study. No monetary or tangible incentive was offered for participation.

The first question is whether relevant demographic characteristics of the sample are clearly identified. The researcher does provide information about the ages and geographic locations of the participants. Also, information about the experience of the teachers is provided. No information is provided about race or socioeconomic status of the participants. However, one might conclude that socioeconomic status is middle class, given that the participants are teachers.

A second question concerns whether the methods of sample selection used by the researchers provide a good representative sample based on the population. The researcher stated she used purposive sampling. The purposive approach to sampling is consistent with a desire to identify those with special knowledge or expertise, e.g., experience with teacher induction during the first few years of entering the teaching profession. As was noted above, the use of such sampling methods as purposive sampling does not necessarily provide a good representative sample of the population. It does not mean that the sample is not representative, but just simply that it may not be representative.

A third question is whether there are any apparent biases in selection of the sample. The researcher noted that all participants graduated from the same university and also the same cohort of students. This suggests not only a sample of convenience but a potential bias in sample selection as well.

The next question is whether the sample size large is enough for the study proposed. The sample size in qualitative research is not based on a specific number but on other factors, such as the representation of the variables of interest in the study. The researcher focused on induction efforts for beginning teachers, and the participants met these criteria.

A fifth question is whether the researcher used appropriate sampling techniques for the purpose and type of research design employed. The researcher used purposive sampling, which is consistent with a qualitative study design. The question is whether the purposive sampling methods used in this study were truly designed to find those who were good representatives of this population, beginning teachers participating in induction methods.

The last question is whether volunteers were used and whether there was an adequate response rate. Qualitative research does not use large numbers of participants, so response rate is not a big issue. However, the research does not indicate whether any other individuals were asked to participate in the study.

In summary, Fry (2007) identified several important demographic characteristics of the participants. However, she left off important ones, including race. The use of the purposive approach to sampling is appropriate with the research design, a qualitative design. There does appear to be some bias in the selection of the sample, based on the report that the participants came from the same cohort of students. There is no minimum in the sample size for a qualitative study, so the sample size is adequate. The use of purposive sampling is appropriate for the qualitative design employed, and volunteers were used; no information was provided as to whether anyone declined to participate.

Summary

The description of the sample used in a research study provides the reader with important pieces of information. It enables those reading the results to determine the efficacy of the study, and it provides necessary details to other researchers interested in replicating the study. We as consumers of research are particularly interested in determining the efficacy of a study. The adequate selection of a sample is important. First, it provides the reader with information about how valid the results may be in applying them to an identified population; second, as practitioners, we are concerned with appropriately applying the results. The methods a researcher may use in selecting a sample include simple random sampling, stratified sampling, cluster sampling, systematic random sampling, and convenience sampling. Convenience sampling provides the least valid approach to selecting a sample.

Sampling error and sampling bias affect the validity of sample selection. Sampling error refers to the researchers' not having obtained an accurate sample of the population; sampling bias concerns a sample that is not representative of the population because the researchers have actively chosen to select individuals in such a way that bias occurs in the sample. For example, samples of convenience typically contain sampling bias.

Sampling methods in qualitative research do not require the same kind of rigor as quantitative research methods. No specific number of subjects has been suggested for conducting qualitative research. Patton (1990) proposed several different sampling methods that can be used in qualitative research. The more commonly used methods include extreme case sampling, typical case sampling, maximum variation sampling, homogeneous sampling, and snowball or chain sampling.

Evaluating the selection or adequacy of a sample includes determining whether the methods of sample selection used by the researchers provide a good representative sample based on the population and whether there are any apparent biases in selection of the sample. Also, we are interested in whether the sample size is large enough for the study proposed and whether the researchers used the appropriate sampling technique for the purpose and type of research design employed.

Exercises

Directions: Locate an article in a professional journal that includes a methods section and describes the sample used in the study. Carefully read the sample description and critique the study based on the questions and guidelines discussed in this chapter.

1. Are relevant demographic characteristics of the sample clearly identified?

2. Do the methods of sample selection used by the researchers provide a good representative sample, based on the population?

3. Are there any apparent biases in selection of the sample?

4. Is the sample size large enough for the study proposed?

5. Does the researcher use the appropriate sampling technique for the purpose and type of research design employed?

6. Are volunteers used? If so, what is the response rate? Also, if the response rate is low, does the researcher attempt to determine if those who volunteer are significantly different from those who do not participate?

12

Evaluating the Methods Section—Procedures

The procedures section in a research article is a step-by-step description of how the study was conducted. This includes a discussion of the research design and methods used in the study. Recall that the scientific method requires that researchers submit their studies to public scrutiny. The procedures section is where considerable focus will be in determining the efficacy of the study. Also, the procedures section gives information to practitioners about how to implement the treatments in the target population. The ability to implement the treatment in the population is one of the more important purposes in conducting research in counseling and education.

In this chapter, I will discuss how the researchers present study variables, particularly the independent variables, if there are any, in the procedures section. Second, I will describe the importance of random assignment to groups in true experimental and quasi-experimental designs. Third, I will discuss internal validity and external validity and their importance in understanding and using results published in professional journals. In this discussion, I will demonstrate how researchers may reduce threats to internal and external validity. Next, I will propose guidelines and questions for evaluating the procedures section. Finally, I will evaluate several research studies presented in the professional literature, using the guidelines presented.

Description of Study Variables

An important consideration for the researchers in the procedures section is to systematically and clearly describe the independent variable (if there is an independent variable). Recall that the independent variable is defined in terms of the researcher's manipulating an event or phenomenon to study its effect on another variable, the dependent variable. Also, there are measurement types of variables that can be considered as independent variables (e.g., IQ). Whatever the independent variable is, the researcher should systematically describe it for the reader. This means that if a particular treatment is used, a step-by-step description is provided in the procedures section. For example, if a researcher is testing the effectiveness of a counseling approach such as cognitive behavioral therapy with those who have been diagnosed with post-traumatic stress disorder, the specific methods used must be described in the procedures section. This includes a discussion of the training received by those providing the counseling or the manipulation. In education, the researcher should describe the teaching method used in detail. Typically, researchers have developed specific training manuals for the interventions that are being tested.

The researcher should also detail how the control group was treated, if there is a control group used. The control group may experience no intervention at all, or it may experience something that is not connected to the independent variables (so there is no possible impact on the dependent variable) but that gives the control group a feeling that it received "special attention" like the experimental group.

Remember from evaluating the hypothesis and purpose statements that certain words can give the reader insight into the type of study conducted. The research design and description of all variables should be consistent with the purpose and the hypotheses presented in the introduction. Consistency can be judged by determining whether the procedures are congruent with the particular words used in the purpose or hypothesis—words like *comparison, relationship*, and *illuminate*. A comparison should involve the use of a research design that allows for the comparison of two or more groups, whereas a correlation-focused study may have multiple dependent variables to correlate with one group. It is important to keep in mind that some studies use several hypotheses and combine comparison, correlational, and/or descriptive approaches.

Random Assignment

Stangor (2004) described random assignment to groups in experimental research. Random assignment is defined as randomly assigning participants to groups (both experimental and control groups). As with random selection, random assignment means that all those selected from the population to participate in a study have an equal chance of being assigned to a particular group. Random assignment to groups is a separate procedure from random selection from the population. Random assignment is accomplished once the researcher has selected participants for the study. Once participants are selected, the researcher can randomly assign each one to a group, including experimental, control, traditional method, and so on.

Not all research methods use random assignment. Descriptive research and qualitative methods do not. However, random assignment to groups does reduce the effects of some threats to validity. The definition of a true experimental study requires that a manipulation occur and that there be random assignment to groups. Random assignment protects against problems with internal and external validity. The intent with random assignment is to ensure that your groups are similar in relevant variables that may affect the outcome or dependent variables. Random assignment is not easily achieved, particularly in the natural environment. For example, if a teacher wishes to test a particular teaching strategy, he or she generally cannot ethically divide the class into an experimental and control group, with one receiving the experimental treatment and the other the control or nothing.

When evaluating the efficacy of the procedure employed in a study, two of the most important considerations are the internal and external validity of the methods. Stangor (2006) defined internal validity as ". . . the extent to which changes in the dependent variable can confidently be attributed to the effect of the independent variable, rather than to the potential effects of confounding variables" (p. 226). More specifically, internal validity refers to how well the study was conducted with the sample and the extent to which extraneous variables were controlled for within the research design. The intent is to reduce all or as many variables as possible (other than the treatment or independent variable) that can influence the outcome or the dependent variable. Clearly, the purpose here is to be able to then state that the independent variable, and not some other extraneous variable, *caused* the outcome.

External validity refers to the extent to which the researchers can replicate the actual events occurring in the natural environment and thus can generalize the results back to the population. Key here is the efficacy of controlling for those factors that influence the researcher's ability to generalize and apply the results to the population from which the sample was drawn.

Information about the internal and external validity of a study can be found in the procedures section. Gelso (1979) suggested that we can understand internal and external validity from the perspective of high or low control over the research conditions. Theoretically, the more control the researchers have over the experimental condition, the higher the internal validity. This means that the researchers have considerable control over the implementation of the study and, potentially, can reduce the effects of extraneous variables by eliminating them through such methods as random assignment, the particular research method, and/or laboratory control over factors that may influence the natural environment.

Conversely, the lower the control the researchers impose through the use of the natural environment, the higher the external validity *may* be, although this is not always the case. The researchers clearly have less control over extraneous variables in the natural setting, where random assignment and fewer opportunities for controlling extraneous variables occur. However, it can be argued that observations and research conducted in the natural environment increase the ability to generalize to the population. The reality is that there needs to be a balance between the natural environment and the amount of control exercised by the researchers. As previously noted, too much control reduces the ability to generalize to the population because a fabricated situation is constructed by the researcher. However, the researcher does not want to concede too much control and reduce the internal validity of the study, which would also hinder the ability of the study to be generalized to the population. If too many variables can be determined to have influenced the outcomes, the researchers are basically left with no new useful information. Parsons and Brown (2002) noted that good internal validity is absolutely necessary to the researcher, even before one can consider external validity (generalizing the results to the population). Consequently, the researchers must balance the amount of control exercised to ensure adequate internal and external validity. The procedures section provides the reader with the information to judge whether the study meets a reasonable level of balance, ensuring that both internal validity and external validity are adequate. It is important to again note here that all research has some flaws in regard to problems with internal and/or external validity. Your job as a reader and user of the research literature is to determine whether the researchers have provided adequate protection of internal and external validity. Researchers have identified potential threats to validity that can provide criteria for determining whether a study has good internal and external validity (Bracht & Glass, 1968; Campbell & Stanley, 1966; Cook & Campbell, 1979). Campbell and Stanley (1966) noted that threats to validity were associated with specific research designs. It may be helpful to quickly review Chapter 4 and the discussion of quantitative research designs before reading the next section. Keep in mind, as the various threats to validity are discussed, that they are typically associated with specific designs. Most threats to validity are associated with research designs; however, a few external threats to validity are a result of how the sample was selected (selection bias and/or error; see Table 12.4).

Table 12.1   Summary of Threats to Internal and External Validity With Pre-Experimental Design

Design	Type of Threat	
	Internal	External
1. One-shot case study	history, maturation, selection, and mortality	Hawthorne Effect; novelty to disruption (possible); experimenter effect (possible), measurement of dependent variable (possible); interaction between time and measurement and treatment effects (possible)
2. One group pretest–post-test	history, maturation, testing, instrumentation, interaction of selection, and other factors, such as maturation	Hawthorne Effect; novelty or disruption (possible); experimenter effects (possible); pretest sensitization, post-test sensitization; measurement of dependent variable (possible); interaction between time and measurement and treatment effects (possible)
3. Static group comparison	history (possible, if the experience studied takes place over an extended time period), maturation (possible), selection, mortality, and interaction of selection with other factors	measurement of dependent variable (possible); interaction between time of measurement and treatment effects (possible)

Threats to Internal Validity

Eight threats to internal validity have been identified (Campbell & Stanley, 1966; Gall, et al., 1996; Moore, 1983; Parsons & Brown, 2002), and these include history, maturation, testing, instrumentation, statistical regression, differential selection, mortality/attrition, and selection-maturation interaction. Several other threats to validity have been identified, but they do not occur as frequently as the eight cited here (Gall, et al., 1996).

The threat of *history* is defined as events occurring during the time of the study that are unrelated to the treatment or independent variables (Campbell &

Table 12.2   Summary of Threats to Internal and External Validity With Quasi-Experimental Designs

Design	Internal	External
1. Time series	history; instrumentation (possible)	pretest sensitization; post-test sensitization; Hawthorne Effect (possible); novelty or disruption (possible); experimenter effects (possible); measurement of dependent variable (possible); interaction between time and measurement and treatment effects (possible)
2. Non-equivalent control group	history (possible if intervention takes place over time) and interaction between selection and other factors	Hawthorne Effect (possible); novelty or disruption (possible); experimenter effects (possible); pretest sensitization; post-test sensitization; measurement of dependent variable (possible); interaction between measurement and treatment effects (possible)
3. Multiple time series	interaction between selection and other factors (possible)	multiple treatment interference; experiment effects (possible); pretest sensitization; post-test sensitization; measurement of dependent variable (possible); interaction between time of measurement and treatment effects (possible)

Stanley, 1966; Gall, et al., 1996; Parsons & Brown, 2002). Whenever studies are conducted over a period of time and there is no random assignment to groups, history can be a threat. Random assignment reduces or eliminates the

Table 12.3   Summary of Threats to Internal and External Validity With True Experimental Designs

Design	Internal	External
1. Pretest–post-test	none	pretest sensitization; post-test sensitization; Hawthorne Effect (possible); novelty or disruption (possible); experimenter effects (possible); measurement of dependent variable (possible); interaction between time and measurement and treatment effects (possible)
2. Post-test only	none	post-test sensitization; Hawthorne Effect (possible); novelty or disruption (possible); experimenter effects (possible); measurement of dependent variable (possible); interaction between time and measurement and treatment effects (possible)
3. Solomon Four Group	none	Hawthorne Effect (possible); novelty or disruption (possible); experimenter effects (possible); measurement of dependent variable (possible); interaction between time and measurement and treatment effects (possible)

effect of history because, theoretically, those randomly assigned to groups will experience similar events or histories. For example, if you have a community that experiences a severe flood during an intervention in the schools with different treatment for different classrooms and schools (the classrooms having been randomly assigned with the use of cluster sampling), then the effects of the flood should theoretically be systematically distributed (some parts of the community would be more or less affected). History is more of a problem for research methods such as descriptive or qualitative approaches. A qualitative approach using case study methods may provide detailed information to the researcher but at the same time be vulnerable to the threat to validity of history. For example, a researcher could study the interaction between second-grade students and their teacher, using a case study approach. Events could occur that might affect the interaction between the teacher and the students. The teacher might experience personal problems at home that affect his or her teaching, and the same could be true for the children.

A second type of threat to internal validity is *maturation* (Campbell & Stanley, 1966; Gall, et al., 1996). Maturation concerns possible physical and/or psychological changes that occur in the participants over the period of the study. This is particularly important for children and adolescents, who have the potential to experience significant changes over a relatively short period of time (e.g., 6 months). The shorter the period of time during which the study is conducted, the less likelihood that maturation will affect the participants. Additionally, the use of random assignment to treatment groups eliminates the threat of maturation. When participants are randomly assigned to groups, all members of the various groups (treatment and control) should, theoretically, experience similar changes in growth. Also, the threat of maturation may be present when the researcher is comparing groups progressing through distinctly different developmental stages. To address this particular issue, researchers generally avoid comparing such groups.

A third threat to internal validity is *testing* (Campbell & Stanley, 1966; Gall, et al., 1996). The threat of testing occurs when participants become sensitized to the intent of the study or the desired responses the researchers are seeking from pretest to post-test. Consequently, the participants perform better on the post-test, not due to the treatment, but because they have become aware of the desired responses, which they detected from taking the pretest. This threat is most problematic when multiple testing occurs due to the research design employed. For example, several quasi-experimental designs use multiple testing occur a period of time (e.g., the time series design).

A fourth threat to validity that is related to testing is *instrumentation* (Campbell & Stanley, 1966; Gall, et al., 1996). Instrumentation concerns the quality of the instrument or the consistency of the instrument. Researchers (Gall, et al., 1996; Moore, 1983) have noted the problem with observational measures and internal validity.

Specifically, it has been found that raters who are observing targeted behaviors or events will score responses differently from the pretest to the post-test. It has been suggested that standardization of measures and ratings is one method that reduces the effects of testing. Also, an instrument that has low reliability results in an increased threat to internal validity. Scores may vary dramatically from pretest to post-test, not as a consequence of the treatment but because of the low reliability of the instrument.

Another threat to internal validity is *statistical regression* (Campbell & Stanley, 1966; Gall, et al., 1996). This is where the research design calls for a pretest and post-test, and changes in scores are likely to *regress* or *move* toward the mean. Typically this occurs with extreme scores or responses and selection of participants because of their extremities. For example, if a teacher has a class of exceptionally bright children and gives a math exam and they all score perfectly, the second time the children take the exam there is an increased likelihood that scores will regress toward the mean. This happens when lower or higher scores are achieved with participants or respondents selected for their extremities. Theoretically, an individual's score on a math exam is based on ability and chance (Gall, et al., 1996). A low score would be a function of bad luck and ability. When the child takes a subsequent math exam on the same material, there is an increased likelihood that his or her scores will be higher. This occurs because, although a person's scores on responses based on ability will be retained, responses due to chance will result in overall scores regressing toward the mean.

Differential selection is a sixth contributor to threats to internal validity (Campbell & Stanley, 1966; Gall, et al., 1996). This threat occurs when the experimental and control groups are selected based on different criteria, or when participants are assigned to groups differentially and not by random assignment. Random assignment to groups eliminates this threat because all groups will have had equal opportunity to be assigned to control and experimental groups. If participants are not randomly assigned to groups, members of the control and experimental groups may differ significantly on relevant variables, which could influence the outcome or responses to the dependent variable.

A seventh threat to internal validity is *attrition*, or experimental *mortality* (Campbell & Stanley, 1966; Gall, et al., 1996). This involves participants dropping out of the study. Participants may drop out of a study for various reasons, and these might be based on the subject's participation in a particular experimental group, which clearly could have an impact on the results. Reasons could include dropping out of a control group because nothing is happening that the participant feels is worthwhile, or moving away from the area where the study is being conducted. Gall, et al. (1996) noted that reducing the effects of experimental mortality may be achieved, again, through random assignment to groups (theoretically, the researcher will have distributed dropouts equally among the groups) and ensuring that rewards for participants are equal for all groups. Researchers additionally may follow up on those who dropped out to determine if, based on relevant variables, they are significantly different from those who continued. Experimental mortality is more likely the longer a study is conducted. People move away or experience other significant events that prevent them from continued participation in a research study.

An eighth threat to internal validity is *selection-maturation interaction* (Campbell & Stanley, 1966; Gall, et al., 1996). In this threat, the issue is that participants are selected based on certain developmental characteristics, which results in groups not being equal at the start of the study. The developmental or maturation characteristics further complicate interpretation of the results: Did the results occur as a consequence of the intervention or changes in maturation? For example, a researcher wants to know the effects of a particular math instruction approach and selects students in fifth and sixth grades. She has the intention of comparing fifth graders' progress (the control group) with sixth graders who are to receive the experimental method. Many of the sixth graders may have begun to enter into formal thinking stages and thus may make more progress in learning math than the fifth graders.

Threats to External Validity

Bracht and Glass (1968) identified 12 threats to external validity (Table 12.4). These 12 threats were categorized into two major groups: population validity and ecological validity. Two threats to population validity have been

Table 12.4   Summary of Threats to External Validity

Type of Threat

Population validity

1. Comparison of accessible population to target population
2. Interaction of personological variables and treatment

Ecological Validity

3. Describing the independent variable explicitly
4. Multiple treatment interference
5. Hawthorne Effect
6. Novelty and disruption effects
7. Experimenter effect
8. Pretest sensitization
9. Post-test sensitization
10. Interaction of history and treatment effects
11. Measure of the dependent variable
12. Interaction of time and measurement

proposed: (a) comparison of the accessible popul;
population, and (b) interaction between "personolo
sonal characteristics) and treatment effects. The 1'
validity include explicit description of the independen
ment interference; the Hawthorne Effect; novelty and
imenter effect; pretest sensitization; post-test sensitization; in...
history and treatment effects; measurement of the dependent variable, .
interaction of time of measurement and treatment effects.

The first threat to population validity, *comparison of accessible population to target population,* concerns the extent to which the researchers use an accessible population that is actually representative of the target population (Bracht & Glass, 1968). The researcher may be interested in a target population that is representative of certain groups residing in the United States, but he or she does not have access to the total population, for geographic and economic reasons. For example, a researcher may be interested in studying the effects of a particular therapy approach in combination with medication for those with major depression. The researcher could not feasibly set up this study in all geographic regions in the country, even though the intended target population is all those with a diagnosis of major depression. Consequently, the researcher may use only those from the Southeast. He or she could randomly select from a list of those from that geographic area who had been diagnosed with the condition. The threat to external validity in this example is whether this particular geographic area has individuals with major depression who are similar to those in other parts of the country. We could speculate about why they may be different: (a) certain ethnic groups migrated to the area and their genetics or physiology may be unique, (b) the weather is different from that in other parts of the country (for instance, it may be more dreary and thus lead participants to feel more depressed), and (c) social service agencies are quite active and provide more services in this area than they do in other parts of the country. These are only a few reasons that the accessible population may not be representative of the target population; many others could be identified. A researcher could randomly select individuals from other parts of the country to survey and determine if the accessible population is significantly different on relevant variables, such as ethnicity. The reality is that a significant number of studies suffer from this threat to external validity for the reasons cited earlier. Consequently, interpreting the results should be accomplished with care when applying them to a group you are working with in a community potentially different from the accessible population.

A second threat to population validity, *interaction between personological variables and treatment,* concerns how specific personal characteristics of participants may interact with treatment and influence the outcome in a not representative of how the population may respond (Bracht & Glass, 1968). An example may be a study focusing on the language development of grade school children, in which the accessible population is only those from affluent suburban communities. These communities may have children who come from families whose parents are well educated and highly verbal. Consequently, these children may perform differently in the experimental interventions than those from urban or rural communities. Moore (1983) suggested that the best method of reducing this threat is to build relevant personological variables into the study design. In our example, the researchers would include children and schools from suburban, urban, and rural communities.

One threat to ecological external validity, *explicit description of the independent variable,* concerns how clearly the researchers describe the independent variable, making it possible for others to replicate the intervention with others in the population (Bracht & Glass, 1968). Others' ability to replicate the independent variable with those from the target population is basically dependent on how well the researchers operationalized the intervention. As mentioned earlier, it is typical to develop an instructional and procedural manual with an intervention. Researchers who use standard approaches to an intervention address this threat to validity. For example, comparing different therapy approaches, such as person-centered and psychodynamic approaches, is a description of the intervention adequate to allow others to replicate it. If no formal manual or approach is available, researchers should provide a detailed description in the procedures section of the intervention.

Multiple treatment interference can potentially occur when the researchers introduce two or more treatments consecutively to the same participants (Bracht & Glass, 1968). The researchers cannot determine which intervention affected the outcome, or if it was both. The problem occurs when others try to implement the intervention with individuals in the population and use only one of the interventions studied. The solution to reducing this threat is to use only one treatment, or compare both interventions separately with the combined treatments.

The *Hawthorne Effect* is a third threat to ecological external validity. If a participant is aware of his or her involvement in a research study, his or her responses to the dependent variables may consequently be altered from the way they would normally be (Bracht & Glass, 1968). Responses may be based on the participants' personality characteristics, whether they typically comply and are cooperative or prefer to act defiantly and resist providing accurate information, even though they agreed to participate. There are times when participants want to see a particular intervention not succeed and may exaggerate their responses. Control group members may attempt to compete with the experimental group to outperform them on dependent variab. solution to this threat is to use a placebo or an intervention that is de. to have no effect on the dependent variable. In a study comparing stress n agement training techniques, in which there are two different methods or t..e researcher is interested in comparing two different stress management training techniques, a third group could be a placebo group. The placebo group might be asked to engage in a neutral activity, such as writing a letter. A fourth group could be a control group, which would experience no activity and would provide a comparison for determining Hawthorne Effects.

Novelty or disruption effects is a fourth threat to external ecological validity (Bracht & Glass, 1968). Any dependent measure gains are a consequence of being exposed to something that is novel (the independent variable) rather than the actual effects of the treatment. This threat is particularly relevant when the treatment is short-term and the novelty does not have a chance to wear off. Theoretically, the novelty will wear off after a period of time; responses to the dependent variables will then be more accurate. When disruption effects occur, they may actually lower responses to the dependent variables. The introduction of a new approach may be so different from previous approaches that it will take time to adjust to the new methods. The solution to this problem is, again, to have a longer intervention time before measuring the dependent variables.

The Hawthorne Effect and novelty and disruption effects are somewhat similar, but they have their differences. The Hawthorne Effect concerns the participants' active efforts to change the outcome because they are aware of their participation. Novelty and disruption effects are more like experiencing a "new toy." It is quite possible that both threats to validity operate in a study.

A fifth threat to external ecological validity, *experimenter effects,* involves the experimenter communicating to the participants, most often subtly, what outcomes he or she would like to achieve (Bracht & Glass, 1968). The researchers may be interested in seeing a particular intervention be successful and may communicate this desire in some way to participants. Also, the researchers may be biased in their scoring of the dependent variables, particularly where the dependent measure requires a judgment on the part of the scorer. For example, classroom observations may be used and be open to interpretation. An approach to avoiding this problem is to reduce the actual influence the researcher has on the implementation of the study by having another implement the study and score any subjective dependent measures. A sophisticated method is to use a double-blind approach, in which those implementing the study are unaware of its intent. In regard to scoring, the researchers can use scorers who are unaware of the intent of the study but are instructed in how to score the dependent variables.

Pretest sensitization is another threat to ecological external validity and involves the participants becoming aware of the desired response to the dependent variable (Bracht & Glass, 1968). In situations where the dependent variable is a self-report, it is possible for pretest sensitization to occur. With self-report measures, it is possible for participants to actually foster learning and subsequently alter their responses (Moore, 1983). The solution to resolving this problem is to use pretest–post-test designs with post-test-only designs (as in the Solomon Four-Group Design). With this design, the researcher can determine the effects of pretesting on responses.

Another threat to ecological external validity, *post-test sensitization*, again concerns a sensitization and learned response to items dealing with the dependent measure (Bracht & Glass, 1968). The opportunity for immediate learning is required and is based on the participants using the materials in subsequent responses. Bracht and Glass (1968) suggested that the best solution for addressing this threat is to use unobtrusive measures in gathering dependent variable information. Unobtrusive measures generally involve minimal contact with participants.

An eighth threat to external ecological validity is *interaction between history and treatment effects* (Bracht & Glass, 1968). This threat refers to how events occurring at the time of the intervention or treatment affect the outcome. For example, if a community had just experienced an economic downturn, this could affect even the responses that are unrelated to the treatment. This threat is a difficult one to evaluate because researchers typically do not address such events in the description of their study. Moore (1983) suggested that extending the study beyond the anticipated impact of the uncontrolled event is a way for the researcher to address this threat. For those of us evaluating the study, it is necessary to rely on the news media to determine if any major events might have affected the study.

Measurement of the dependent variable, a ninth threat, concerns how effectively the researcher operationalized the dependent variables (Bracht & Glass, 1968). The instrument chosen by the researchers may have been poorly constructed, with low reliability and/or validity. (Validity in regard to an instrument refers to how well the instrument measures the concept that it was intended to measure; see Chapter 13 for further explanation about the reliability and validity of instruments.) The best solution for reducing this threat is for researchers to choose instruments that have good reliability and validity.

The last threat to ecological external validity, *interaction between time of measurement and treatment effects,* involves the effects of treatment being greatest just after the intervention is implemented. Consequently, the actual long-term effects are unclear (Bracht & Glass, 1968). Typically, researchers administer post-tests just after the intervention when, theoretically, the impact of the intervention is greatest. To avoid this threat, researchers administer a follow-up assessment of the dependent variables several months after the intervention to determine long-term impact.

Five questions are suggested as a guide for evaluating the methods section (procedures) of a research article:

1. What type of research design was used in the study?

2. Is the research design consistent with the purpose and hypothesis presented in the introduction?

3. Are the independent variables clearly defined? Are the independent variables so clearly defined that they can be replicated using the information provided in the procedures section?

4. Identify any threats to internal validity. How are they threats?

5. Identify any threats to external validity. How are they threats?

Evaluation of Examples From the Literature

Study 1 Quantitative Research

Henderson, et al. (2007) described the procedures section as follows:

The process of approval for human subjects research by the University's institutional review board was followed and approval was obtained. The conditions of each session were assigned randomly, and the participants did not know which group they would be attending. Participants in the experimental (n=19) and control conditions (n=17) were tested separately in small groups of five to ten individuals. Using the example of various Pennebaker, et al. written disclosure studies (Pennebaker, 1997a, 1997b; Pennebaker & Seagal, 1999; Pennebaker & Susman, 1988), the drawing sessions took place across 3 consecutive days, with all participants drawing for a total of 20 minutes each session.

At the beginning of the first session for each condition, the lead investigator briefly explained the purpose of the study and written informed consent was obtained. This included informing participants of the sensitive nature of the study and providing them with a list of individuals or psychological service providers to contact if they felt distressed at any time during or after the experiment.

All participants completed the time one measures for PDS, BDI-II STAI, SMS, PILL, and a demographic questionnaire immediately before drawing at the first session. With the exception of the demographic questionnaire, the same measures were completed immediately after the last drawing session (time two) and at a 1-month follow-up (time three). When participants in both conditions finished the self-report measures, they were given a large envelope containing one blank sheet of paper and an instruction sheet specific to their condition. For simplicity and standardization, a box of crayons and a pencil were also provided. A trained research assistant instructed them to open their envelopes and follow along as the specific instructions provided within their envelope were read aloud by the assistant.

The participants in the mandala condition were asked to draw a large circle on their paper and then fill the circle with representations of feelings or emotions to their trauma using symbols, patterns, designs, and colors (but no words) that felt right to them. In the control condition, participants were instructed to draw an object over the next 3 days. Each day they were given a different drawing assignment (cup, bottle, or pens) and told to make their drawing as detailed as possible. The research assistant instructed the participants to draw for 20 minutes. Their drawing and the instruction set were put in the envelope before leaving. Participants were thanked for their participation and reminded to return the following day.

At the end of the third session, a trained research assistant debriefed participants after they completed the second set of dependent variable measures (i.e., the PDS, BDI-II, STAI, and SMS) and the drawing. However, this debriefing did not involve telling participants the true nature of the study for fear of biasing the results at the follow-up session. Therefore, this was an abbreviated debriefing that focused more on how they were doing and ascertaining whether there were any problems they have experienced. A full debriefing as to the nature of the study and the expected results was provided to the participants after the completion of the third set of dependent variable measures at the 1-month follow-up. The researchers waited a month to ask about the symbolic meaning of the mandala drawings because having the participants put their feelings in words could have confounded results. This information was used for a brief examination of the qualitative features and symbolic meaning of the mandalas. (p. 150)

The first question to address in evaluating the methods section (procedures) is to identify the type of research design used in the study. The researchers described the use of assigning participants randomly to either the control or experimental group. Also, the researchers described in detail the intervention used with the experimental group. The researchers used a pretest–post-test research design. The research design is consistent with the hypotheses presented. For example, it was hypothesized that those randomly assigned to a mandala drawing condition would experience significantly better psychological and physical health compared to those in the control group, who did not experience the intervention. The independent variable, the mandala condition, is described in relatively good detail. The description of what the participants in the experimental group were asked to do is stated concisely, e.g., they were asked to "draw a large circle . . ." (p. 151). Specific instructions to participants were not provided, and this would have been helpful to understand the exact presentation made to the participants in the experimental condition. The experimental condition would be somewhat difficult to replicate without the exact instructions given to the participants.

Many threats to internal validity are addressed with a true experimental design involving the use of random assignment to groups. The instruments, Beck Depression Inventory, The State-Trait Anxiety Inventory, and others were given on pretest–post-test, and consequently, the participants may have developed hypotheses about what the investigator was attempting to assess. Participants could have altered their responses based on this information from taking the pretest to taking the post-test. The only control for this threat is the use of post-test-only designs or Solomon Four-Group Designs. No information is provided on how the participants were recruited, and there were only 36 total participants in both the experimental and control groups. This appears to be a sample of convenience and potentially results in a threat to external validity, population validity—an experimentally accessible population versus the target population. The target population appears to be those with PTSD. There may be several other threats to external validity, ecological validity: novelty and disruption effects and pretest sensitization. Novelty and disruption effects may be a consequence of simply being exposed to a new program and a novel experience, drawing mandalas. The researcher uses a pretest–post-test design, and there potentially is pretest sensitization.

The questions to address when evaluating the methods and procedures section of a qualitative research study are similar to those posed in evaluating a quantitative study, but there are still some differences. It is important to identify the type of research design used and the consistency of the design with the purpose of the study. There is no independent variable, so a question about the independent variable is not necessary. However, there should be a clear description of the procedures used to collect the data and information, e.g., phenomenological methods. The potential threats to validity of qualitative research are significant, and typically a researcher does not address such issues because the intent is to focus more on external validity and what happens in the natural environment. Bogdan and Biklen (2007) concluded that the use of generalizability in qualitative research is different than what is termed to be generalizability in quantitative research. They concluded that qualitative researchers are interested in obtaining universal conclusions of social processes specifically related to human functioning. A question to address with qualitative research is whether the researcher can obtain data or information that can result in universal conclusions based upon his or her methods. Qualitative research can involve immersion into the environment that is being studied to obtain an in-depth understanding. A criticism of such efforts is that a researcher can inject his or her own biases into the study (Bogdan & Biklen, 2007). Another question is whether the researcher has impacted the outcome with his or her own biases.

Research questions to address when evaluating a qualitative study and the methods-procedures:

1. What type of research design was used in the study?

2. Is the research design consistent with the purpose presented in the introduction?

3. Does the researcher attempt to identify universal processes, which can result in broader generalization?

4. Did the researcher introduce any bias into his or her procedures based on the procedures used?

Study 2 Qualitative Research

An example of description of qualitative research and the methods and procedures section is provided by Fry (2007), who described her procedures in the following way:

The researcher plays an integral role in qualitative research, serving as the "principal instrument" (Merriam, 1998, p. 20) for data collection and analysis. This role allows a qualitative researcher to "obtain the intricate details about phenomena such as feelings, thought processes, and emotions" (Strauss & Corbin, 1998, p. 11). Toma (2000) explained that another benefit of qualitative research occurs when the researcher is subjective rather than objective as traditionally called for in research with human subjects. Subjectivity allows "researchers and subjects to collaborate to determine meaning, generate findings, and reach conclusions" (p. 177). Toma suggested such research partnerships generate good qualitative data because when researchers "care deeply about what and who they are studying" (p. 177), they are more likely to become "insiders" (p. 183) who get to know and negotiate meaning about their research topic.

At the start of this study I already cared about the four participants. In addition to working with them during the earlier investigation of student teaching induction (Fry, 2006), when the participants were pre-service teachers, I was their professor and field supervisor. Through the experiences we shared, I developed personal relationships with each. I hoped they would be successful beginning teachers and cared about their personal well-being. In addition to undertaking new research about a timely topic, this investigation allowed me to continue to be supportive of these four young teachers long after the time when a university professor's involvement in a beginning teacher's career typically ends. My attachment to this research topic was not just limited to an interest in the research participants. I spent my 1st year teaching in a district that provided an effective induction program. I was far more successful teaching in the district where I received induction support. Thus, I am predisposed to see induction as useful because of my own experiences.

Influenced by Toma's (2000) guidelines, I designed this investigation as ?
was "genuinely interested in the subject—both in terms of the overall phe
the people who can set light on it" (p. 180). I have shared the nature of my interest, .
is also a source of potential bias in this study. Accordingly, I also used a systematic
research protocol for data collection and analysis to enhance the credibility, dependabil-
ity, and confirmability of the findings (Lincoln & Guba, 1985). This protocol, along with
the relationship I had with the participants (Toma, 2000) was designed to reduce the
impact of my bias on the investigation. Ultimately, as Bogdan and Biklen (1998) aptly
explained, "data...provide a much more detailed rendering of events than even the
most creatively prejudiced mind might have imagined prior to the study" (p. 34).

A case study research design was selected for this investigation. According to Yin
(1994), case study is the proper research design when a phenomenon's variables cannot be
separated from its context. In the case of this study's participants, there was no way to separate their response to their induction support from the context of their teaching positions,
relationships with their colleagues, and other variables unique to each teacher. Because of
the numerous independent variables that influence beginning teachers' responses to induction, an experiment that isolated the impact of induction was not possible. A case study
approach, however, provided insight into beginning teachers' responses to their induction
support. This approach was also selected based on Merriam's (1998) definition of a case as
"a phenomenon that is inherently bounded, with a finite amount of time for data collection
or a limited number of people who could be interviewed or observed" (p. 27).

Phone interviews, emails, teacher journals, and exit interviews were used to answer
the research questions. The principal data for this investigation were collected through
monthly interviews with each participant. The interviews were semi-structured, and four
questions provided the initial framework.

1. How is teaching going so far this year/since the last time we talked?
2. How did your student teaching experiences prepare you for your 1st year of
   teaching?
3. What additional experiences (in student teaching) might have been helpful?
4. Is there anything you would like to bring up that I haven't asked about?

Depending on how detailed the response was, I would ask follow-up questions. After
the first three interviews, it became clear that the second and third questions provided less
meaningful information than I anticipated when I designed the investigation. Instead of
investigating beginning teachers' induction experiences and retroactive evaluation of
their student teaching experiences, which was my initial objective when I began, my
emphasis switched to induction based on the themes that emerged in the data.

Since the participants' induction experiences provided such intriguing data, I replaced
the second and third questions. The new questions follow-up on aspects of each participant's induction experience based on information they shared in previous interviews. I
implemented this new questioning technique for the fourth set of interviews. The questions were different for each participant and each subsequent interview (p. 220).

Fry provided an example of how questions were altered as a consequence of earlier responses. She goes on to describe her methods and procedures as:

> Participant-initiated emails and participants' teaching journals provided additional data. These additional data were collected because they helped me understand the interviews more fully. Participant-initiated emails and journal entries often addressed topics that were discussed in interviews.
>
> For example, a week after our April interview, Shari sent me an email with the subject, "I need some help!!" In the text of the message she explained that she had been invited to apply for a job in another school district and asked for my opinion about how she should proceed. Her email provided additional details about her contract-renewal—something we discussed in an earlier interview. The additional information helped to clarify questions I had after reviewing my interview notes. The email contact was beneficial because it kept me informed about Shari's induction experiences in the time between our monthly interviews. Exit interviews served as the final data point, providing a sense of closure for the investigation. (p. 221)

The first question concerns what type of research design was used in the study. Fry noted that she used a case study approach, a qualitative method. The use of a case study design is consistent with the purpose of discovering the quality of induction methods for beginning teachers. The researcher stated that she wanted to understand the quality of induction for beginning students, and a qualitative method can give detailed information about the process. The researcher acknowledges that she was very familiar with the cases (participants) and attempted to develop an argument for using them in her study, e.g., citing literature that supports this approach, but it is not a clear argument. She cited one author, Toma, who suggested that such research can best be accomplished when the researcher is subjective because he or she can enter the world of the participant. Interest in a topic and entering the world of the participant are components of a qualitative design, but this researcher acknowledged more than simply interest and stated she wanted the participants to be successful (almost like functioning in parental role versus a research role). An important question is whether she addresses this bias in the discussion section and notes the limitations of the methods. She concluded in the section of limitations of the study that: "I hesitate to declare my close relationship with the participants a limitation of the study because it was an intentional part of the research design" (p. 234). It appears she did express a bias with her methods.

Summary

The procedures section of the methods is a step-by-step, detailed description of what the researcher did to complete the study. It is the research methods used. One purpose of the procedures section is to clearly identify the variables of interest (dependent and independent). A second purpose is to provide information to the reader about the research design used, so an assessment can be made as to the rigor of the study and the potential for any threats to internal and external validity.

Exercises

Choose an article and review the procedures sections. Your review should address the following questions relevant to quantitative research:

1. What type of research design was used in the study?

2. Is the research design consistent with the purpose and hypothesis presented in the introduction?

3. Is the independent variables clearly defined? Is the independent variable so clearly defined that it can be replicated using the information provided in the procedures section?

4. Identify any threats to internal validity. How are they threats?

5. Identify any threats to external validity. How are they threats?

Questions for qualitative research study:

1. What type of research design was used in the study?

2. Is the research design consistent with the purpose presented in the introduction?

3. Does the researcher attempt to identify any universal processes that can result in broader generalization?

4. Did the researcher introduce any bias in his or her procedures based on the procedures used?

13

Evaluating the Methods Section—Instruments

The instrumentation is that area of the methods section where the researchers systematically describe the dependent measures used in the study. There are a number of different ways to measure the dependent variable, and the type of research design and the purpose of the study influence what measures are used. As with the procedures section, the instrumentation section must spell out clearly which instruments were used and how they were administered so that others who wish to replicate the study or want to use similar methods in actual practice can do so. Also, a clear description of the instruments allows those reading the study to determine the quality of the measures used and whether they are appropriate to the intent of the study. Researchers have noted the importance of achieving objectivity and obtaining reliable and accurate measures in the tests they use (Gall, et al., 2002; Moore, 1983).

Standardization of Instruments

An important consideration in assessing the objectivity and quality of a dependent measure is the extent to which the procedures and scoring methods are standardized (Gall, et al., 2002; Moore, 1983). Standardization in administering the dependent measure theoretically provides more objective data. A manual for administering the dependent variable is a major method of establishing standardization. Manuals may include what is told to those the test or measure, time allotted for responses, follow-up questions if certain answers are given, and so on.

Another consideration in standardizing the dependent variable is consistent, systematic scoring methods. The test developers generally include standardized scoring methods in the manual for a standardized instrument. There are generally two types of approaches to scoring in a formal measure: criterion-referenced and norm-referenced. Criterion-referenced scores are based on a predetermined level of performance, a criterion. An example from education might be an elementary school-age child demonstrating the ability to multiply single digits, with a criterion of 100 percent success.

A second type of score for the dependent variable, as mentioned, is the norm-referenced approach. In this approach, scores are interpreted based on the comparison of one group's performance with other groups', all of whom represent a clearly defined population. An example might be a language or vocabulary test, in which children at different grade levels are used to develop normative scores.

Culture, Gender, and Diversity Bias

Researchers and practitioners have noted the importance of using measures of the dependent variable that are culturally, gender-, and diversity-issue appropriate (Drummond, 2000; O'Bryant & McCaffrey, 2006). Anastasi and Urbina (1997) stated, ". . . no single test can be universally applicable or equally 'fair' to all cultures" (p. 342). Use of an inappropriate test or dependent measure can result in test bias and problems with interpreting outcomes. Several potential problems in testing have been identified when researchers use samples from populations such as those from minority backgrounds, individuals with disabilities, and other populations who are characterized by different worldviews (diversity) than that for which the instrument was originally intended and developed (Drummond, 2000; Hinkle, 1994). Possible sources of problems include the establishment of equivalents across diverse groups; lack of appropriate norms among diverse groups; differences in language and meanings of test items in different cultures, genders, and so on; and varying attitudes among diverse groups toward test taking. Drummond (2000) noted the importance of using culturally and racially sensitive instruments. He also noted the APA Standards for Educational and Psychological Tests, which acknowledge the relevance of using instruments that are sensitive to diversity.

Reliability of Instruments

Researchers have noted that one of the most important considerations in determining the quality of the dependent measures is the reliability of the instruments and dependent variables (Drummond, 2000; Gregory, 2007; Heiman, 1995; Urbina, 2004). Gregory (2007) stated that reliability ". . . refers to the attribute of consistency in measurement" (p. 96). He further noted that there are not many psychological tests that are totally consistent but that they can vary quite readily. He further described this variability in the following way: "The concept of reliability is best viewed as a continuum ranging from minimal consistency of measurement (e.g. simple reaction time) to near perfect repeatability of results" (p. 96). A particular test score contains both a true score and error. Error refers to all the potential effects that alter the true score, such as the limitations of the test (if the items being presented are unclear, considerable interpretation may be needed by the responder); time of day in responding to the measure (responses to tests given late at night may be affected by respondents' fatigue); lack of consistent administration procedures; human errors in scoring; and so on. Several methods have been proposed to determine the degree of reliability and, conversely, the amount of error, and these include test-retest reliability, alternate-form reliability, scorer reliability, and internal consistency. These various forms of determining reliability measure different types of error. Reliability is reported as a correlation expressed as the degree of the relationship between two sets of scores. Possible scores in these correlations can range from -1.0 to +1.0. A higher positive correlation indicates a strong relationship between the two sets of scores, whereas a negative correlation denotes an inverse relationship between scores. Generally, scores of .80 and higher are considered strong indicators of reliability in a particular test or measure (Moore, 1983; Urbina, 2004).

Test-retest is one approach to determining reliability; it involves the measurement of the consistency of the scores over a period of time. The researchers administer the dependent measure at one point and then again at another time. The distance between administrations should not be too close (e.g., an hour apart). The respondents may remember the question and their answers. Nor should the retest be too long after the initial test; if, for instance, the retest is a year after the test, the concept measured may change and not be a consequence of lowered reliability of the instrument. This method of determining reliability addresses such problems as consistency in administering the measure.

Alternate-form reliability concerns the consistency of a measure based on content, for instance when two forms of the measure are administered to a sample and reliability coefficients are obtained between them (Drummond, 2000; Urbina, 2004). The intent is to have alternate forms of a test that consistently measure the same concept. Alternate forms allow a researcher to measure something at different times, and control for the effects of testing (testing occurs when a test taker recalls items on a test and his or her performance is possibly influenced by pretest).

Scorer reliability, or intertester reliability, means that objective observational data is collected and, therefore, requires several scorers to interpret responses. To avoid subjective bias with only one scorer, researchers will use several scorers to ensure adequate reliability. Intertester reliability is the extent to which a scoring key is developed and used with consistency. Correlation scores are obtained between raters scoring the same target variables. Low correlations between scorers indicate low reliability and consistency. This also concerns any other type of scoring procedure, such as machine scoring, in which errors can occur with the reading of smudged responses on a computer-generated scoring sheet.

The last type of reliability is *internal consistency,* which is the most frequently reported type of reliability. It involves the extent to which the items in a measure correlate or are related to each other or to their homogeneity. More specifically, this type of reliability refers to how consistent the responses are within a measure of a particular construct or concept.

Validity of Instruments

Gregory (2007) described the importance of validity and stated, "Psychometricians have long acknowledged that validity is the most fundamental and important characteristic of a test" (p. 120). Validity is defined as the degree to which a test measures what it is designed to measure. For example, if a test is designed to measure intelligence, then the items are evaluated by the extent to which they measure this dependent variable. A further delineation of validity is defined in terms of how test scores are interpreted and whether the interpretation is an accurate representation of the construct identified (Urbina, 2004). Urbina noted that this definition and condition of validity is most important.

One specific value of validity is difficult to obtain and report (Gregory, 2000; Urbina, 2004). Generally, the establishment of validity is obtained through comparisons with test results and actual behavior or outcomes. Gregory further noted that the accumulation of evidence for the validity of a test may be determined to be weak, acceptable, or strong.

Three types of validity have been identified as important in developing an "argument" for the strength of test validity: construct validity, content validity, and criterion-related validity (Gall, et al., 2002; Gregory, 2007; Heppner et al., 1992; Urbina, 2004). The most general type of validity is *construct validity* because it supposedly concerns the degree to which a test measures an intended theoretical concept or construct. Urbina (2004) has identified three components of construct validity, which include the following sources of evidence: content-related sources, convergence and divergence sources, and criterion-related sources. Content-related sources include determining the relevance and representativeness of the items on the test. There are a number of different sources for convergence and divergence evidence, which include factor analysis, structural equation modeling techniques, correlations among tests, and differentiation in scores based upon certain variables such as age, where differences in scores would be expected. The last source, criterion-related, is composed of obtaining evidence of prediction of a particular construct, or accuracy in identifying a construct in practice. Other types of validity are used to support the discovery of construct validity. As mentioned earlier, validity is the degree to which a test measures the intended concept or construct. It has been noted that there is no single source for determining construct validity, but it is more often a consequence of gathering evidence from other types of validity (Urbina, 2004).

Content validity is a basic type of validity that concerns the extent to which responses on test items represent a particular content. For example, if a counselor wants to measure aggression in a client, the content validity is the degree to which the items represent client aggressive behaviors, such as yelling, hitting, and so on. Content validity is generally determined by having experts in a particular content area rate the degree to which the items represent the content or concept intended (Gregory, 2007). One method is to have experts rate whether items should be included in a particular test. Correlations among the experts provide a numerical value that illustrates the degree of content validity. The higher the positive correlation (closer to +1.0), the better the content validity.

A third type of validity is *criterion-related validity*, which involves how well a test predicts outcomes based on a particular behavior or skill. This type of validity is established by determining a set of criteria that predicts future outcomes. Correlations may be used to establish criterion-related validity. Correlations with scores on the test are made with actual outcomes of the set criterion. Concurrent validity is another type of criterion-related validity, defined as the extent to which a particular test relates or correlates with an accepted standard test that has an intended similar construct or concept. This approach is used when developing a new test while correlating scores to an accepted standard test.

Approaches to Measuring the Dependent Variable

A number of different methods and approaches to measuring the dependent variable in quantitative research methods have been suggested. They include direct observation and behavioral measures, self-report and inventories, ratings of others' behavior, physiological approaches, and interviews (Eid & Diener, 2006; Gall, et al., 1996; Heiman, 1995; McMillan, 2004; Merrell, 1999). Qualitative researchers typically employ a few of the methods used in quantitative research, such as direct observation and interview, together with triangulation methods to increase the reliability and validity of their observations and data collection (Berg, 2004; Taylor & Bogdan, 1984).

Direct observation and behavioral measures involve a focus on observable behavior. Merrell (1999) stated as follows: "Direct observation of behavior is one of the cornerstone tools for the assessment of behavior, social, and emotional problems" (p. 48). Trained observers or scorers are used to record or evaluate behavior of the target sample and target behavior (the dependent variable). This approach to measuring the dependent variable may be used in both quantitative and qualitative research methods. Heppner, et al. (1992) noted that there are several advantages to using direct observational methods rather than approaches like self-reports; for example, the measurement is of direct behavior and not inferred or projected outcomes. Consequently, the measurement (theoretically) is more objective. There are limitations with direct measures. Even though direct measures are considered more objective, there remains the possibility of bias among the observers or raters. This may be particularly true in cases where there is only one rater rather than several raters. Also, Heppner, et al. stated that individual views or idiosyncrasies of the raters may influence what is observed and thus influence the reliability of the measure.

Self-report and inventories are probably the most frequently used method of measuring the dependent variable in psychology, counseling, and education. This approach to measuring the dependent variable is more frequently used in quantitative than qualitative research. In self-report approaches to measuring the dependent variable, respondents or study participants are generally asked to rate the extent to which an identified behavior, attitude, or feeling is present. There are hundreds of inventories and self-report measures from which a researcher can choose to measure the dependent variable (Conoley & Impara, 1995; Eid & Diener, 2006). There are self-report measures of stress, coping strategies, career interests, a host of attitude measures, self-esteem, and so on. Items on these scales may involve the use of simple yes-no responses, Likert-type gradations (rating the extent of agreement with statements based on choices like *agree* or *disagree*), rank order, forced choice (choosing one of two items) or open-ended responses. The following is an example of a Likert-type scale.

Directions: Please read the following statements and rate them based on the scale provided.

1. All teachers are above average in intelligence.

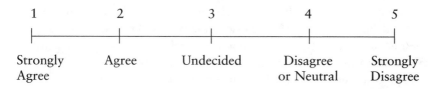

1	2	3	4	5
Strongly Agree	Agree	Undecided	Disagree or Neutral	Strongly Disagree

An example of an instrument requiring ranking of responses is demonstrated in the following example of a possible scale designed to measure work ethic.

Directions: Read each set of statements (a through f) and **rank** the statements in terms of how well each statement represents your values or how you feel. **Rank** in order of 1 to 6, with **1 being most representative** of your values and **6 being least representative** of your values.

   a. People should spend more time in leisure activities.

   b. I believe one should not do a sloppy job.

   c. If one works hard enough one is likely to make a good life for oneself.

   d. It is important for one to show respect for one's supervisor.

   e. I think it is important to be on time for work.

   f. One should not work overtime because it cuts into family time.

Heppner, et al. (1992) have noted the advantages and disadvantages of self-report and inventories. One of the most important advantages to researchers in using self-report and inventories is the ease and time of administering them (see Table 13.1). Self-report approaches generally do not require extensive training to administer, and for the most part are brief. A second advantage is that the researcher can assess non-observable events such as cognitions and feelings that generally cannot be measured through direct observation.

Heppner, et al. (1992) suggested that the most serious problem with self-report measures is the possibility of distortion or bias by the responder (see Table 13.1). Respondents may deny or repress feelings or cognitions that are troublesome or incongruent with how they see themselves. Another reason respondents may show bias in their responses may be because they wish to give socially desirable responses, to present themselves in a more positive way, or attempt to respond the way they perceive the researcher wants them to on the self-report. A second problem with self-report measures is that respondents may not be aware of certain feelings, attitudes, or behaviors they possess and thus cannot accurately indicate what occurs in actual practice (Heppner, et al., 1992). For example, a researcher interested in how Alzheimer's disease affects behavior may find that it is difficult for the person with Alzheimer's to report, because of the effects of the condition on self-awareness. Consequently, a different approach to measuring dependent variables with this population may be more appropriate.

Ratings of others' behavior is a third method of measuring a dependent variable. This method of assessment is used in both quantitative and qualitative research approaches. This approach basically involves the use of some standardized method of scoring the behavior of others in some systematic way. An example is a music teacher evaluating the singing ability of a student. The standardized method here is the student's attempt to replicate specific musical notes. In counseling, an example is the assessment of a client's psychological functioning (e.g., the Global Assessment System [GAS]). Heppner, et al. (1992) noted that the use of experts in ratings of others increases the effectiveness of the rating method. One advantage then is that the use of experts increases the accuracy of the measurement. A second advantage of this approach is that it is generally not very time-consuming and is simple to administer (Table 13.1).

A possible problem with ratings of others is that raters may interject their own biases into the process (see Table 13.1). For example, if a counselor rates a client's progress and is seeking a particular outcome, the ratings may be biased. One method of reducing individual rater bias is to use multiple raters and determine interrater reliability.

A fourth approach to measuring the dependent variable is through the use of *physiological methods*. Physiological measurement involves the assessment of such responses as heart rate, blood pressure, galvanic skin response, and immune system response. A major advantage is that such measurement is generally considered objective and accurate (see Table 13.1). One problem with this method of measuring the dependent variable is that it is generally time-consuming (see Table 13.1). A second problem is that the equipment for measuring the variable of interest is expensive. Third, measurement generally must take place in a very controlled environment, typically in a clinic.

Another approach to measuring the dependent variable is through the use of *interviews*. Interviewers ask respondents a set of questions; this may involve relating brief or detailed responses. Interviews are used frequently in qualitative methods and less frequently in quantitative research studies because they do not allow for easy quantification of the responses. Heppner, et al. (1992) stated that one advantage of the interview method is the flexibility of how information and data are collected (see Table 13.1). Researchers can alter the questions asked based on the responses given and

Table 13.1   Approaches to Measuring Dependent Variables

Approach	Description	Strength	Limitation
Direct observation	Trained observers or scorers are used to evaluate behavior.	The measurement is more objective.	Possibility of bias among the observers or raters.
Self-report inventories	Rate the extent to which an identified behavior, attitude, or feeling is present.	Ease and time of administration, do not require extensive training, and achieve access to non-observable events.	Possibility of distortion bias by the responder attempting to achieve socially desirable responses; responder may not be aware of certain feelings, attitudes, or behaviors.
Ratings	Use of some standardized method of scoring behavior of others.	Measurement is not time-consuming, increases the accuracy of the measurement.	Rater may interject own biases into the process.
Physiological methods	Assessment of responses such as heart rate, blood pressure, galvanic skin response, immune system response.	Measurement is objective and accurate.	Method is generally time-consuming; measuring the variable of interest is expensive.
Interviews	Interviewers ask respondents a set of question that may involve brief or detailed responses.	There is flexibility in the way information and data are collected; in-depth information may be collected.	The method is time-consuming and costly; it is difficult to achieve a standard approach to scoring responses.

adjust to the flow of the interview. Another advantage of the interview method is that in-depth information may be gathered, as opposed to the superficial information available from structured self-report measures.

Problems with the interview method are that it is time-consuming and costly (Heppner, et al., 1992). The interviewer must take the time to develop a relationship with the interviewee before there is a focus on the topic of interest (see Table 13.1). The interviewer generally receives in-depth training, which is expensive to complete. Another problem with the interview method is a difficulty in achieving a standard approach to scoring responses in a systematic way.

Guidelines and Questions for Evaluating the Instruments—Quantitative Research

1. Is there a clear and adequate description of the instrument?

2. What types of measures were used in the study (direct observation and behavioral measures, self-report and inventories, ratings of others' behavior, physiological approaches, and/or interview)? Identify any problems or limitations with the types of measures used.

3. To what extent are the instruments standardized, and what types of standardized scoring were used (criterion-referenced or norm-referenced)?

4. Does the instrument appear to be appropriate for the sample (e.g., are there any cross-cultural, gender, and/or diversity biases)? Explain.

5. Is the reliability of the instruments reported? What type of reliability is reported?

6. Is the reliability reported for the instruments adequate? Explain.

7. What types of validity are reported for the instruments used?

8. Is the validity of the instruments adequate? Explain.

Evaluating Examples From the Research Literature—Quantitative Research

Study 1 Quantitative Research

We can go back the study used in previous chapters, Henderson, et al. (2007), which focused on the use of mandalas for healing those with post-traumatic stress disorder. The researchers used five measures in this study; however, only two are used to illustrate how to evaluate the instruments. Henderson, et. al. (2007) described their instruments in the following way:

The PDS (Foa, 1995) is a 49-item self-report measure to aid in the detection and diagnosis of PTSD. Participants report on PTSD symptoms that they have experienced within the last month. This measure not only yields PTSD diagnostic information but also provides an index of PTSD symptom severity. Items are rated with regard to presence (i.e. yes, or no) and with regard to symptom severity. Symptom severity scores are rated from below 10 (mild), 10–20 (moderate), 21–35 (moderate-to-severe), to above 35 (severe) (Foa, 1995).

PDS symptom severity scores were used as the primary means of indicating changes in the severity of participants' traumatic symptoms from baseline (Time 1) to completion of the intervention (Time 2) to 1-month follow-up (Time 3). The coefficient alpha for the PTSD symptom severity scores was .87 in the current study (p. 149).

The first question is whether there is a clear and adequate description of the instrument. It is noted to be a self-report measure, the Post-traumatic Stress Disorder Scale (PDS), and it was designed to identify the levels of severity of post-traumatic stress. However, no items are presented to illustrate the scale, nor is there any information about how the different levels of severity are differentiated. As has been noted above, one of the advantages in using self-report and inventories is the ease and time of administering them, and that it can assess non-observable events such as cognitions and feelings that generally cannot be measured through direct observation. The most significant problem with self-report measures is the potential for distortion or bias by the respondent.

The next question to address is the extent to which the instruments are standardized and what types of standardized scoring were used (criterion-referenced or norm-referenced). No information is provided about the standardization of the PDS, nor is there any information about whether the scores are based on and compared with criterion-referenced or norm-referenced scores.

Another question is whether the instrument is appropriate for the sample (e.g., are there any cross-cultural, gender, and/or diversity biases). Participants in the study were prescreened for post-traumatic experiences or stressors. However, no information is provided about whether the instrument is appropriate and/or sensitive, based on culture or gender differences. Also, the reader of the article has not seen examples of the items, and this gives the reader minimal information about the appropriateness of the instrument for diverse groups.

The next two questions concern reliability. One question is whether the reliability of the instruments is reported. Little information is provided on the reliability of the instrument. The researchers do report the coefficient alpha for the instrument to be .87 in the current study. Coefficient alpha concerns the internal consistency of the instrument, and .87 is an adequate level of internal consistency. A problem is that no other reliability from previous studies is reported, nor is any other reliability reported, such as test-retest. The last question concerns the validity of the instrument. Again, no information is provided on the validity of the instrument, as with the information provided on the reliability. Both of these issues are significant problems in the use of this instrument in the study. The reader cannot judge whether this instrument is reliable and valid, so the results are easily identified as questionable.

Another scale or instrument used in this study was the State-Trait Anxiety Inventory (STAI). Henderson, et. al. (2007) described the instrument as follows:

> The State-Trait Anxiety Inventory (STAI; Speilberger, 1983) is a 40-item, self-report measure that assesses levels of transitory feelings of anxiety, worry, and fear (state), and the more stable (trait) tendencies to feel worried and react anxiously. The STAI was included in this study to assess changes in both state and trait anxiety levels from baseline to follow-up at Times 2 and 3. Coefficient alphas of .90 and .92 were found in the current study for state and trait anxiety. (p. 149)

Again, the first question is whether there is there a clear and adequate description of the instrument. The researchers describe the instrument as assessing different levels of anxiety, worry, and fear (which they defined as state anxiety) and more stable reactions of feeling worried and anxious, which they termed a trait. This description provides some information on the intent of the instrument but does not provide information about actual items that illustrate the content. Again, this is a self-report measure and one advantage is the ease and time of administering them. Also, since the focus is on non-observable events (anxiety and cognitions), it can still be assessed through self-report. The problem is the potential for bias and/or distortion by the respondent.

The second question concerns whether the instrument is standardized. There is no mention of whether the SMS is standardized, and there is no information about comparing scores to criterion- or norm-referenced data. No information is provided on the appropriateness of the instrument with diverse groups. Again, the coefficients alpha are reported (the internal consistency of the instrument), which were found to be .90 and .92, respectively, for state and trait anxiety. Finally, no validity is reported for the instrument. Based on the information provided to the reader, it is difficult to conclude that either instrument evaluated (the PDS or the STAI) gives the researcher a strong basis for making decisions about the findings with such limitations in the reported quality of the instruments.

Guidelines and Questions for Evaluating the Instruments—Qualitative Research

The questions for evaluating qualitative research are similar for three questions. They do not cover issues like standardization of the instruments or reliability or validity, since these involve the use of numerical values. Fry (2007) described the use of the following instrument in her qualitative study:

Phone interviews, emails, teacher journals, and exit interviews were used to answer the research questions. The principal data for this investigation were collected through monthly interviews with each participant. The interviews were semi-structured, and four questions provided the initial framework.

1. How is teaching going so far this year/since the last time we talked?

2. How did your student teaching experiences prepare you for your 1st year of teaching?

3. What additional experiences (in student teaching) might have been helpful?

4. Is there anything you would like to bring up that I haven't asked you about?

Depending on how detailed the response was, I would ask follow-up questions. After the first three interviews, it became clear that the second and third questions provided less meaningful information than I anticipated when I designed the investigation. Instead of investigating beginning teachers' induction experiences and retroactive evaluation of their student teaching experiences, which was my initial objective when I began, my emphasis switched to induction based upon the themes that emerged in the data. (p. 220)

Since the participants' induction experiences provided such intriguing data, I replaced the second and third questions. The new questions follow-up on aspects of each participant's induction experience based on information they shared in previous interviews. I implemented this new questioning technique for the fourth set of interviews. The questions were different for each participant and each subsequent interview. Participant-initiated emails and participants' teaching journals provided additional data. These additional data were collected because they helped me understand the interviews more fully. Participant-initiated emails and journal entries often addressed topics that were discussed in interviews. (p. 221)

The following are questions to address in evaluating qualitative research:

1. Is there a clear and adequate description of the instrument?

2. What types of measures were used in the study (direct observation and behavioral measures and/or interview)? Identify any problems or limitations with the types of measures used.

3. Does the instrument appear to be appropriate for the sample (e.g., are there any cross-cultural, gender, and/or diversity biases)?

The first question is whether there is an adequate description of the instruments. The instruments used in this qualitative study included interviews, journals, and e-mail messages. The journals and e-mail messages may be categorized as self-report. The researchers provided considerable information about the interviews and how they were conducted, including the questions that were asked. Minimal information was provided about the participant-initiated e-mails and journals. No detail is given about how the e-mails or journals were solicited or formatted, e.g., their content or focus.

Interviews, e-mails, and journals were used in data collection. As noted above, interviews are used frequently in qualitative methods, and one advantage of the interview method is the flexibility regarding how information and data are collected. The researchers can alter the questions asked based on the responses given, and therefore they can adjust the flow of the interview to the responses. There are several problems and limitations with the interview method. Interviews can be time-consuming and costly. Also, they may involve considerable time to train the interviewers to obtain quality data. A limitation of interviews is that it is difficult to standardize responses, and this hinders objective interpretation to some degree.

The next question is whether the instruments were appropriate for the participants. There is little information about the demographic characteristics of the participants, except that they were all women, there were four participants, and they received their degrees from a university in the western United States. It is difficult to determine adequately if the instruments were appropriate, given this sparse information.

Summary

The instrumentation section is where the researchers describe how they operationalized the dependent variables. The information presented here can provide the reader and consumer of research with important information about the efficacy of the study. Inadequate and/or inappropriate measures can affect the results obtained and, consequently, the validity of the study. Several questions and guides are useful in determining whether a study is valid. We typically are concerned with whether the researchers have provided a clear description of the instruments used and what types of measures were employed. Also, it is important to know whether an instrument is standardized and if any potential diversity biases exist. Most important, the researchers should report the reliability and validity of the instruments used. Without information on the reliability and validity of the instruments used in a quantitative study, it is difficult to conclude whether the study results obtained are accurate.

The questions for evaluating the instruments in qualitative research include several questions similar to those that are used in quantitative research.

Exercises

Select a quantitative research article and answer the following questions.

1. Is there a clear and adequate description of the instrument?

2. What types of measures were used in the study (direct observation and behavioral measures, self-report and inventories, ratings of others' behavior, physiological approaches, and/or interview)? Identify any problems or limitations with the types of measures used.

3. To what extent are the instruments standardized, and what types of standardized scoring were used (criterion-referenced or norm-referenced)?

4. Does the instrument appear to be appropriate for the sample (e.g., are there any cross-cultural, gender, and/or diversity biases)? Explain.

5. Is the reliability of the instruments reported? What type of reliability is reported?

6. Is the reliability reported for the instruments adequate? Explain.

7. What types of validity are reported for the instruments used?

8. Is the validity of the instruments adequate? Explain.

Select a qualitative study and answer the following questions:

1. Is there a clear and adequate description of the instrument?

2. What types of measures were used in the study (direct observation and behavioral measures and/or interview)? Identify any problems or limitations with the types of measures used.

3. Does the instrument appear to be appropriate for the sample (e.g., are there any cross-cultural, gender, and/or diversity biases)?

14

Evaluating the Results Section

Reading and understanding the results section is probably the most daunting part of evaluating a research article for those who are somewhat intimidated by research and the use of math and statistics. Students have frequently commented to me that they "skip over" the results section, with all its statistical procedures and numbers. They are intimidated by statistics and prefer to read the discussion section, which summarizes the results with words rather than numbers. I encourage you and challenge you to become more comfortable reading the results sections of journal articles.

Those who are conducting and writing these sophisticated research articles typically have extensive backgrounds in statistics or employ a consultant who has considerable expertise with statistics. There are entire graduate-level courses in statistical procedures such as analyses of variance, regression, structural equation modeling, nonparametric statistics, and so on. Therefore, it would not be reasonable to assume that one chapter on reading statistics and results would conclude with the reader's having gained considerable expertise in statistical methods. However, the intent of this chapter, in keeping with the purpose of this book, is to prepare you to feel more comfortable in identifying and understanding basic statistical concepts and procedures in your efforts to evaluate the efficacy of a particular research report.

This chapter is separated into two major parts. The first part addresses the understanding and evaluation of quantitative research, and the second focuses on interpreting and evaluating qualitative research results. I also propose guidelines for evaluating the results section, followed by an evaluation of examples from the research literature using these guidelines.

Part I: Quantitative Research Results

Results obtained through quantitative research methods are presented mathematically. Recall from Chapter 3 that there are two major categories of statistical methods employed in quantitative research: descriptive and inferential statistics. Descriptive statistics are used to report results based on the sample, whereas inferential statistics are designed to make it possible to infer, from the results of a study (and the sample of the population), back to the larger population, and generalize back to the target population.

Descriptive Statistics

Descriptive statistics have been described as efforts by researchers to systematically summarize the data collected (Urdan, 2005). The idea is for the researchers to present data descriptively in a way that is easy to understand and that conceptualizes general characteristics of the sample's responses. Descriptive statistics address the sample only and are in no way connected to understanding or generalizing back to the population. Generally, descriptive statistics are presented first in the results section of an article, followed by inferential statistics. The important issue for the researcher is which methods to use in presenting descriptive statistics. Most commonly presented methods are mean and standard deviation. It is rare to use mode and median. Tables and graphs can be used to visually illustrate descriptive statistics.

Inferential Statistics

The ultimate purpose of conducting a quantitative study is to test hypotheses, and this involves using statistical methods that allow the researchers to infer, from data gleaned from the sample, information that can be applied to the larger population. Inferential statistics are methods that allow the researchers to do this. Numerous inferential statistical methods are used; see Chapter 3 for a review.

An important question to address when reading the results section is whether any violations of assumptions were made. This gives the reader information about whether the researcher used appropriate statistics, parametric or nonparametric. Review Chapter 3 for a detailed description of potential violation of assumptions. Recall that no specific number of violations of assumptions has been associated with the decision to use particular statistical methods.

Inferential statistics, as stated earlier, are used to make decisions or reach conclusions about whether results obtained from a sample can be applied to the target population. All the methods discussed as inferential statistics are associated with quantitative research methods. The majority of the methods used in inferential statistical procedures involve making comparisons between groups. The intent of using inferential statistics is to answer hypotheses or research questions as they relate to the population of interest, and the decision for the reader of quantitative research is whether the researcher addressed what was intended with the statistics used.

Summary

Understanding and evaluating a research article that employs and reports quantitative research may appear to be a daunting task, but there are several important points to focus on that may reduce the confusion and difficulty in reading and using such research information. Much of the research you will read in psychology and education will be based on collected data that fits a normal curve. Data that is based on the normal curve allows researchers to analyze outcomes with sensitive and more powerful statistical methods, as opposed to data that violates the assumption of normality, therefore requiring that nonparametric statistical methods be employed.

Descriptive statistical methods are used by researchers to summarize the data collected based on the sample in a particular research study. This includes calculating measures of central tendency (mean, median, mode) and measures of variability (standard deviation, and so on). Inferential statistical methods are used by researchers to generalize results back to the population of interest. These types of statistical methods are used to support or refute stated hypotheses. There are two major types of inferential statistical methods: parametric and nonparametric. Parametric statistical methods require adherence to certain assumptions about the data collected (e.g., normality, independence, and so on). When these assumptions are violated, the researcher must employ nonparametric statistical methods. The choice of statistical methods is also influenced by the purpose of the study: specifically, whether it is a comparison or descriptive study.

Guidelines for Evaluating the Results Section—Quantitative Research

As stated earlier, the presentation of information in the results section of an article is probably where the differences between quantitative and qualitative methods are most noticeable. Consequently, I have suggested several guidelines for evaluating quantitative research in Part I. Listed below are the guidelines and questions for evaluating the results section in an article based on quantitative research.

1. What descriptive statistics were used? Do they adequately describe the sample?

2. Were any violations of assumptions present, considering the types of data collected?

3. What types of inferential statistics were used? Are the inferential statistics used adequate to answer the research hypotheses or questions?

Evaluating Examples From the Research Literature—Quantitative Research

Quantitative Study Example

A review of the study by Henderson, et al. (2007) shows that they completed an analysis of covariance (ANCOVA). The researchers used ANCOVA to control for differences between the two groups at three different observation times. They described their statistical calculations as follows:

A series of one-way analyses of covariance (ANCOVA) comparing the experimental and control groups were conducted for all outcome measures at Time 2 and at 1-month follow-up. Because the two randomly assigned groups had different initial levels of trauma symptom severity, depression, anxiety, and health symptom severity at Time 1, the use of ANCOVA as opposed to analysis of variance was warranted. Using ANCOVA permitted the researcher's to detect mean differences between treatment groups at Times 2 and 3, while controlling for differences at baseline. Although baseline differences between groups were not statistically significant, they were large enough to warrant the use of ANCOVA. As indicated by Table 1, all variables were correlated with themselves over time, and this also spoke to the importance of using ANCOVA to control for baseline levels of the outcome variables.

The covariate for each ANCOVA was the value for the respective outcome variable at the beginning of the study, before the mandala-drawing manipulation (or control drawing manipulation). Controlling for baseline levels of traumatic symptoms as measured by the PDS, participants in the mandala condition were experiencing fewer symptoms of trauma than those in the control condition at 1-month follow-up ($F(1, 35) = 6.615$, $p < .015$).

Whereas there were differences between the two groups with respect to PTSD symptoms, there were no significant differences on the other measures (i.e., the BDI-II, State-Trait Anxiety Inventory, SMS, or PILL), suggesting that the mandala-drawing exercise was specific to symptoms of traumatic stress (see Table 3) (151).

The first question to address is what descriptive statistics were used and do they adequately describe the sample. The researchers write in the last paragraph: "Whereas there were differences . . ." and note that means and standard deviations were described in Table 3. Means and standard deviations for the control and experimental groups were provided on the various assessment instruments, such as the Beck Depression Inventory (BDI), State-Trait Anxiety Inventory (STAI), Spiritual Meaning Scale (SMS), and the Pennebaker Inventory of Limbic Languidness (PILL).

The second question concerns whether there were any violations of assumptions present, considering the types of data collected. All the measures used were based upon interval types of data, so the issue of normality was not violated (although no chi-square goodness-of-fit was calculated). Linearity was not violated since no regression analysis was calculated. Independence of scores also was not violated because comparisons were made between groups at different times and not within groups. Finally, homogeneity of variance was not violated because the standard deviations between control and experimental groups were not noticeably different (more than three times different). However, no calculations of the F Maximum Test for homogeneity of variance were included.

The last question to address is the evaluation of the types of inferential statistics that were used and whether the inferential statistics used were adequate to answer the research hypotheses. The researchers used an ANCOVA to compare differences. The Henderson, et al. (2007) hypothesis was stated as follows: "It was hypothesized that individuals assigned to a mandala-drawing condition would show a significant increase in psychological and physical health relative to control group participants both immediately after the intervention and at a 1-month follow-up" (p. 151). The use of the ANCOVA allowed for comparisons at different times and controlled for an extraneous variable (differences in symptoms at onset) between the experimental and control group.

The researchers provided information through descriptive statistics about the sample through reporting means and standard deviations. There were no clearly noted violations of assumptions, and the researchers, Henderson, et al. (2007) used inferential statistics, ANCOVA, to adequately answer the hypothesis.

Part II: Evaluating the Results Section— Qualitative Research

The results sections in qualitative research studies will look quite different from those in quantitative studies. The results section is probably where you will find the biggest differences from quantitative research, in the presentation and the kinds of results. Whereas in quantitative research numbers and statistical procedures are cited, qualitative research is characterized by descriptions. It has been noted that qualitative research methods are based on language to communicate research results (Gall, et al., 2002). Consequently, analysis and reporting of data in qualitative research are communicated through linguistic methods, or language.

Miles and Huberman (1994) suggested three steps in the analysis of qualitative data: data reduction, data display, and drawing conclusions. Data reduction involves describing the circumstances or context or units of the analysis or the data segments to code. Data display is how the researcher presents examples of the data collected, which may include graphs and charts. Last, the researcher wants to provide conclusions, and this may be achieved through concrete examples of the data that demonstrate the themes, concepts, and/or theories identified. The reader of qualitative research is most often interested in this last step, drawing conclusions, because this is where the researcher attempts to compose understanding of the data collected and come up with conclusions.

Miles and Huberman (1994) suggested the following systematic tactics for developing meanings and drawing conclusions in qualitative research: counting, noting patterns or themes, determining plausibility, clustering, creating metaphors, differentiation or splitting, noting relationships between variables, and making conceptual theoretical coherence. Counting, according to Miles and Huberman (1994), involves counting the number of times a theme or pattern emerges from data analysis. There are decisions made as to whether the number of times a particular theme or construct emerges in analysis is consistent and frequent enough to state that it is important or significant. The number of times a theme or construct is expressed may then be reported in a qualitative research article. A second approach to analyzing data is noting patterns or themes, and this involves identification of commonalities among data collected (Miles & Huberman, 1994). Certainly, when studying human beings in counseling or education, there may seem to be chaos in the information collected. The qualitative researcher may review pages of transcripts of interviews or review notes on observations to identify common patterns that consistently emerge. We as human beings have the ability to see patterns, and to predict and control our lives and environments, we use information from identified patterns.

Another strategy for analyzing qualitative research data is determining plausibility (Miles & Huberman, 1994). Basically this refers to determining whether data collected and constructs formulated make sense. A researcher may conclude that the data makes sense or appears to be plausible in explaining certain phenomena. For example, if a researcher interviewed several people who reported seeing unidentified flying objects (UFOs), that researcher might consider whether or not the experiences reported are plausible.

Clustering is the fourth strategy for analyzing qualitative research data (Miles & Huberman, 1994). This strategy involves clustering together experiences or phenomena that have common characteristics. It is an attempt to go beyond identifying patterns and may place similar patterns into larger categories. Miles and Huberman stated that clustering may be interpreted to be movement to higher levels of abstraction. An example might be young children, for example 2-year-olds, showing outbursts that might be interpreted as a pattern of temper tantrums. Clustering several common patterns or experiences together may result in identification of "characteristic" 2-year-old behavior; specifically, in addition to tantrums the behavior may involve the expression of need for control and exercise of control over the child's environment.

Creating metaphors is another strategy for analyzing qualitative data (Miles & Huberman, 1994). Keeping in mind that analysis of qualitative data is based on a linguistic model, you may consider the use of metaphors as an attempt to describe and organize data beyond simply literal interpretations.

A sixth strategy for analyzing qualitative data is differentiation, or splitting (Miles & Huberman, 1994). Differentiating involves dissecting variables into smaller parts to further clarify concepts and themes. This is, in a sense, an attempt at moving from simple to more complex variables by noting variability and differences. Differentiation is used when a researcher wants to understand and break larger concepts and variables into component parts. An example in counseling might be an attempt to clarify conflict in a marital therapy. The general theme might be identifying conflict, and differentiation might address types of conflict, such as conflict over finances.

Another tactic is noting relationships between variables, which involves discovering any relationships between two or more variables (Miles & Huberman, 1994). Teachers, for example, may develop feelings of powerlessness with certain administrative approaches (e.g., authoritarian, criticism-based). The relationship between these two processes may be analyzed (e.g., the relationship between the teacher's feelings of powerlessness and the administrator's critical and authoritarian behaviors).

An eighth tactic in analyzing qualitative research is making conceptual theoretical coherence of variables of focus (Miles & Huberman, 1994). This tactic is one of the more frequently used and involves attempting to make sense of data in relation to concepts and theories. Data is analyzed, and there is an attempt to discover examples from the data that support concepts and/or theory. The theory of attachment (infant attachment) might be a focus in a qualitative study. The researcher would focus on videotapes of interactions between an infant and its mother, comparing it to videotapes of interactions between an infant and a stranger. Detailed descriptions of the inter-actions in the two types of dyads would be developed based on this tactic.

Based on these tactics for drawing conclusions, the qualitative researcher will provide concrete examples of the data in the results section. The display of these tactics will be organized based on the methods used.

Summary

Analysis and reporting of results in qualitative research are based on lin-guistic structures and communicating results through language. There are three important steps and components that should be included in the results section of a qualitative research study: data reduction, data display, and drawing conclusions. This last step is important in reading qualitative research and gives the reader information about the conclusions reached. Such conclusions are reported in terms of tactics used for analyzing data. There are a number of different tactics for analyzing qualitative research data, and these include counting, noting patterns or themes, determining plausibility, clustering, creating metaphors, differentiation or splitting, not-ing relationships between variables, and making conceptual theoretical coherence. Finally, the researchers should illustrate the themes, concepts, and/or phenomena with concrete examples from the data.

Guidelines for Evaluating the Results Section—Qualitative Research

Listed below are the guidelines and questions for evaluating the results section in an article based on qualitative research.

1. What tactics or strategies for coding and interpreting the data are made? Are they clearly described?

2. Are concrete examples of the data clearly linked to identified themes, con-cept, and/or theories? Are these examples adequate?

Evaluating an Example From the Results Section—Qualitative Research

In her study of first-year teachers and induction processes, Fry (2007) reported using descriptive and interpretative categories in her data analysis. One major theme or category identified was time and collegiality, and the following example was provided:

"Everyone keeps telling me the 1st year is the hardest, and it better be because otherwise I don't want to do this." (Stella, September 14, 2004). Stella, Shari, Becca, and Laura faced challenges common to beginning teachers. All four began the school year working long hours; 10–12 hour days during the week plus 10 or more hours on the weekend were common. Stella reported being so exhausted that she went to bed as early as 7:45 p.m. during the first month of school. Each participant experimented with different strategies to make their schedules more manageable. By late October, they had found more balanced approaches. (p. 224)

Negotiating a balance between work and collegial relationships proved problematic for Stella as well. Stella taught in a school where two veteran teachers were assigned as mentors for all of the new teachers in her building. . . . Stella and her assigned mentor did not form a strong connection, but Stella did find an authentic mentor in one of her building administrators. They connected on a personal as well as professional level, and their relationship provided Stella with comfort and support. (p. 225)

A second theme that was reported was "the transition from student teacher to teacher." Fry (2007) provided the following examples from the results section:

For Stella, the biggest challenge stemmed from teaching 5th grade after student teaching in a 2nd grade class. The students had higher skill levels and abilities, and initially, Stella struggled with planning and teaching. In our first interview she said: "I was ready to quit the Tuesday after we started . . . everything was overwhelming. I know I student taught the first day (of school) but it's different when it's all on you. I need to get my feet under me, but they're just not there yet." (September 14, 2004). (p. 226)

A third theme identified by Fry (2000) was mentoring and administrative support. She provided several examples of this theme:

"If I had it all to do over again, I would ask for a mentor who has been around for longer and has things figured out." (Laura, October 26, 2004). Stella, Shari, and Laura were each assigned a mentor teacher. Shari and Laura's mentors were teachers at the same grade level, while Stella was assigned one of two teachers who served as mentors for every new teacher in her school. Becca's school district had no mentoring program. As Laura's quote at the beginning of this section suggests, her mentor was new to the grade level at which they both taught. The mentor also was in her 4th year of teaching, which is just one year beyond the induction years. (pp. 227–228)

Fry (2007) presented her data conclusions with several different themes and systematically used concrete examples from her collection methods. She clearly explained the connection to the themes.

Exercises

Directions: Select a study from the research literature that uses a quantitative design and evaluate the results section based on the questions listed below.

1. What descriptive statistics were used? Do the researchers adequately describe the sample?

2. Were any violations of assumptions present, considering the types of data collected?

3. What types of inferential statistics were used? Are the inferential statistics used adequate to answer the research hypotheses or questions?

Directions: Select a study from the research literature that uses a qualitative design and evaluate the results section based on the questions listed below.

1. What tactics or strategies for coding and interpreting the data are made? Are they clearly described?

2. Are concrete examples of the data clearly linked to identified themes, concepts, and/or theories? Are these examples adequate?

15

Evaluating the Discussion Section

The discussion section is designed to summarize the intent of the research project and present implications for actual practice. We are particularly interested in this section because, as practitioners, we want to know what works and how it may be applied. The discussion section should address the practical significance of the results (Heiman, 1995; LaFountain & Bartos, 2002; Moore, 1983). In a sense, the researchers must go beyond the numbers and statistics reported in the results section and interpret the findings so that they may be of practical application.

In this chapter, I address the important components that should be included in a discussion section: restatement of the purpose; presentation of the implications of the findings and how they relate to theories, others' findings, and actual practice; alternative explanations; citation of the potential limitations of the study and the results; and discussion of possible directions for future research (LaFountain & Bartos, 2002; Moore, 1983; Vierra & Pollock, 1988). Next, I present guidelines or questions to be used in evaluating the efficacy of a discussion section. Finally, there are examples provided using the guidelines and questions presented here.

Ideally, the researchers will restate the purpose of the study at the beginning of the discussion section. This is done to remind the reader of the purpose and link it with the results. This approach theoretically ensures that the purpose and the hypotheses or research questions are answered.

Second, the researchers should summarize the results, without using any numbers or statistics, and relate them to previous research, theories, and practice. In summarizing the results, the researchers need to be succinct and note

193

the significant points of the findings. It is important that the researchers address how the research questions or hypotheses relate to the findings. Additionally, the researchers need to relate the results to theory or practice in a clear and understandable manner. Finally, the researchers will want to relate the results to previous research that either supports or refutes prior findings.

The researchers may need to propose alternative explanations when the results do not meet expected outcomes or are not consistent with the theories addressed. It is important that the researchers systematically address any results in which there is some discrepancy from what was expected based on other research or based on the hypotheses presented. In addition, this analysis should include speculation regarding why such alternative findings were obtained.

A fourth issue to be addressed in the discussion section is a review of the potential limitations of the study. The researchers specifically review the research methods employed and the method of selecting participants, which may have resulted in limitations or threats to internal and external validity. In evaluating this section of the discussion, it is necessary to review the potential threats to validity based on the research design used and the methods of selecting participants. Almost every study has limitations, and the researchers' acknowledgment of possible limitations demonstrates an understanding of the cautions that should be taken in interpreting the results.

Generally, the last point for the researchers to address in the discussion section is to suggest further issues to study. This section is of interest to other researchers who may want to investigate the topic of research. However, as consumers of research, we are also interested because a discussion of future areas of investigation allows insight into what else needs to be accomplished and provides further information about the limits of what is known about the topic of interest.

Guidelines for Evaluating the Discussion Section

1. Do the researchers clearly restate the purpose and research hypotheses or questions?

2. Do the researchers clearly discuss the implications of the findings and how they relate to theories, others' findings, and actual practice?

3. If relevant, do the researchers provide alternative explanations of the results obtained when there is discrepancy with other sources or expected outcomes?

4. Do the researchers identify potential limitations of the study and the results?

5. Do the researchers identify possible directions for future research?

Evaluating Examples From the Research Literature

Quantitative Research Study

The comparison by Henderson, et al. (2007) of an intervention for post-traumatic stress provides an example for analysis. They stated, in the discussion section, the following:

In our study, we examined the benefits that individuals suffering from clinical levels of traumatic distress could gain from processing their trauma through the creation of mandalas. Although it was hypothesized that there would be significant improvements in numerous health outcomes, the only outcome for which there was significant relative improvement was PTSD symptom severity. Such results are only partially consistent with studies relying on verbal processing tasks (Sloan & Marx, 2004a, 2004b), because gains in the current study were specific to trauma symptom severity, whereas gains in verbal processing tasks appear to be more broadly ranging. Results of the current investigation are nevertheless noteworthy, because the condition of interest in the current study was PTSD and participants were selected who had elevated levels of traumatic distress, although not necessarily elevated levels of depression, anxiety, or physical symptoms, or decreased levels of meaning in life. Therefore, the mandala-drawing exercise seemed effective in ameliorating symptoms of the clinical condition for which participants were specifically chosen. The current mandala-drawing exercise and similar ones should be investigated as ways of supplementing or substituting for verbal processing treatments for trauma victims, particularly those who, because of personality features or cognitive factors, are unable or unwilling to process traumatic experiences through verbal means. (pp. 152–153)

Two obvious weaknesses of this study are the small sample size and the differences in the numbers of males and females. The Henderson, et al. (2007) project was a small initial study to test the feasibility of this line of research, and similar studies with greater sample size and more balanced gender distribution need to be conducted. Furthermore, although the participants were undergraduate college students with post-traumatic stress disorder (PTSD), it would be beneficial to have a sample from a larger population of individuals suffering from more severe levels of trauma. Another shortcoming was the lack of direct comparison of a mandala-drawing task with other control groups, such as a predrawn mandala coloring condition, another art therapy condition, and a writing condition. Another condition might be desirable, in which individuals would be asked to reflect on their trauma, but not allowed to symbolically depict or write about that trauma. Ideally, all or some of these conditions could be examined in future studies, and the different health benefits for different manipulations might be uncovered.

Extending this line of research with children and adolescents who are victims of abuse would be an area of great interest. Some children, depending on age and educational opportunities, lack the ability to adequately and effectively express traumatic experiences through written or verbal language. Furthermore, children are often shamed into secrecy by their abusers and are fearful to disclose incidences of abuse. Mandalas drawn by such children could serve the need of expression of traumatic experiences in a simpler and less threatening way than writing or talking about the events. The current findings suggest that research in such areas would prove fruitful.

Scientific research into Jungian theory is uncommon. Jung's theories are often criticized as being too vague or complex and difficult to understand and, therefore, better left to the realms of art or religion (Slegelis, 1987). It seems as though Jungian theory has been unable to gain respect among more scientific schools of thought because of this lack of scientific research.

Similarly, the field of art psychotherapy has lacked the credibility and respect of more scientific fields due to a lack of empirical research. Future research ought to be conducted that might bridge the worlds of the artistic and the scientific in an effort to increase awareness of healing techniques derived from Jungian theory and art psychotherapy.

The researchers do restate the purpose by starting with the discussion with "we examined the benefits" and a summary of the hypothesis, "it was hypothesized that there would be significant improvements" (p. 153). The second question concerns whether the researchers connect the findings to other research findings and theory. The researchers do make connections to previous research: "Such results are only partially consistent with studies relying on verbal processing tasks (Sloan & Marx, 2004a, 2004b)" (p. 151). The researchers do attempt to connect the results to alternative explanations or concepts by stating: "The current mandala exercise and similar ones should be investigated as ways of supplementing or substituting for verbal processing treatments for trauma victims, particularly those who, because of personality features or cognitive factors, are unable or unwilling to process traumatic experiences through verbal means" (p. 154). They attempted to suggest that their findings may be best used with those who do not process experiences through verbal means, but still recognize the relevance of this approach.

The researchers have a separate section addressing the strengths and weaknesses of the study. They noted that one weakness was the small sample size and the fact there were so many more females than males. They also acknowledged that they used college students, who may not be representative of the larger population. Finally, they suggested that the use of a more similar control group experience would have provided clearer results.

The researchers also have a separate section for directions for additional research. They suggested expanding the population studied to include children and adolescents with PTSD. They note that the use of art with children may be particularly useful because children like this type of medium of expression.

Qualitative Research Study

Fry (2007) cited in her discussion section the findings of her study on first-year teacher induction. She stated:

This study examined the induction experiences of four 1st-year teachers and how they responded to available induction support. The findings indicated that these 4 beginning teachers had different support needs. The participants also received variable forms of support. The one common experience seemed to be the inadequate nature of the induction support each participant received.

Smith and Ingersoll's (2004) research on induction appears to be the most comprehensive in the literature, yet the quantitative data set they used did not ask questions about whether or not the forms of induction were meaningful. In the current investigation, the participant who received the best induction combination (best meaning the combination that has the greatest likelihood of reducing attrition) was dissatisfied with her induction experience. Therefore, Table 1 highlights the support each teacher received using the forms of induction Smith and Ingersoll analyzed in order to provide a framework for discussing the present investigator's results. As discussed in the literature review, basic induction (mentoring and supportive communication from an administrator) has no statistically significant impact on reducing the predicted level of attrition (with no induction support, predicted attrition was 40%; with basic induction predicted attrition was 39%). When basic induction was combined with Level II, the predicted level of attrition was reduced to 27%, and when combined with II and III, the rate was reduced to 18%.

Comparing this summary of the participants' induction experiences to Smith and Ingersoll's (2004) levels of induction support presents an interesting synthesis. Based on the number of support components, it appears that Stella received the "best" induction. However, she only found two of the components worthwhile: administrator communication and common planning time. Laura received three induction components, but mentoring was problematic because her assigned mentor was new to teaching at her grade level and only a 4th year teacher. Although she found the communication from her administrator supportive, the frequency, form and duration were inadequate. Shari's mentoring and common planning time were somewhat helpful, but she found the communication from administrator too supportive.

Instead, she would have preferred critical feedback in addition to praise. Becca shared the latter concern, and her common planning time was rarely spent with the other teachers at her grade level because of their unsuccessful team dynamics. In conclusion, for the four 1st-year teachers in this study, the amount of induction support received did not correspond to satisfaction in terms of their perceptions of the effectiveness of their induction support. Nevertheless, all four continued teaching after their 1st year.

There has been a growing trend in professional development to avoid "one size fits all" approaches where veteran teachers and beginners all receive the same forms of training. This trend recognizes teachers' developmental spectrum and endeavors to provide salient professional development (Marzano, 2003).

This same approach may be appropriate for induction. The participants in this study indicated a range of competencies and self-perceived deficit areas. For example, Stella, who was comfortable with her approach to classroom management, would have benefited more from induction meetings about implementing guided reading groups instead of classroom management sessions. Meanwhile, Laura would have liked further opportunities to learn about classroom management as well as guided reading. Just as teachers are encouraged to differentiate their diverse students in K–12 classrooms, school districts should differentiate professional learning opportunities for beginning teachers (p. 232).

In summary, I present the following list of suggestions for how Stella, Shari, Becca, and Laura's induction experiences could have been strengthened. In regard to mentoring: assign new teachers caring, eager, and capable mentors who have a common planning period and teach at the same (or close) grade level/content area. The mentors should be veteran teachers with at least one year experience at the grade level they are currently teaching (p. 233).

Practical Support

Encourage a school climate where beginning and veteran teachers comfortably ask colleagues and administrators for help so beginning teachers are confident asking for help.

Researcher Reflections

When I designed this study, I intentionally adapted a research design that allowed me to be subjective, care about my participants, become an insider, and make meaning of the study's data with participants (Toma, 2000). What I did not anticipate was that I would essentially become part of the phenomenon I was investigating: the participants' induction experience.

Limitations of the Study and Suggestions for Future Study

Because of limitations to this study, the results may not be generalizable to a larger population. Stella, Shari, Becca, and Laura were all graduates of the same elementary education teacher preparation.

Program

The participants were also all female, between 22–24 years of age, and taught in a rural or suburban school districts. The limitations created by the small, heterogeneous sample in this investigation suggest a need for future investigations about 1st-year teacher responses to induction experiences using more diverse participants. Qualitative and quantitative methods can be used to investigate how beginners value their induction experiences.

Such research has the potential to help school districts refine their induction efforts to better meet beginning teachers' needs.

I hesitate to declare my close relationship with the participants a limitation of the study because it was an intentional part of the research design. (p. 228)

The five questions to address in evaluating the discussion start with whether the researcher clearly restated the purpose and research hypotheses or questions. Fry (2007) started the discussion with the statement: "This study examined the induction . . ." (p. 226). A second question concerns whether the researcher discussed the implications of the findings. The researcher provided a summary of the findings and suggested specific approaches to improve teacher-induction procedures. The researcher did not provide any alternative explanation of the results and noted the similarity to other study outcomes only. The researcher suggested that the results may not be generalizable because of the small sample size and specific characteristics of the sample. However, she went on the state that her close relationship with the participants was a limitation of the study. Despite noting the limitation, the researcher retracted this caution by stating it was her intention to develop a close relationship with the participants. Finally, the researcher did identify potential areas for future research that include a combination of qualitative and quantitative methods to further understand teacher-induction procedures.

Summary

The discussion section is where the researchers attempt to summarize and make sense of the results. First, the researchers should restate the purpose of the study and summarize the findings. Next, the researchers should link the findings to theories and/or previous research and discuss any alternative explanations for the results that are not consistent with their own conclusions. It is important for any limitations to be noted and for future research areas to be identified.

Exercises

Directions: Locate an article in the professional literature addressing a topic you are interested in exploring. Evaluate the discussion section based on the questions addressed in this chapter. Try to explain and justify your answers based on specific examples from the article you have chosen.

1. Do the researchers clearly restate the purpose and research hypotheses or questions?

2. Do the researchers clearly discuss the implications of the findings and how they relate to theories, others' findings, and actual practice?

3. If relevant, do the researchers provide alternative explanations of the results obtained when there is discrepancy with other sources or expected outcomes?

4. Do the researchers identify potential limitations of the study and the results?

5. Do the researchers identify possible directions for future research?

III

Application of
Research and Evaluation

16

Developing a Research Proposal and Conducting Research in Practice

There has been considerable debate in the counseling and educational literature over the extent to which research should be emphasized in the training and actual practice of counselors and educators (Border, Bloss, Cashwell, & Rainey, 1994; Heppner, Kivlighan, & Wampold, 1992; Kanfer, 1990; Love, Bahner, Jones, & Nilsson, 2007; Merlo, Collins, & Bernstein, 2008; Sexton, 1996; Sexton & Whiston, 1996; Townend & Grant, 2006). Despite this debate, there has been a recent emphasis on the importance of research in practice, or evidence-based practice (see Chapter 7). The importance of accountability in practice is pressuring professionals to care about research and link research to practice. There is a distinct conflict between the training that educators (those training practitioners) have and the training that those practitioners would prefer to receive. Educators assume that training their students to be scientist-practitioners is appropriate, whereas practitioners would rather focus on becoming practitioner-scientists. Graduate-level training for counselors has, for the most part, focused on the scientist-practitioner model (Hoshmand & Polkinghorne, 1992; Kanfer, 1990; Townend & Grant, 2006).

Three problems have been noted with the scientist-practitioner training approach (Heppner, et al., 1992; Hoshmand & Polkinghorne, 1992; Szymanski, Ozegovic, Phillips, & Briggs-Phillips, 2007). One problem has been identified as the possible lack of effective training in research and scientific methods, which results in minimal scholarship activity by practitioners (Szymanski, et al., 2007). A second problem that has been identified is the question of how useful and applicable research reported in the literature may be to actual practice (Hoshmand & Polkinghorne, 1992). A third problem that has been suggested as one that limits the use of research in practice is the appropriateness of research designs and whether they represent sterile, controlled research laboratories or the natural environment (Whiston, 1996).

Szymanski, et al. (2007) suggested a novel approach to fostering the development of research skills for those primarily interested in practice. They proposed the importance of an academic research training environment (RTE). The components of an RTE are faculty modeling of research activity; reinforcement of student interests; practical application of statistical methods; and opportunities to link research knowledge to practice (Szymanski, et al., 2007). The last component is particularly important to fostering student research self-efficacy. This means requiring and promoting research activities during field experiences. Such efforts foster student understanding and comfort level with conducting research in a practice setting.

At this point in our discussion (and at this point in the text), I hope that the importance of using research and the scientific approach in practice is clear, but I want to cite several additional views that have emphasized the importance of practitioners using a scientific approach to practice. Increasingly, counselors and educators are being required to demonstrate the effectiveness of their work, such as with student performance or client outcomes (Odom, Brantlinger, Gersten, Horner, Thompson, & Harris, 2005; Sexton, 1996; Sexton & Whiston, 1996). Funding sources (taxpayers and insurance companies), government organizations, and consumers themselves (parents of students and clients in counseling) are demanding demonstrations of effectiveness. Those interested in demonstrations of effectiveness want solid, objective evidence and not simply professional opinion (e.g., "We believe our interventions to be effective"). Other research has suggested, and I have noted in earlier chapters, that the research process is valued in our society as one of the most important sources of knowledge in decision making (Kettlewell, 2004; Sexton, 1996; Sexton & Whiston, 1996). The dilemma for counselors and educators is not necessarily *whether* research methods should be used, but *how they can be most efficiently and effectively used* to inform the work we do and provide documentation that what we do is effective.

A second reason the research process is important to our professions is simply that professions are in part defined by having an organized body of knowledge (Brown & Srebalus, 1996; Merlo, et al., 2008). Developing an organized body of knowledge is best achieved through the mutual interaction of research and practice. In essence, science informs practice and practice informs science, creating evidence-based practice.

A third reason for the practitioners to conduct research is to maintain enthusiasm for the work. There has been considerable writing and research on professional "burnout" for educators and counselors. I personally believe that one method of reducing burnout is to develop and participate in research. One reason for burnout is a feeling of ineffectiveness and monotony. Developing and conducting research provides the hope of finding alternative methods to practice and the possibility of changing the issues and problems confronting the professional. Additionally, conducting research and finding effective methods of practice may lead to professional advancement opportunities—it demonstrates initiative.

Practitioner-Researchers

Hopefully, at this point in your understanding and reading of this text, other courses you have taken and personal experience have led to an appreciation of the important link between research and practice. In this chapter, I describe the process of developing, participating in, and conducting research, mainly from a practitioner's perspective, the practitioner-scientist approach. Consequently, I will describe how to develop and conduct a research project. This will be based on a step-by-step process. Second, I describe how practitioners in counseling and education can implement research in a practical way and still meet the daily demands of the employment setting.

Developing a Research Proposal

There are slightly more steps in developing a research proposal than are found in an article published in a professional journal. Keep in mind that a research proposal is essentially your map (a detailed and readable map) for conducting the study. Consequently, the more detail you have in your steps, the better. (See Table 16.1.)

The first step is identifying a problem or an issue to address. As mentioned earlier, the practitioner-scientist approach should be a mutual exchange between research and practice, and this is also quite true in identifying a problem or issue. Wiersma and Jurs (2005) noted the importance of identifying a good research problem. There are several different methods of developing a research problem. These include a review of theories that have the potential

Table 16.1   Steps in Developing a Research Plan

Step 1	Identify a problem or issue to address.
Step 2	Identify current status of the problem from other research.
Step 3	Operationalize the problem or issue.
Step 4	Develop purpose statement and/or hypotheses.
Step 5	Select research design and procedures.
Step 6	Operationalize dependent variable and select measures.
Step 7	Identify population and sample and determine sample selection procedures.
Step 8	Conduct the study and collect data.
Step 9	Analyze the data.
Step 10	Report the data.

to explain a phenomenon, discussions with colleagues, observing issues confronted in practice, and a review of current professional literature and current issues. Charles (1995) suggested several helpful considerations when identifying research topics. These include (a) personal interest in the topic, meaning a topic that will be rewarding and motivating to see through to completion, (b) an important topic, meaning one that will answer the "So what?" question we ask in evaluating others' research, (c) the amount of time required to complete the project—will it be possible to conduct the study, given your current day-to-day job demands?, and (d) are there any costs to conducting the study (in particular, will it require considerable amounts of money)? Wiersma and Jurs (2005) cautioned against choosing a research problem that is more philosophical or abstract, which makes it difficult to research. A simple example is whether there are ghosts. One can investigate people's attitudes toward whether there are ghosts, but studying the physical evidence of a ghost is a much more philosophical and abstract idea.

Once you have identified a problem or issue you wish to investigate, your next step is to determine what currently exists in this area in the research literature. Has any research been conducted on the topic? Were the findings what you would have hypothesized? (Review Chapter 2 for searching the literature.) In determining the status of current research on the topic, you will gain information that will help you make a decision to pursue a research project or not. In your review, you will want to use your recently acquired skills in evaluating journal articles and determine whether the studies are of relatively solid quality and whether they address the issues you are interested in studying.

If you determine that you wish to pursue a study, the literature review will provide you with a basis for developing other sections of your proposal, such as operationalizing the problem, hypotheses, and so on. Another benefit in becoming informed about a particular research topic is that you will become more knowledgeable and be able to share this information with others.

A third step in developing your proposal is operationalizing the problem or issue so the study may be conducted. This step may also be defined in terms of developing the purpose statement. This step is not an easy one; it requires a clear identification of the problem so the research variables may be developed from the target problem. If the purpose statement is poorly constructed, it will be difficult to successfully complete the other steps. For example, if you saw a problem with children learning science, you could focus on developing a teaching method or on how the children learn or on both. The perspective you choose to use to define the problem will influence your efforts in developing and refining the proposal. To operationalize the problem, you must develop a concrete expression of it so that it may be observed and measured. Many problems can be discussed in the abstract, but to be studied they must be conceptualized concretely. You will need to determine the population of interest and complete a clear statement of the intent of your study (the purpose statement). This includes identifying the type of study (e.g., comparison, descriptive, relationship). Review Chapter 10 for information about constructing a good purpose statement. Also, you will need to identify clearly the variables of interest (dependent and independent) if it is a true experimental or quasi-experimental design.

An example of an abstract statement of the problem and, potentially, an operationalizeable statement of the initial research idea, for a study of children learning science might be: "There is a need for innovative curriculum for teaching science to elementary school children." A concrete statement of the problem might be: "The purpose of this study is to determine whether an authentic curriculum method will increase elementary students' understanding of science better than traditional methods of instruction."

The next step is to develop your hypotheses. In stating the hypotheses, you will want to think about the types of hypotheses based on previous research literature, a theory, or personal clinical experience. An example of linking theory to a hypothesis can be found in writing about the conceptual change, integration of cognitive and sociocultural developmental views, and approach to learning (Mason, 2007; Vosniadou, 2007). Vosniadou (2007) described how children begin to learn from birth: "Cognitive developmental research has shown that the knowledge-acquisition process starts soon after birth and that infants organize the multiplicity of their sensory experiences under the influence of everyday culture and language into narrow but relatively coherent frameworks that allow distinct types of explanations and predictions and embody causal notions and epistemological commitments know, as 'naïve theories'" (p. 58). Vosniadou (2007) noted that the teaching of science is typically restricted to the school environment. Such an approach is not consistent with how humans learn, developing hypotheses from experience, known as authentic learning. A possible hypothesis of such a study might be: "Elementary school children receiving science instruction based upon a conceptual change, authentic learning approach will have higher standardized test scores on science than those receiving a traditional science instruction method."

As with the evaluation of a research article and the hypotheses developed by researchers, you will want to ensure that your hypotheses are testable. This will be partly addressed in the development and operationalizing of your purpose statement. The study must be able to be conducted and operationalized in such a way as to measure the dependent variables. If you are conducting the study alone, you may want to discuss your hypotheses with others, either peers or individuals who regularly conduct research. Even though the hypotheses may make sense to you, they may not be clear to others, and having others read your hypothesis will provide you with feedback about the clarity and conciseness of your hypotheses.

The next step is the development of your research methods, procedures, and research design. This is a most important step in your study: How you establish the methods will determine to a considerable degree the efficacy of your study. Designing a research study has been noted to be a problem-solving process (Heiman, 1995) because you are attempting to come up with an effective method for testing out hypotheses. Heiman (1995) suggested four considerations in designing a study: the intent or nature of the hypotheses; the focus or nature of the behavior to be studied; concerns over validity; and ethical and practical considerations.

The first consideration in determining a research design is to think about the purpose and hypotheses of your study. As stated earlier, we want consistency between the purpose or hypotheses and the research design. Thus, if you are conducting a study to identify and clarify an event or phenomenon, you will probably choose a descriptive or qualitative research design. To determine relationships between variables and issues, you will be collecting data that focus on two or more variables and conducting correlational analyses. For studies in which you wish to compare outcomes from those receiving services with outcomes from those not receiving services, you will want to decide between using a true experimental design and using a quasi-experimental design. To decide which designs make sense for you to use based on your purpose, it may be helpful to refer back to Chapters 3 and 4. There are a number of other texts that can also provide a detailed step-by-step discussion on the procedures for conducting research and choosing particular research designs (Charles, 1995; Isaac & Michael, 1987; Heiman, 1995; Heppner, et al., 1992; Ponterotto & Casa, 1991). Many of these texts are designed primarily to teach methods of conducting research.

According to Heiman (1995), a second consideration in selecting a procedure is the characteristics of the variables you are studying. For example, if you are studying the effects of gender on learning math, you cannot randomly assign subjects or participants to groups—you cannot randomly assign someone to a particular gender. Therefore, you must choose a design that takes into consideration this restriction, a quasi-experimental design or a descriptive-causal comparative design.

Heiman (1995) noted that issues of validity are a third consideration in determining your research design. Recall the discussion in Chapter 12 of internal and external validity and how the use of a particular research design influences the validity of a study. Typically, we will want to balance the threats to internal and external validity. For example, if there is a high internal validity and a large amount of control by the researcher, there should be less control and a more natural measurement of the variables of interest (external validity). Heppner, et al. (1992) stated: "A study that exerts a high amount of experimental control will most likely depart from a naturalistic setting, and a study that examines variables in a highly naturalistic setting can have only limited experimental control" (p. 68). A researcher, particularly in applied professions like counseling and education, must balance the amount of control employed to achieve as high a level of validity, both internal and external, as possible.

A fourth consideration is that of ethics and practice (Heiman, 1995). Our professional ethics state that we should do no harm, so we want to plan studies that do not harm those whom we serve, clients (counseling) and/or students (education). Procedures have been developed to protect the rights of subjects in research studies (Office of Protection From Research Risks, 1993). Also, most important for the practitioner are practical considerations. The research design must not take up considerable amounts of time, particularly if it interferes with performing day-to-day duties and job requirements.

To summarize, I would suggest a research design for the practitioner that is straightforward, not complex, not time-consuming, and, probably most important, fits well into the day-to-day practice of his or her profession. The use of qualitative research designs and quasi-experimental designs is probably most appropriate for practitioners in counseling and education and is also less intrusive (Townend & Grant, 2006). There are several reasons why these designs may be more appropriate for practitioners to use in counseling and education. One reason is that the sample size need not be as high as is typically required in quantitative methods. For example, case study research, which may be used in both qualitative and quasi-experimental methods, may involve only one participant. A second reason is that random assignment is not necessary or is frequently not used with these designs; this is desirable because random assignment is not possible in the natural environment.

The next step in developing a research proposal is the selection of instruments, or the operationalization of the dependent variable. The type of instrument or operationalization of the dependent variable will depend to some degree on the research design used, quantitative or qualitative. For quantitative research methods, in which numbers of quantification are important, you will want to consider the following issues: objectivity; standard conditions of administering the test; and the use of normative comparisons, reliability, and validity (Gall, Gall, & Borg, 2006). Objectivity refers to the use of self-report, observations, the use of others for scoring, and so on. Self-report measures have the potential for respondent bias but offer ease in administration. Standard conditions for administering the test reduce test error. Normative comparisons allow for, theoretically, more valid interpretations of results. Reliability addresses how consistent the measure is. Validity addresses the degree to which you are actually measuring what you want or intend to measure. There are several important sources to consult when attempting to identify an appropriate test. These include *The Twelfth Mental Measurements Yearbook* (Conoley & Impara, 1995) and *Tests in Print* (Murphy, Conoley, & Impara, 1994). Typically, you will be able to find these books in the references section of your library. They provide descriptions of the tests and information about test properties such as reliability and validity.

There are several important considerations in selecting a test. One is to ensure that the test measures the dependent variable of interest. A second is that the test must be appropriate for use with the population or sample you are using. One approach to finding a measure that best fits the dependent variable is to review the literature for other studies investigating a similar dependent variable. It is helpful if there is a measure that is commonly accepted as measuring the dependent variable of interest. For example, to measure depression, a frequently used measurement tool is the Beck Depression Inventory, BDI-II (Seignourel, Green, & Schmitz, 2008).

In qualitative research, observational, recording, and interview methods are typical. There is no attempt to quantify the responses; instead, the object is to develop categories of response, or themes. Use of observational methods requires that the researcher has a focus (e.g., groups and their interaction in a specific context or dyads in a work setting, such as supervisor-supervisee). Recall from Chapter 5 that a common approach to understanding and interpreting qualitative research is to determine your unit of analysis or data collection: social practice, episodes, encounters, roles, relationships, and so on (Lofland, Snow, Anderson, & Lofland, 2006). You should determine your unit of analysis prior to data collection so you can focus on the variable of interest.

A key approach to data collection and operationalization of the dependent variable in qualitative research is triangulation. This involves the use of multiple sources of data collection to identify the themes or constructs of interests. This means that you might possibly have several observers reviewing the same phenomena or coding audio- or videotaped sessions.

Another step in developing and planning a research study is to systematically select your sample from your identified population. If you are teaching third-grade students and wish to study how an innovative science program might compare to a more traditional method, your population may be all third-grade students in the United States. Once you have determined the population, your next consideration is how to effectively select a sample that is manageable and accessible. As a practitioner, you will not typically have unlimited time to contact multiple sites to obtain permission to recruit subjects or participants for a study. If you use a qualitative or quasi-experimental design with your own class, your study will be much more manageable, but, as we discussed in Chapter 11, this will result in several limitations to the study and threats to external validity. Even so, it may still be important to conduct such a study to determine the effectiveness of a new approach and bring about the potential for change in how subjects are taught.

Another approach is to collaborate with colleagues in other schools in your district or other parts of your state or throughout the United States and have them attempt to implement a similar research design using basically the same methods. Consequently, you would have a larger sample than simply your own classroom with which to test your technique. Also, expanding the study to other schools allows for greater generalization and addresses some of the threats to external validity.

A third approach is to switch teaching the subject of the study with another teacher in your school and provide the intervention with that classroom. This may be accomplished through a mutual exchange: The other teacher teaches your class, and you teach his or hers. This reduces the bias of other factors influencing the outcome of the study in cases when the only access you have to the sample is your work with them regarding the intervention. In actual practice, it is not unusual for teachers to team-teach or switch classes, so (theoretically) it should not be too disruptive.

In counseling and education, practical approaches to conducting research would include the use of case study methods when using both qualitative and quasi-experimental designs. You may work with a client or a student and find that a new, innovative approach is warranted, and you want to test it out systematically. A case study approach may be the most sensible approach. You could certainly implement the new technique with several clients. Generally, it is not feasible to switch with other counselors and take on their clients, as teachers can do with their classes. Clients become attached to counselors and are not easily "traded" to other counselors.

An important consideration in any study conducted with clients or students is consent to participate. Your ethical responsibilities as a researcher are to ensure that anyone whom you ask to participate in a research study has *freely* given *informed* consent. Those working with children (minors) must obtain informed consent from a parent and assent from the child. An important step in ensuring ethical research is processing any request through an institutional human subjects committee.

Practical Considerations in Conducting Research

There are several practical considerations that must be addressed when conducting research as a practitioner-scientist. One issue concerns the devotion of time to the project. It is critical that you set aside time to conduct the study. It may not involve significant amounts of time if you have incorporated the study carefully into your practice, but it will require attention on a consistent basis. A second consideration is the support from your administration and your colleagues. Conducting research without consulting your supervisor or administration could create problems for you (e.g., they may wonder how you are spending your time). A third consideration is the development of a well-thought-out, written plan for your study. The plan should clearly outline your steps, and it may be helpful to develop a timeline for implementation of those steps. A fourth issue is how you will code and analyze the data. If you are using a qualitative study, you may want to consult with a faculty member at a local university who is familiar with coding qualitative information and/or familiar with some of the computer programs for coding qualitative data, such as QSR NUD*IST (Nonnumerical, Unstructured Data—Indexing, Searching and Theorizing) (QSR International, 1997). For studies conducted with quantitative methods, again, you may want to consult with a faculty member at a local university who can assist in data analysis if you want to complete more complex calculations such as analyses of variance (ANOVAs). There are several computer programs that can be used in the analysis of quantitative data, including the Statistical Program for the Social Sciences (SPSS) and the Statistical Analysis System (SAS).

Summary

In summary, it may not be as difficult as you might think to conduct research during the daily practice of your profession in counseling or education. Your key considerations are the devotion of time to the project and plans to systematically evaluate the data collected. It is important to construct a plan of action for conducting your study. I have found that having a detailed plan alerts me to gaps in my design or potential problems. One of the most important issues is to select a topic that is interesting and potentially exciting to you. It will maintain your interest and provide increased satisfaction to you in your daily activities.

17

Development and Application of Program Evaluation Research

Our society, including political and social institutions, has increasingly required more accountability in social service and educational programs. Stufflebeam and Shrinkfield (2007) noted the importance of evaluation and stated: "Evaluation arguably is society's most fundamental discipline. It is oriented to assessing and helping improve all aspects of society" (p. 4). Gall, Gall, & Borg (2006) discussed the importance of evaluation and stated: "The main reason is that public administrators have come to view evaluation as an important tool in policy analysis and program management" (p. 542). I would suggest that we as professionals should be interested in the quality and outcomes of the services and professional activities we provide, as well as in the importance of providing funding sources with information about the effectiveness of education and counseling programs. Program evaluation is a systematic approach to gathering information about our professional practices and gives us a tool for improving our programs. It also is different in intent from traditional research, although one might use similar methods at different points in the process. Gall, et al. (2006) noted the similarities between research and evaluation and also outlined differences. First, they cited the similarities by stating: "In practice, evaluators make substantial use of the research designs, measurement tools, and data analysis techniques that constitute the methodology of educational research" (p. 543). Despite the use of many methods in educational research, there are differences. Gall, et al. (2006) outlined three differences between research and evaluation. One difference is that the actual impetus for the evaluation is initiated by someone other than the researcher, and the use of the outcome information is to make decisions about policies, programs, or management activities (Gall, et al., 2006. A program evaluator is frequently hired or requested to complete an evaluation by an organization, an administrator, or a governmental body to assist in making specific decisions. Conversely, a research study is conducted to uncover information about a particular phenomenon or issue. Research is much more broadly based in focus, and the focus is on the researcher's interests. A second difference, according to Gall, et al. (2006), is the degree to which the results are generalized. Evaluation is designed to answer a specific set of questions for a particular group, organization, or agency. Research, on the other hand, is intended to generate outcomes that provide results on a much broader scale, to generalize back to a large target population. The third difference between evaluation and research concerns the emphasis on value judgments (Gall, et al., 2006). Evaluation is engaged in making conclusions that may involve judgment about the worth of a program, whereas research is intended to uncover evidence that is more in the nature of discovery.

Definitions of Program Evaluation Research

Several definitions of program evaluation research have been offered, but they share common components (Gall, et al., 2003; Rossi & Freeman, 1993; Stufflebeam & Shinkfield, 2007). For example, Rossi and Freeman (1993) defined program evaluation as ". . . a systematic application of social science

Table 17.1   Similarities and Differences Between Research and Evaluation

	Research	*Evaluation*
Purpose	Test theories and develop practices and procedures	Decision making and information for social programs
Audience	Professional and scientific community	Specific group or communities such as funding sources or governmental agencies
Method	True experimental, quasi-experimental, nonexperimental (descriptive) qualitative, and so on	True experimental, quasi-experimental, nonexperimental (descriptive) qualitative, and so on

research procedures in assessing the conceptualization and design, implementation, and utility of social intervention programs" (p. 19). More specifically, they suggested that program evaluation involved efforts to improve through planning and through monitoring the effectiveness of health, education, and human service programs. Gall, et al. (2006) defined educational evaluation as ". . . the process of making judgments about the merit, value or worth of educational programs" (p. 542). The Joint Committee on Standards for Educational Evaluation (1994) proposed a definition stating that "evaluation is the systematic assessment of the worth or merit of an object" (p. 3). Stufflebeam and Shinkfield (2007) suggested that evaluation is ". . . the systematic assessment of an object's merit, worth, probity, feasibility, safety, significance, and/or equity" (p. 13). The commonality of these definitions is an assessment of the worth and/or merit of an object or program.

Professional Standards for Program Evaluation

Standards for conducting program evaluation have been proposed (Joint Committee on Standards for Educational Evaluation, 1994) and these standards were first developed in the early 1980s. There are 30 standards that fall into four general categories: utility, feasibility, propriety, and accuracy. These standards were established to guide the evaluator in setting up high-quality, professional evaluations. The standards for utility, according to Stufflebeam and Shinkfield (2007), concern whether the information gained from an evaluation addresses the needs of the identified audience. Feasibility standards address whether the evaluation is realistic to conduct (Stufflebeam & Shinkfield, 2007). Feasibility also includes the cost of conducting the evaluation—is the cost too high or inflated? The third general category of standards is propriety, which concerns the extent to which an evaluation and its results are legally and ethically conducted with regard for those affected by the results (Stufflebeam & Shinkfield, 2007). Finally, accuracy, according to Stufflebeam and Shinkfield (2007), is the extent to which the information and data collected accurately reflect the program being assessed or evaluated.

Types of Evaluations

Three major different types of evaluation have been identified: need, formative, and summative (Gall, Gall, & Borg, 2006; Stufflebeam & Shinkfield, 2007). Assessments of needs are designed to identify the discrepancy between actual conditions and what is sought or desired (Borg, et al., 2003). A focus on needs may include assessment of particular types of education programs or counseling services such as crisis services or special school services like after-school programs. Rossi and Freeman (1993) defined needs assessment as the ". . . systematic appraisal of type, depth, and scope of problems perceived by study targets or their advocates" (p. 90). Typically, a needs assessment is conducted prior to designing more comprehensive programs. One would not want to develop a program, even if it were a great program, if the need was not there. This is particularly true today, given social and political oversight of programs and the scrutiny over expenditure of public funds.

A second type of evaluation, process or formative evaluation, concerns whether a program is implemented as designed, e.g., how well was the program implemented? Focusing on evaluation of effort or process does not generally address whether a program is effective, but it does answer important questions about the amount and quality of effort needed to implement a program.

A third type of evaluation is evaluation of outcome, also referred to as a summative evaluation. Evaluation of outcome concerns how successful a program is in achieving designated goals. Typically, summative evaluation results are provided to policymakers such as politicians (Stufflebeam & Shinkfield, 2007), whereas formative evaluation results are generally given to those who are implementing the program.

Evaluation Models

A number of different models of conducting evaluations have been proposed (Stufflebeam & Shinkfield, 2007). These designs may utilize both quantitative and qualitative methods of data collection. One model of evaluation that has been developed is the case study model (Stake, 1994; Stufflebeam & Shinkfield, 2007). Stufflebeam and Shinkfield (2007) described case study evaluation this way: "A case study evaluation's signature feature is an in-depth examination of the case and issuance of a captivating, illuminative report" (p. 309). Case study research typically involves the use of qualitative methods most frequently, and a much deeper investigation into the processes of a program. However, as Stufflebeam and Shinkfield (2007) noted, the case study evaluation method generates considerable data and information, and the evaluator must organize and present the information to help the decision makers use the findings.

Another evaluation model is the consumer-oriented approach (Scriven, 1991; Stufflebeam & Shinkfield, 2007). Stufflebeam and Shinkfield (2007) describe this model as being consumer-oriented, and the importance of the outcome data are interpreted in terms of how those who are receiving the services or program are affected. So the evaluation is focused on determining the worth or value of a program. The use of checklists in evaluating programs is a key component of this model (Scriven, 2005).

Another evaluation model is the context, input, process, and product evaluation (CIPP) model (Stufflebeam, 2003). Stufflebeam and Shinkfield (2007) describe the CIPP model as focused on both formative and summative evaluation. Questions are asked about the object of evaluation, such as: "What needs to be done? How should it be done? Is it being done? And Is it succeeding?" (p. 327). Stufflebeam and Shinkfield (2007) described the CIPP model this way: ". . . the model's intent is to supply evaluation users—such as policy boards, administrators, and project staffs—with timely, valid information of use in identifying an appropriate area for development; formulating sound goals, activity plans, and budgets" (p. 327). It is a broad approach to evaluation that focuses on improvement of programs and accountability. It originally was developed to evaluate schools and has since been expanded to be used in various arenas (Stufflebeam & Shinkfield, 2007).

There are several other evaluation models, and I want to give you a brief introduction to some of these, but the purpose of this book and this chapter is essentially an introduction to evaluation. There are a number of different resources that address these models and other models in much greater detail (Chen, 2005; Davidson, 2005; Sufflebeam & Shinkfield, 2007).

Steps in an Evaluation

There are systematic steps in conducting program evaluation, just as there are with scientific research (Gall, et al., 2003; Stufflebeam & Shinkfield, 2007). Steps in conducting a program evaluation include forming the evaluation team, identifying relevant stakeholders, determining the focus of the evaluation, identifying the evaluation questions to be answered, selecting the evaluation methods and designs, selecting the measures for the evaluation, collecting the data, organizing and analyzing the data, and reporting the results to relevant stakeholders. (See Table 17.2.)

The first step in the evaluation process is the formation of an evaluation team. Stufflebeam and Shinkfield (2007) discussed potential roles for evaluation team members, such as measurement and evaluation specialist; subject matter specialist; evaluation manager, and so on. It is desirable to have an evaluation team rather than a sole individual conducting an evaluation, particularly when the organization being evaluated is a large one, or when there is a large amount of evaluation material to be collected. There are several reasons for using an evaluation team: the use of evaluation team provides a more varied perspective and, theoretically, more objectivity; and a team may be needed to share the volume of work and activities involved. Some have suggested that relevant stakeholders should be included in an evaluation team (Houser, Anderson, & Wang, 1995; Whyte, 1990).

The Joint Committee on Standards for Educational Evaluation (1988) proposed standards for personnel who conducted evaluations. Twenty-one standards were proposed that focus on four general categories, as do the general standards: utility, feasibility, propriety, and accuracy. Further, the Joint Committee stated that ". . . evaluations (must) be conducted legally, ethically, and with due regard for the welfare of evaluatees and clients of the evaluations" (p. 269).

An important question is whether those conducting the evaluation are "insiders" or "outsiders." An insider, someone who works for the organization, may have a good understanding of the issues confronting an organization. Also, an insider may obtain cooperation from others quite readily because of his or her relationships with members of the organization. A problem may be the objectivity of an insider who may have a vested interest in finding certain outcomes. An outsider typically brings a more objective view but may need more time understanding the dynamics of the organization. Also, he or she may not be accepted or trusted by members of the organization and may therefore have difficulty obtaining the desired information. A solution to the limitations of insiders and outsiders is to form an evaluation team that includes both insiders and outsiders.

The second step in the evaluation process is the identification of relevant stakeholders. Stakeholders are all those who may potentially be affected by the results of an evaluation. For example, if a school system is evaluating the

Table 17.2   Steps in Program Evaluation

Step 1	Formation of the evaluation team
Step 2	Identification of relevant stakeholders
Step 3	Determination of a focus for the evaluation
Step 4	Identification of evaluation model and methods
Step 5	Selection of evaluation methods and designs
Step 6	Selection of measures for the evaluation
Step 7	Collection of the data
Step 8	Analysis of the data
Step 9	Reporting of the results to relevant stakeholders

effectiveness of a particular curriculum in elementary grades, relevant stakeholders would include parents, teachers, aides, administrators, community members, and children. Stakeholders may be used in the development of the evaluation; in (obviously) conducting the evaluation; and in interpreting the results. It has been suggested that if relevant stakeholders are not included in planning an evaluation, they may sabotage the process (Gall, et al., 2002).

The third step is the determination of a focus for the evaluation. Gall, et al. (2002) suggested that determining the focus of the program evaluation should involve identifying the relevant characteristics of the program that will be studied and evaluated. Relevant program characteristics may include the evaluation of quality of staff, the achievement of program goals, the use of resources, the effectiveness of management, and so on. Typically, an evaluation does not include all components of a program because they would be too time-consuming and costly to evaluate, so it is important to determine the exact focus of the evaluation, which is typically obtained from the source requesting the evaluation and from the relevant stakeholders.

A fourth step in an evaluation is the identification of the evaluation questions to be answered. Questions to be answered may be predetermined by the source requesting the evaluation (e.g., a governmental organization or administration). Even when the evaluation questions are predetermined, an evaluator or the evaluation team will want to discuss the questions with those requesting the evaluation to ensure that there is an understanding of those questions.

The next step in the evaluation process is to select the evaluation models and designs. Several models of evaluation have been proposed: decision making (Stufflebeam, et al., 2005); consumer-driven (Scriven, 1987); needs assessment (Cook, 1989); and responsive evaluation (Stake, 1994). Each of these approaches uses specific methods in conducting the evaluation and data collection. For example, Stufflebeam's (2005) decision-making model uses surveys and interviews, and Stake's (1994) transaction model uses case studies and interviews. I will not go into extensive detail describing these models, but I will state that when you decide to conduct an evaluation, you will want to identify a particular model that meets the needs of the intent of the evaluation. Stufflebeam and Shinkfield (2007) provide a systematic discussion of the various models and provide an analysis and classification of the models. They note that some evaluations are not valid or well founded, and they term these evaluations "pseudoevalautions." The various proponents of these evaluation models have written extensively about their methodologies and procedures, and it is important to become familiar with the method you choose to use. It is not my intent in this chapter to provide detailed information about the different models; to comprehensively cover the models would require considerably more than just one chapter. Also, the models are described elsewhere in great detail (Guba & Lincoln, 1992; House, 1993; Rossi & Freeman, 1993; Stufflebeam & Shinkfield, 2007).

The sixth step, as in traditional research, is to select measures for the evaluation. As with traditional research, the program evaluators will want to choose instruments and measures that assess the intended variables. This is accomplished by operationalizing the outcome variables of interest, for instance, a reading program in which the children's reading scores on a particular test are used. The program evaluator may use many of the same types of measures as those used in traditional research, such as surveys, observations, and interviews. There are certain methods that are preferred, such as interviews, surveys, and observations, which are frequently used. It is not unusual for evaluators to develop an instrument that is specific to the program being evaluated—reliability and validity may therefore be compromised to some degree. However, there are methods to reduce problems with reliability and validity. Evaluators should field-test new measures and check reliability and validity before the measure is used in the actual evaluation. An evaluator may use qualitative methods, which have benefits to gathering and using the data. Gall, et al. (2002) observed that qualitative methods do not always allow for in-depth understanding of stakeholders' perceptions.

The seventh and eighth steps are the collection and analysis of the data. Collection of data should be accomplished systematically, with timelines identified to ensure completion of the required tasks. It is helpful in conducting an evaluation, whether accomplished through a team or by a sole evaluator, to develop a written plan and dictate who will take care of which components of the data collection.

Evaluators will analyze data based on methods similar to those used in traditional research. Both descriptive and inferential statistical methods may be used. For qualitative methods of evaluation, the researcher may also use methods of analysis similar to research approaches, such as using computer programs to analyze and search for common themes in interview transcripts. Key in choosing methods of analyzing data and information gathered is considering the questions to be answered during the evaluation. For example, if an evaluator is interested in determining if a particular science teaching method is best, he or she may choose to use a correlated t-test to compare differences pre- and post-test, comparing the same group at two different times.

The ninth and final step is reporting the results to relevant stakeholders. An evaluation report will usually look much different from a journal article. Generally, the report begins with a statement of the purpose of the evaluation. No citation of previous research is provided. The rationale presented in the report is simply that the evaluation was requested by a specific source with a particular purpose in mind. There may be several reports developed, one for each stakeholder group, as each may have different needs and interests in the findings. The questions to be addressed in the evaluation will be restated. Because they are visual, tables and graphs are particularly helpful in presenting program evaluation results. An important consideration in preparing evaluation results for different stakeholder groups is to write in language that is appropriate for the population reading it. Conclusions are arrived at regarding the initial questions asked, and recommendations are specific to the program being evaluated. This is different from the way conclusions and recommendations are made in professional research articles.

As with traditional research, the program evaluation report will include a clear description of the procedures used. Thus the instruments will be described, as well as the ways in which participants were contacted.

Summary

Recently there has been considerable pressure from governments and consumers for social and educational programs to demonstrate effectiveness, including the influence of evidence-based practice. A key approach to documenting effectiveness is through the use of program evaluation. The field of evaluation has progressed significantly over the past three decades because of the pressures for documenting effectiveness. Professional evaluators have suggested certain criteria for conducting evaluations (Joint Committee on Standards for Educational Evaluation, 1994).

Several types of program evaluation methods have been proposed: needs assessment, formative, and summative. As in traditional research, program evaluation research is based on systematic methods, and there are sequential steps to conducting an evaluation: formation of the evaluation team; identification of relevant stakeholders; determination of the focus of the evaluation; and so on. Counselors and educators will be likely to participate in and/or conduct program evaluation research on a regular basis in the completion of their job duties. Consequently, it is important for them as professionals to become familiar with the methods and approaches to program evaluation. A good way to become familiar and knowledgeable about program evaluation is through participation as a evaluation team member. Having program evaluation skills will enhance your professional skills and future career opportunities.

18

Current and Future Issues in Counseling and Educational Research

Counseling and education practitioners are confronted more and more with pressure to incorporate research into practice. Sociopolitical influences increasingly require demonstration of effectiveness in practice. At this point in the discussion, I hope that you have a broad appreciation of the importance of the study and application of research in the practice of your profession. In this chapter, I hope to solidify your (positive) attitudes toward a practitioner-scientist or a scientist-practitioner (if you prefer) model for your profession and alert you to current and future issues confronting counseling and educational research. Therefore, there is discussion of the following issues: the relevance of the practitioner-scientist view, the connection of the practitioner-scientist/scientist-practitioner view with evidence-based practice, and how to conduct and implement research from a cross-cultural and diversity perspective.

The Practitioner-Scientist Model

There has been considerable debate over why the scientist-practitioner model has not worked for professionals practicing in the fields of counseling and education (Berninger, Dunn, Shin-Ju, & Shimada, 2004; Bernstein &

Kerr, 1993; Hoshmand & Polkinghorne, 1992; Kanfer, 1990; Love, Bahner, Jones, & Nilsson, 2007). This tension, as has been noted earlier, centers on training programs that expect practitioners to embrace research and share a worldview of research similar to that of those training the practitioners, the university faculty members of the training institutions (Barnette, 2006). However, others have noted problems with this view and that practitioners cannot pragmatically share such a worldview concerning how much time and effort should be devoted to conducting research in a practice setting (Bernstein & Kerr, 1993; Heppner, Kivlighan, & Wampold, 1992; Love, et al., 2007). A variation of the scientist-practitioner model is the *practitioner-scientist model*. In the practitioner-scientist approach, the emphasis is on practice, but practice that is based on a perspective and foundation of science and evidence-based research.

Several researchers have offered helpful viewpoints in understanding and potentially implementing the practitioner-scientist model (Hoshmand & Polkinghorne, 1992; Kanfer, 1990; Love, et al., 2007; Luebbe, Radcliffe, Callands, Green, & Thorn, 2007). Hoshmand and Polkinghorne (1992) stated that ". . . the test for knowledge is whether it serves to guide human action to attain goals . . . the test is pragmatic" (p. 58). As Gelso (2006) suggested, training in the scientist-practitioner model need not be rigidly implemented, with equal emphasis on research and practice. In addition, Heppner, et al. (1992) suggested that there can be much different configuration than a simple 50/50 split of time between practice and research—80 percent focus on practice and 20 percent on research, for instance. The issue, as I see it, for practitioners in counseling and education is to find the pragmatic and realistic proportion of emphasis on practice and research. Related to the issue of emphasis is a further clarification and definition of what it means to operate from a practitioner-scientist model, and this will need to come from practitioners who realistically use and conduct research in their practices.

Kanfer (1990) proposed steps to bridging science and practice based on a problem-solving approach. These steps include (a) identifying the problem; (b) operationalizing the problem; (c) identifying principles, theories, and research that are applicable to solving the problem; (d) identifying desired outcomes; (e) selecting a strategy; (f) implementing and monitoring the strategy; and (g) returning to (c) if the desired outcomes are not achieved. Basically, Kanfer (1990) suggested continuous, systematic hypothesis testing and experimentation to resolve practice issues. Key in this approach is the search for information, scientific research information, that will form the basis of the intervention or strategy. You can use the newly developed skills acquired from the research published in the professional literature to identify relevant and potentially effective strategies to test.

Love, et al. (2007) proposed a creative approach to integrating science and practice. They suggested early learning experiences with research during academic training. Faculty and student research teams can facilitate the development of research self-efficacy and provide support through the process. Also, they noted the importance of an academic environment that supports and encourages research activities. One aspect of such an environment is faculty modeling successful integration of research into practice. Another important aspect of the academic environment, according to Love, et al. (2007) is working as a team on research projects. These researchers found that team effort on a research project resulted in higher research self-efficacy ratings.

Luebbe, et al. (2007) provided an interesting view of differentiating more traditional science views and evidence-based practice (EBP) views. The differentiation is focused on understanding the definitions and practical aspects of two different scholarly activities: empirically supported treatment (EST) and evidence-based practice. They defined EST as ". . . an empirically supported treatment is a product derived from randomized clinical trials" (p. 645). They differentiated the two views, science views and EBP views. They defined EBP this way: "Evidence-based practice in psychology is a process that incorporates the retrieval and examination of scientific evidence. Further, EBP presents a method for finding and evaluating the best available research evidence, whether it means randomized clinical trials (the foundation of EST) or other forms of high quality evidence" (p. 645). Essentially, EST is a subset of evidence-based practice in which clinical trials provide important evidence to facilitate in the decision making, whereas EBP is a broader process focused on discovering the best available research evidence, including evidence not found in EST. EBP may include in the best available evidence (research results from several research sources), not just clinical trials. The use of an EBP process for practitioners focuses the effort on collecting and evaluating scientific information, which fits well with a practitioner-scientist orientation.

As a practitioner, you cannot take time to search out scientific information for each individual you work with in a counseling or educational setting. However, several criteria may be helpful to employ when considering the use of the scientific approach: (a) note whether progressively difficult situations arise that are resistant to change and in which repeated attempts with traditional methods are unsuccessful; (b) determine if there are multiple situations or persons who share similar issues and could benefit from a new approach or intervention; (c) if you are working with certain ethnic, racial, gender, or other variables, decide whether traditional strategies are applicable or whether less traditional methods may be more appropriate; or (d) focus on a particular interest of your own that will be exciting and stimulating to explore.

In summary, the practitioner-scientist issue concerns a need to clarify the definition and characteristics of a practitioner-scientist model. Practitioners and academics (those training practitioners) also need to identify practical methods of implementing a practitioner-scientist model based in reality, one that is not an unachievable ideal.

The Relevance of Research to Practice

The issues presented here are not mutually exclusive; they are distinctly related. The second issue confronting counselors and educators, beyond an orientation of practitioner-scientist or scientist-practitioner, is the relevance of research to practice. The issue of making research relevant to practice has been a consistent debate over the past several decades (Berninger, et al., 2007; Pfeiffer, Burd, & Wright, 1992; Sexton, 1996; Sexton & Whiston, 1996). It has been noted that practitioners typically have negative attitudes toward research (Barnette, 2007). Several reasons may be cited for these negative attitudes, attitudes that contribute to the problem of connecting research to practice. One reason is the use of highly technical language typically presented in professional journals, as you most likely have experienced in reading articles for earlier chapters of this book. This has been a problem in a lot of the counseling and educational literature. Researchers typically are academics and, therefore, write research articles for other academics and not for practitioners. However, in applied fields such as counseling and education, the purpose (for the most part) of research published in professional journals is the application of the knowledge gained, and application is most likely to be accomplished by practitioners. Thus those publishing professional journals will need to address this problem of making published research more readable (this does not mean less sophisticated or complex).

The second problem concerning the issue of relating research to practice is an attempt to find the best methods of research. Traditional scientific methods, which were developed from the natural sciences and use a laboratory model, have dominated the social sciences until recently. In applied fields like education and counseling, laboratory research results may not be as applicable as field-based research methods. There has been a significant increase in the use of qualitative methods, which typically involve efforts to study naturally occurring events. However, there has been a reluctance to accept field-based research, to some degree because of the suspected limitations (e.g., threats to internal validity). The recent introduction of evidence-based practice processes is helping to change the efforts to link research to practice.

It has been noted that there has been a conflict surrounding the practitioner's view that research reported in the professional literature is based on laboratory research methods and not the natural environment. This conflict has led some researchers to propose alternative research designs. Hoshmand (1989) suggested that acceptance of any alternative research designs in the social sciences (and other disciplines) has been slow, but some progress has been made recently. The major argument concerns loss of control when one does not use traditional laboratory methods, which (theoretically) increases threats to internal validity. In reality, until recently it has been difficult for researchers to get research published in professional journals when the research is not based on traditional scientific methods. There are concerns over loss of control, for instance when a study is conducted in the natural environment, where the researcher typically has little control over extraneous variables.

Several researchers have proposed interesting ideas on how to address this issue of the use in the social sciences of traditional quantitative methods versus nontraditional and/or qualitative designs (De Anda, 2007; Ferguson & Bibby, 2004). De Anda proposed a model for conducting research that involves the use of quasi-experimental methods. She suggested using a single-group, pretest–post-test design, and collecting data over several groups at different times to include in comparisons. The comparison would be a correlated t test, but with the use of several groups over a period of time. She noted that it is possible to use the interventions with different groups over a period of time, which would help in controlling for threats, such as history. For example, a researcher could study a particular teaching method with students in high school algebra and conduct a pretest–post-test analysis. An important additional step is to try the teaching method with additional algebra classes over a period of time.

In Chapters 16 and 17, I discussed ways for practitioners to systematically implement research and evaluation in actual practice situations. I also noted that certain methods are more feasible to implement than others (e.g., quasi-experimental designs and qualitative designs). However, it is important to be aware that this issue of whether traditional or alternative methods are better exists and that it may create problems in gaining acceptance of results obtained by alternative methods.

In summary, there are two problems with the issue of relating research to practice. First, the use of highly technical writing in professional journals that describes research and is designed to be read by academics creates problems when relating research to practice. Second, the fields of counseling and research need to develop methods of conducting research that are considered relevant and useful to the practitioner, methods that may not necessarily be based on traditional laboratory methods.

Conducting Research From a Cross-Cultural and Diversity Perspective

We live in a world that is becoming more and more diverse, with fewer homogeneous groups, and we are confronted with the issue of how to provide counseling and educational services to a diverse target population. The issues surrounding research from a cross-cultural and diversity perspective are based on concerns such as who should conduct cross-cultural research and how research results can be ethically applied to a diverse population (population research).

The first issue, who should conduct cross-cultural research, has received spirited debate (Fitzgerald, 2006; Ponterotto, 1993; Sue, 1993). Parham (1993) questioned whether those from White racial backgrounds could effectively conduct minority research. Fitzgerald (2006) cited several concerns in conducting cross-cultural research. First, there are issues in the use of measurements for two reasons. One is that the stimuli of the measurements may not be sensitive to different cultures, e.g., the translation of the instrument may not be consistent. Second, the instrument may not be appropriate for the cultural population. Another issue centers on assumptions made in making comparisons, that is, a cultural group is relatively homogeneous. Fitzgerald (2006) pointed out that there can be more differences within cultures than between cultures. Ponterotto (1993) noted that White researchers may experience concerns over rejection and challenge in conducting research focusing on minorities. The question then becomes, should only those from minority backgrounds conduct minority and cross-cultural research? Sue (1993) noted increased tension among different racial and ethnic minority groups. Consequently, can researchers from one racial or ethnic group conduct research that addresses all groups? Several investigators have suggested that one group may not be "qualified" to conduct cross-cultural research, and it has been proposed that the best solution is for researchers from different racial backgrounds to collaborate in developing and conducting research (Atkinson, 1993; Mio & Iwamasa, 1993).

Another concern is whether research results can be ethically applied to diverse populations, which is particularly relevant to you as a practitioner. As has been noted previously in Chapter 8, "Ethics and Research," the application of research results may cause harm to a population, particularly if the results portray a particular ethnic group negatively. Population research may be a problem when the interpretation of the results is based on a particular orientation, such as that of the dominant majority. It has been suggested that to avoid interpreting and applying research results inappropriately, which could possibly harm a population, there should be training in and awareness of cross-cultural issues for practitioners (LaFromboise & Foster, 1992).

Summary

Several issues confront counseling and educational research: the application of the practitioner-scientist view; the relevance of research to practice and how to use alternative research designs; and how to conduct and implement research from a cross-cultural and diversity perspective. There are not any easy solutions to these issues. However, as a practitioner, it is important for you to be aware of the issues when you go about the practice of your profession. It will be essential for you to continue reading and using the professional literature so that you can practice your profession ethically and effectively. At this point in your training, it is hoped that you have a certain amount of respect for the research process, tempered with a critical eye, so that you can systematically assess what will be potentially useful to you in the practice of your profession.

Glossary

accessible population All individuals of the target population who can feasibly be accessed for participation in a study.

alpha level The level of (statistical) significance set by the researcher for rejecting the null hypothesis.

alternative hypothesis A statistical hypothesis based on a rejection of the null hypothesis.

analysis of covariance (ANCOVA) A statistical calculation comparing differences of means between two or more groups that statistically controls for one or more extraneous variables. The results are reported in adjusted means for the groups, based on the influence or effects of the extraneous variables.

analysis of variance (ANOVA) A parametric inferential statistical procedure designed to compare differences between the means of two or more groups.

baseline The natural level of performance as measured from the dependent variable of the sample prior to introduction of the independent variable or an intervention.

case study A detailed investigation of an individual, group, organization, or other assemblage.

chi-square A nonparametric inferential statistical procedure designed to determine whether collected data (nominal data) is significantly different from what was expected.

cluster sampling A sampling technique in which a sample is chosen of naturally occurring groups or intact units, and all individuals in the group are studied.

concurrent validity The degree to which responses on a new test correspond to responses on an established test. Also, the extent to which scores on a test correspond to the present behavior of an individual.

confounding variable A variable other than those being studied, which could potentially affect the research outcome. Extraneous variable.

construct A concept that is proposed to explain commonalities among phenomena or theories.

construct validity The degree to which scores on a test measure an actual construct that they are intended to measure.

content validity The extent to which the test items represent the concepts that they intend to measure.

control group A group used in an experimental study that receives no treatment and that is compared to an experimental group, based on dependent measures.

convenience sample A sampling technique that is based on availability of the sample (e.g., a sample that is easy to access).

correlation coefficient An expressed strength of relationship between two variables and the direction of the strength of the relationship.

correlational research A type of study that focuses on clarifying the extent of correlationships between two variables.

criterion-related validity The degree to which scores obtained on a dependent measure correlate to an identified standard or observable behavior.

dependent variable The variable that is "affected" by the independent variable.

descriptive research Research that involves defining existing conditions or characteristics.

descriptive statistics Statistical methods used to summarize the results of a sample.

directional hypothesis A hypothesis that is based on previous research, theory, or personal experience and that involves predicting the direction of the outcome.

ecological validity The degree to which research results obtained in a certain situation can be generalized back to the natural environment.

effect size The degree to which an independent variable influences the dependent variable.

ethnographic research Qualitative research methods that focus on exploring and describing cultural and/or social phenomena.

evidence-based practice An organized process of systematically gathering research evidence to support the choice of a particular practice.

experimental group The group in an experiment that receives the intervention or manipulation (the group that receives the independent variable).

experimental mortality The degree to which study participants drop out during the course of the study.

external validity The degree to which results from an experiment can be generalized to other individuals beyond the study.

extraneous variable A variable in a study that has the potential to influence results but that is not the focus of the study.

face validity The extent to which a measure or technique appears to measure what it is designed to measure.

factor analysis A statistical procedure in which clusters of items are highly correlated and form factors that relate to a criterion.

formative evaluation Evaluation that involves assessing the effort and quality needed to implement a program. It does not concern the effectiveness of the program but how well the program is implemented.

Hawthorne Effect A change in the outcome or dependent variable as a consequence of receiving special attention (e.g., awareness of being in a research study might have an effect that would not be related to the independent variable).

historical research A research method that is designed to study past phenomena or events to understand current situations.

hypothesis A formally stated prediction of outcome that is based on previous research, theory, or personal experience.

independent variable Generally, the variable that is manipulated and affects another variable, the dependent variable. There are also measurement types of independent variables that are not manipulated but are hypothesized to affect another variable.

indirect proof Refers to seeking clarification about the validity of a theory through scientific methods, but never obtaining direct proof supporting a theory or hypothesis.

inferential statistics Parametric statistical procedures that are used to make inferences about results from a sample to a population.

informed consent The research subject's agreement to participate in a study after a researcher has performed his or her ethical and legal duty to inform potential subjects about their freedom to choose to participate in the study and what that participation would entail.

internal consistency The extent to which items on a test correlate to each other. It refers to respondents to a test making consistent types of responses to items on a test.

internal validity The degree to which a researcher controls for and reduces the effects of extraneous variables that can affect study outcomes so that they represent true outcomes.

interrater reliability The degree to which raters agree in their scores of the same observable behavior.

interval scale A measurement scale that is expressed in equal units with no true zero. Most mathematical operations may be performed on interval data.

intervening variable A variable that influences that relationship between the independent and dependent variables. There would be a different outcome between the independent and dependent variables without the intervening variable's influence.

levels of significance The probability that results obtained from one sample (experimental) group will differ significantly from those obtained from another (control) group.

mean The arithmetic average of scores.

measurement scales Units of measurement defined in terms of nominal, ordinal, interval, and ratio data.

measures of central tendency A mathematical expression that summarizes scores and distribution of scores based on a sample.

measures of variability Mathematical expression of how scores in a distribution vary from one another.

median A score in a distribution of scores that is exactly at the 50th percentile.

metasearch engine A computer search engine that combines requests into several search engines so the user can access results from several different sources without searching individual sources.

mode The most frequently occurring score in a distribution.

multiple analysis of variance (MANOVA) A statistical calculation used to compare differences between means of two or more groups and differences between two or more dependent variables (the dependent variables correlate in some way).

multiple regression A statistical procedure in which the magnitude of the relationship between a predicted variable and two or more predictor variables is calculated.

multiple time series design A quasi-experimental design that involves several groups receiving treatment in which multiple assessments of the dependent variable occur.

nominal scale A scale in which data or scores identify categories, such as gender and ethnicity.

nondirectional hypothesis A predication that there is a difference between research groups (e.g., the control and experimental groups) but no direction is indicated.

nonparametric statistics Inferential statistics that are based on data that are not necessarily normally distributed.

normal distribution A frequency distribution of scores, typically represented by a bell-shaped curve and symmetrically shaped around the mean.

null hypothesis A prediction that no differences or relationships exist between the dependent variables and the effects of any independent variables among groups studied.

ordinal scale The organization of data that is represented by rank order (e.g., military rank).

parameters Numbers that define certain characteristics of the population.

parametric statistics Inferential statistics used to analyze data that are normally distributed.

paradigm A pattern of defined scientific practices.

Pearson correlation coefficient A mathematical expression of the strength of the relationship between two or more variables. Scores may range from -1.0 to +1.0.

plagiarism Occurs when someone uses another's ideas or writings as his or her own. Plagiarism can be intentional or unintentional.

population The group of individuals that is identified as having certain characteristics of interest to the researcher. A sample with well-defined characteristics is drawn from a population.

population validity The degree of accuracy with which results from a particular study may be generalized to the population of interest.

post-hoc comparisons Mathematical procedures used with certain inferential statistical methods (ANOVAs) to determine whether significant differences exist between three or more groups.

predictive validity The degree to which one measurement or set of data predicts what actually, naturally occurs.

process evaluation The method of collecting information that will be used to evaluate how effectively a program is being implemented.

program evaluation The methods employed to evaluate the goals, objectives, and outcomes of social programs.

qualitative research Established approaches to studying social phenomena using language to define and describe the outcomes. No numbers or mathematical operations are employed in qualitative research approaches.

quantitative research Well-established research methods that employ numbers and mathematical procedures to express and explain research outcomes.

quasi-experimental research An experimental method in which there is a manipulation of the independent variable but no random assignment.

random assignment The method of assigning individuals from a sample to experimental and/or control groups. The basis of this method is that everyone chosen for a sample must have an equal chance of being in any of the groups.

random selection A collection of methods of selecting study participants (a sample) from a population. These methods include simple random sampling, systematic random sampling, stratified random sampling, and others.

range A measure of variability that is expressed in terms of the lowest and highest scores in a distribution of scores.

ratio scale Data or scores that include a true zero in which scores are equidistant. Ratio scales allow for computing with any mathematical calculations.

regression toward the mean A change in the extreme scores, with subsequent testing to more moderate scores, as a result of chance influences not consistently expressed.

reliability The degree of consistency in data or scores, either within scores or over time.

sample A group or unit selected from a larger target population. The sample is intended to be representative of the larger population.

search engine A program designed to search the Internet (the World Wide Web) for information.

science The acquisition of knowledge, a systematic approach, and an objective analysis with opportunities for conclusions about how our world may function.

single-subject experimental design The use of a single subject with a manipulation or experiment conducted over a period of time. In addition, there are multiple measurements of the dependent variable (e.g., behavioral observations of the dependent variable).

Spearman correlation A linear correlation between nonparametric data (pairs of ranks).

split-half reliability A type of test of reliability that involves the calculation of a correlation between two different parts of a test (e.g., calculating the correlation between all odd questions and all even questions).

standard deviation A standard measure of the degree to which scores vary from the mean.

stratified random sampling A method of selecting participants for a study in which certain characteristics are identified as relevant to control. Participants are then chosen randomly to reflect these characteristics of the population. Stratification may be proportional or nonproportional.

structural equation modeling A statistical technique that is used in theory testing.

systematic random sampling A method of selecting a sample in which every nth participant is chosen from an accessible population.

t-test A parametric statistical procedure that involves the comparison of two means.

test-retest reliability A measure of test reliability that involves the correlation or consistency between two different administrations of the same test at two different times.

time series design A research design that involves a manipulation with one experimental group and uses multiple measurements of the dependent variables over a period of time.

triangulation The convergence of data collection through several methods or procedures

true experiment A study that includes two conditions: (a) random assignment to experimental groups, and (b) a manipulation of the independent variable.

type I error A decision based on statistical calculations in which rejection of the null hypothesis is made when the hypothesis should not be rejected (e.g., when the null hypothesis is true).

type II error A decision based on statistical calculations in which the null hypothesis is accepted when it should be rejected.

validity The degree to which a method or procedure measures what it is intended to measure.

variable A construct or concept that can be measured or operationalized and that can be quantified.

variance The degree to which scores are dispersed about the mean. It is calculated by squaring the standard deviation.

Wilcoxon signed-rank test A nonparametric statistical procedure to determine the differences between two groups, based on an identified dependent variable.

References

Admi, H. (1996). Growing up with a chronic health condition: A model of an ordinary lifestyle. *Qualitative Health Research, 6*(2), 163–183.

Alcoholics Anonymous. (1952). *Twelve steps and twelve traditions.* New York: Alcoholics Anonymous World Services.

American Counseling Association. (1995). *Code of ethics and standards of practice.* Alexandria, VA: Author.

American Counseling Association. (2005). *ACA code of ethics.* Alexandria, VA: Author.

American Psychiatric Association. (1994). *Diagnostic and statistical manual of mental disorders* (4th ed.). Washington, D.C.: Author.

American Psychological Association. (1992). American Psychological Association ethical principles of psychologists and code of conduct. *American Psychologist, 47,* 1597–1611.

American Psychological Association. (2003). *Ethical principles of psychologists and code of conduct.* Washington, D.C.: Author.

American Psychological Association (2006). Evidence-based practice in psychology. *American Psychologists, 61*(4), 271–285.

American Psychological Association Presidential Task Force on Evidence-Based Practice. (2006). Evidence-based practice in psychology. *American Psychologist, 61*(4), 271–285.

Anastasi, A., & Urbina, S. (1997). *Psychological testing* (7th ed.). Upper Saddle River, NJ: Prentice Hall.

Anderson, D., Wang, J., & Houser, R. (1993). Issues and needs of persons with disabilities in Hawaii: An exploration of racial/ethnic group differences. *Journal of Rehabilitation, 59,* 11–16.

Ary, D., Jacobs, L., & Razavieh, A (2002). *An introduction to research in education.* Belmont, CA: Wadsworth.

Atkinson, D. (1993). Who speaks for cross-cultural counseling research? *Counseling Psychologist, 21*(2), 218–224.

Baban, A. (2007). The nature and relevance of qualitative research in the era of evidence-based practice. *Cognition, Brain, Behavior, 11*(2), 223–228.

Baban, A., & Craciun, C. (2007). Changing health-risk behaviors: A review of theory and evidence-based interventions in health psychology. *Journal of Cognitive and Behavioral Psychotherapies, 7*(1), 45–67.

Babbie, E. (1992). *The practice of social research* (6th ed.). Belmont, CA: Wadsworth.

Babbie, E. (2006). *The practice of social research.* (11th ed.). Belmont, CA: Wadsworth.

Baldwin, S., Wampold, B., & Imel, Z. (2007). Untangling the alliance-outcome correlation: Exploring the relative importance of therapist and patient variability in the alliance. *Journal of Consulting and Clinical Psychology, 75*(6), 842–852.

Bandura, A. (1977). Self-efficacy: Toward a unifying theory of behavior change. *Psychological Review, 84,* 191–215.

Barnette, V. (2006). A scholarly work commitment in practice. *Counselling Psychology Quarterly, 19*(3), 253–263.

Barton, C., Sulaiman, N., Clarke, D., & Abramson, M. (2005). Experiences of Australian parents caring for children with asthma: It gets easier. *Chronic Illness, 1*(4), 303–314.

Baumrind, D. (1964). Some thoughts on ethics of research: After reading Milgram's "Behavioral study of obedience." *American Psychologist, 19,* 421–423.

Beauchamp, T., & Childress, J. (2001). *Principles of biomedical ethics.* New York: Oxford University Press.

Berg, B. (2004). *Qualitative research methods for the social sciences* (5th ed.). Boston: Pearson.

Berninger, V., Dunn, A., Shin-Ju, C., & Shimada, S. (2004). School evolution: Scientist-practitioner educators creating optimal learning environments for all students. *Journal of Learning Disabilities, 37*(6), 500–506.

Bernstein, B., & Kerr, B., (1993). Counseling psychology and the scientist-practitioner model: Implementation and implications. *Counseling Psychologist, 21*(1), 136–151.

Best, J., & Kahn, J. (1998). *Research in education* (8th ed.). Boston, MA: Allyn & Bacon.

Best, J., & Kahn, J. (2003). *Research in education* (9th ed.). Boston: Allyn & Bacon.

Berg, B. (2004). *Qualitative research methods for the social sciences* (5th ed). Boston: Pearson.

Blanton, D., & Dagenais, P. (2007). Comparison of language skills of adjudicated and nonadjudicated adolescent males and females. *Language, Speech, and Hearing Services in Schools, 38*(4), 309–314.

Bogdan, R., & Biklen, S. (2007). *Qualitative research for education: An introduction to theories and methods* (5th ed.). Boston: Allyn & Bacon.

Bohon, L., Santos, S., Sanchez-Sosa, J., & Singer, R. (1994). The effects of a mental health video on the social skills knowledge and attitudes of Mexican immigrants. *Journal of Applied Social Psychology, 24,* 1794–1805.

Border, L., Bloss, K., Cashwell, C., & Rainey, L. (1994). Helping student apply the scientist-practitioner model: A teaching approach. *Counselor Education and Supervision, 34,* 172–179.

Bracht, G., & Glass, G. (1968). The external validity of experiments. *American Educational Research Journal, 5,* 437–474.

Brannen, J. (1992). *Mixing methods: Qualitative and quantitative research.* Brookfield, VT: Avebury.

Bredart, S., Lampinen, J., & Defeldre, A. (2003). Phenomenal characteristics of cryptomnesia. *Memory, 11*(1), 1–11.

Brown, D., & Srebalus, D. (1996). *Introduction to the counseling profession* (2nd ed.). Boston: Allyn & Bacon.

Brown, E. (2006). Good mother, bad mother: Perceptions of mothering by rural African-American women who use cocaine. *Journal of Addictions Nursing, 17*(1), 21–31.

Brunelle, N., Cousineau, M., & Brochu, S. (2005). Juvenile drug use and delinquency: Youths' accounts of their trajectories. *Substance Use & Misuse, 40*(5), 721–734.

Campbell, D. T., & Stanley, J. C. (1966). *Experimental & quasi-experimental designs for research.* Chicago: Rand McNally.

Castro, F., & Coe, K. (2007). Traditions and alcohol use: A mixed methods analysis. *Cultural Diversity and Ethnic Minority Psychology, 13*(4), 269–284.

Charles, D. (1995). *Introduction to educational research* (2nd ed.). White Plains, NY: Longman.

Charmaz, K. (2006). Measuring pursuits, marking self: Meaning construction in chronic illness. *Journal of Qualitative Studies on Health and Well-Being, 1*(1), 27–37.

Chen, H. (2005). *Practical program evaluation: Assessing and improving planning, implementation, and effectiveness.* Thousand Oaks, CA: Sage Publications.

Clark, V., & Creswell, J. (Eds.). (2008). *The mixed methods reader.* Thousand Oaks, CA: Sage Publications.

Conoley, J., & Impara, J. (1995). *The twelfth mental measurement yearbook.* Lincoln: University of Nebraska Press.

Cook, D. (1989). Systematic need assessment: A primer. *Journal of Counseling and Development, 67,* 462–464.

Cook, T., & Campbell, D. T. (1979). *Quasi-experimentation: Design and analysis issues for field settings.* Chicago: Rand McNally.

Coolidge, F. (2006). *Statistics: A gentle introduction* (2nd ed.). Thousand Oaks, CA: Sage Publications.

Cox, C., & Cohen, B. (2000). Mandala artwork by clients with DID: Clinical observations based on two theoretical models. *Art Therapy, 17*(3), 195–201.

Creswell, J., Clark, J., Gutmann, V., & Hanson, W. (2008). An expanded typology for classifying mixed methods research into designs. In V. Clark and J. Creswell (Eds.), *The mixed methods reader* (pp. 159–196). Thousand Oaks, CA: Sage Publications.

Culatta, B., Reese, M., & Setzer, L. (2006). Early literacy instruction in a dual-language (Spanish-English) kindergarten. *Communication Disorders Quarterly, 27*(2), 67–82.

Curlette, W. (2006). A framework for research studies: Mixed methods through combining Bayesian statistics and qualitative research in individual psychology. *The Journal of Individual Psychology, 62*(3), 239–249.

Curry, N., & Kasser, T. (2005). Can coloring mandalas reduce anxiety? *Journal of the American Art Therapy Association, 22,* 81–85.

Curry, S., Sporer, A., & Pugach, O. (2007). Use of tobacco cessation treatment among young adult smokers: 2005 National health interview survey. *American Journal of Public Health, 97*(8), 1464–1469.

Daehler, M., & Bukatko, D. (1985). *Cognitive development.* New York: Knopf.

Daly, C. (2006). The sound of science: The power to bless or burn. *Southern Medical Journal, 99*(12), 1416–1418.

Davidson, E. (2005). *Evaluation methodology basics: The nuts and bolts of sound evaluation.* Thousand Oaks, CA: Sage Publications.

Davison, G., & Lazarus, A. (2007). Clinical case studies are important in the science and practice of psychotherapy. In S. O. Lillienfield & W. T. O'Donohue (Eds.), *The great ideas of clinical science: 17 Principles that every mental health professional should understand.* New York: Routledge.

De Anda, D. (2007). Intervention research and program evaluation in the school setting: issues and alternative research designs. *Children & Schools, 29,* 87–94.

Denzin, N. K. (1978). *The research act.* Chicago: Aldine.

Denzin, N. K., & Lincoln, Y. S. (Eds.). (1994). *Handbook of qualitative research.* Thousand Oaks, CA: Sage Publications.

Denzin, N. K., & Lincoln, Y. S. (Eds.). (2000). *Handbook of qualitative research* (2nd ed.). Thousand Oaks, CA: Sage Publications.

DeTienne, D., & Chandler, G. (2007). The role of gender in opportunity identification. *Entrepreneurship Theory & Practice, 31*(3), 365–387.

Driver, S., O'Connor, J., Lox, C., & Rees, K. (2004). Evaluation of an aquatics programme on fitness parameters of individuals with a brain injury. *Brain Injury, 18,* 847–859.

Drummond, R. (2000). *Appraisal procedures for counselors and helping.* St. Paul, MN: Merrill.

Eid, M., & Diener, E. (2006). *Handbook of multimethod measurement in psychology.* Washington, D.C.: American Psychological Association.

Esterling, B., L'Abate, L., & Murray, E. (1999). Empirical foundations for writing In prevention and psychotherapy: Mental and physical health outcomes. *Clinical Psychology Review, 19*(1), 79–96.

Erickson, K., Hatton, D., Roy, V., Fox, D., & Renne, D. (2007). Literacy in early intervention for children with visual impairments: Insights from individual cases. *Journal of Visual Impairment & Blindness, 10*(2), 80–95.

Farber, N. (2006). Conducting qualitative research: A practical guide for school counselors. *Professional School Counseling, 9*(5), 367–375.

Farynaiarz, J., & Lockwood, L. (1992). Effectiveness of microcomputer simulations in stimulating environmental problem solving by community college students. *Journal of Research in Science Teaching, 29,* 453–470.

Felce, D., de Kock, U., Mansell, J., & Jenkins, J. (1984). Providing systematic individual teaching for severely disturbed and profoundly mentally handicapped adults in residential care. *Behavior Research and Therapy, 22,* 299–309.

Ferguson, E., & Bibby, P. (2004). The design and analysis of quasi-experimental field research. In G. Breakwell (Ed.), *Doing social psychology research* (pp. 93–127). Leicester, England: British Psychological Society.

Fitzgerald, H. (2006). Cross cultural research during infancy: Methodological considerations. *Infant Mental Health Journal, 27*(6), 612–617.

Forsyth, D., & Leary, M. (1997). Achieving the goals of the scientist-practitioner model: The seven interfaces of social and counseling psychology. *Counseling Psychologist, 25*(2), 180–200.

Fry, S. (2007). First-year teachers and induction support: Ups, downs, and in-betweens. *The Qualitative Researcher, 12*(2), 216–237.

Frye, N. (1965). Varieties of literary utopias. In F. Manuel (Ed.), *Utopias and utopian thought* (pp. 25–49). Boston: Houghton Mifflin.

Gall, M., Borg, W., & Gall, J. (1996). *Educational research: An introduction* (6th ed.). White Plains, NY: Longman.

Gall, M., Gall, J., & Borg, W. (2002). *Educational research: An introduction* (7th ed.). White Plains, NY: Longman

Gall, M., Gall, J., & Borg, W. (2006). *Educational research: An introduction* (8th ed.). Boston: Pearson Education.

Gallo, L., Bogart, L., Vranceanu, A., & Matthews, K. (2005). Socioeconomic status, resources, psychological experiences, and emotional responses: A test of the reserve capacity model. *Journal of Personality and Social Psychology, 88*(2), 386–399.

Gamble, V. N. (1993). A legacy of distrust: African Americans and medical research. *American Journal of Preventive Medicine, 9*(6), 3–38.

Gelso, C. J. (1979). Research in counseling methodological and professional issues. *Counseling Psychologist, 8*(3), 7–35.

Gelso, C. J. (1993). On the making of a scientist-practitioner: A theory of research training in professional psychology. *Professional Psychology Research and Practice, 24,* 468–476.

Gelso, C. (2006). On the making of a scientist-practitioner: A theory of research training in professional psychology. *Training and Education in Professional Psychology, 5,* 3–16.

Gliner, J., & Morgan, G. (2000). *Research methods in applied settings: An integrated approach to design and analysis.* Mahwah, NJ: Lawrence Erlbaum Associates.

Goldfried, M. (1984). Training the clinician as scientist-professional. *Professional Psychology: Research and Practice, 15,* 477–481.

Gortmaker, V., & Brown, R. (2006). Out of the college closet: Differences in perceptions and experiences among out and closeted lesbian and gay students. *College Student Journal, 40*(3), 606–619.

Gostin, L. (1991). Ethical principles for the conduct of human subject research: Population-based research and ethics. *Law, Medicine, and Health Care, 19*(3–4), 191–201.

Gowers, S. (2006). Evidence based research in CBT with adolescent eating disorders. *Child and Adolescent Mental Health, 11*(1), 9–12.

Grbich, C. (2007). *Qualitative data analysis: An introduction.* Thousand Oaks, CA: Sage Publications.

Greenberg, J., Evans, A., Harris, K., Loyo, J., Ray, T., Spaulding, C., & Gottlieb, N. (2007). Preschooler feeding practices and beliefs: Differences among Spanish- and English-speaking WIC clients. *Family & Community Health, 30*(3), 257–270.

Gregory, R. (2007). *Psychological testing: History, principles, and applications.* Boston: Allyn & Bacon.

Guba, E. (1990). *The paradigm dialog.* Thousand Oaks, CA: Sage Publications.

Guba, E., & Lincoln, Y. (1992). *Effective evaluation: Improving the usefulness of evaluation results through responsive and naturalistic approaches.* San Francisco: Jossey-Bass.

Hamilton, D. (1992). Traditions, preferences, and postures in applied qualitative research. In N. Denzin & Y. Lincoln (Eds.), *Handbook of qualitative research* (pp. 60–69). Thousand Oaks, CA: Sage Publications.

Hardin-Jones, M. & Chapman, K. (2008). The impact of early intervention on speech and lexical development for toddlers with cleft palate: A retrospective look at outcome. *Language, Speech, and Hearing Services in the Schools, 39*(1), 89–96.

Hatinen, M., Kinnunen, U., Pekkonen, M., & Kalimo, R. (2007). Comparing two burnout interventions: Perceived job control mediates decreases in burnout. *International Journal of Stress Management, 14*(3), 227–248.

Heiman, G. (1995). *Research methods in psychology.* Boston: Houghton Mifflin.

Henderson, P., Rosen, D., & Mascaro, N. (2007). Empirical study on the healing nature of mandalas. *Psychology of Aesthetics, Creativity, and the Arts, 1*(3), 148–154.

Henry, R., Anshel, M., & Michael, T. (2006). Effects of aerobic and circuit training on fitness and body image among women. *Journal of Sport Behavior, 29*(4), 281–303.

Heppner, P., Kivlighan, D., & Wampold, B. (1992). *Research design in counseling.* Pacific Grove, CA: Brooks/Cole.

Hinkin, T., Holtom, B., & Klag, M. (2007). Collaborative research: Developing mutually beneficial relationships between researchers and organizations. *Organizational Dynamics, 36,* 105–118.

Hinkle, J. (1994). Practitioners and cross-cultural assessment: A practical guide to information and training. *Measurement and Evaluation in Counseling and Development, 27,* 103–115.

Hollowood, T., Salisbury, C., Rainforth, B., & Palobaro, M. (1994). Use of instructional time in classroom serving students with and without severe disabilities. *Exceptional Children, 61*(3), 242–253.

Hoshmand, L. (1989). Alternate research paradigms: A review and teaching proposal. *Counseling Psychologist, 17*(1), 3–79.

Hoshmand, L., & Polkinghorne, D. (1992). Redefining the science-practice relationship and professional training. *American Psychologist, 47*(1), 55–66.

Hosie, H. (1994). Program evaluation: A potential area of expertise for counselors. Special section: Critical issues in research in counselor education and supervision. *Counselor Education and Supervision, 33*(4), 349–355.

House, E. (1978). Assumptions underlying evaluation models. *Educational Researcher, 7,* 4–12.

House, E., (1993). *Professional evaluation: Social impact and political consequences.* Newbury Park, CA: Sage Publications.

House, E. (1994). The future perfect of evaluation. *Evaluation Practice, 15,* 239–247.

Houser, R., Anderson, D., & Wang, J. (1995). Participatory Action Needs Assessment: A unified approach to needs assessment within the state/federal VR system. *Journal of Applied Rehabilitation Counseling, 26,* 55–58.

Houser, R., Wilczenski, F., & Ham, M. (2006). *Culturally relevant ethical decision-making in counseling.* Thousand Oaks, CA: Sage Publications.

Hunsley, J. (2007). Addressing key challenges in evidence-based practice in psychology. *Professional Psychology, 38*(2), 113–121.

Isaac, S., & Michael, W. (1987). *Handbook in research and evaluation.* San Diego: EdITS Publishers.

Isaksson, G., Lexell, J,. & Skar, L. (2007). Social support provides motivation and ability to participate in occupation. *Occupation, Participation and Health, 27*(1), 23–30.

Iverson, G., Brooks, B., Collins, M., & Lovell, M. (2006). Tracking neuropsychological recovery following concussion in sport. *Brain Injury, 20*(3), 245–252.

Jick, T. (2008). Triangulation as the first mixed methods design. In V. Clark and J. Creswell (Eds.), *The mixed methods reader* (pp. 105–118). Thousand Oaks, CA: Sage Publications.

Joint Committee on Standards for Educational Evaluation. (1988). *The personnel evaluation standards.* Newbury Park, CA: Sage Publications.

Joint Committee on Standards for Educational Evaluation. (1994). *The program evaluation standards* (2nd ed.). Thousand Oaks, CA: Sage Publications.

Jones, J. (1981). *Bad blood: The Tuskegee syphilis experiment.* New York: Free Press.

Kaiser, A. (2007). Addressing challenging behavior: Systematic problems, systematic solutions. *Journal of Early Intervention, 29*(2), 114–118.

Kamps, D., & Abbott, M. (2007). Use of evidence-based small group reading instruction for English language learners in elementary grades: Secondary tier intervention. *Learning Disability Quarterly, 30*(3), 153–168.

Kanfer, F. (1990). The scientist-practitioner connection: A bridge in need of constant attention. *Professional Psychology: Research and Practice, 21*(4), 264–270.

Kartalova-O'Doherty, Y., & Doherty, D. (2008). Coping strategies and styles of family carers of persons with enduring mental illness: A mixed methods analysis. *Scandinavian Journal of Caring Sciences, 22*(11), 19–28

Kelly, G. (1955). *The psychology of personal constructs* (Vols. 1 and 2). New York: W. W. Norton.

Kelman, H. (1967). Human use of human subjects: The problem of deception in social psychological experiments. *Psychological Bulletin, 67*(1), 1–11.

Kettlewell, P. (2004). Development, dissemination, and implementation of evidence-based treatment: Commentary. *Clinical Psychology: Science and Practice, 11*(2), 190–195.

King, L., Burton, C., Hicks, J., Drigotas, S. (2007). Ghosts, UFOs, and magic: Positive affect and the experiential system. *Journal of Personality and Social Psychology, 92*(5), 905–919.

Klomegah, R. (2007). Predictors of academic performance of university students: An application of the goal efficacy model. *College Student Journal, 41*(2), 407–415.

Koronyo-Hamaoui, M., Danziger, Y., Frisch, A., Stein, D., Leor, S., Laufer, N., Carel, Fennig, S., Minourni, M., Apter, A., Goldman, B., Barkai, G., Weizman, A., & Gak, E. (2002). Association between anorexia nervosa and the hsKCa3 gene: A family-based and case control study. *Molecular Psychiatry, 7,* 82–85.

LaFountain, R., & Bartos, R. (2002). *Research and statistics made meaningful in counseling and student affairs.* Pacific Grove, CA: Brooks/Cole.

LaFromboise, T., & Foster, S. (1992) Cross-cultural training: Scientist-practitioner model and methods. *Counseling Psychologist, 20*(3), 472–289.

LaFromboise, T., & Howard-Pitney, B. (1995). The Zuni life skills development curriculum: Description and evaluation of a suicide prevention program. *Journal of Counseling Psychology, 42,* 479–486.

Landau, J., Druen, P., & Arcuri, J. (2002). Methods for helping students avoid plagiarism. *Teaching of Psychology, 29*(2), 112–115.

Landrum, T., Cook, B., Tankersley, M., & Fitzgerald, S. (2007). Teacher perceptions of the useability of intervention information from personal versus data-based sources. *Education and Treatment of Children, 30*(4), 27–42.

Lane, D., & Corrie, S. (2006). *The modern scientist-practitioner: A guide to practice in psychology.* New York: Routledge.

Leary, D. (2001). One big idea, one ultimate concern: Sigmund Koch's critique of psychology and hope for the future. *American Psychologist, 56,* 425–432.

Leary, M. (2001). *Introduction to behavioral research methods* (3rd ed.). Boston: Allyn & Bacon.

Leong, F., & Zachar, P. (1991). Development and validation of the scientist-practitioner inventory for psychology. *Journal of Counseling Psychology, 38*(3), 331–341.

Leong, C., Tse, S., Loh, K., & Hau, K. (2008). Text comprehension in Chinese children: Relative contribution of verbal working memory, pseudoword reading, rapid automatized naming, and onset-rime phonological segmentation. *Journal of Educational Psychology, 100*(1), 135–149.

Lincoln, Y., & Guba, E. (1985). *Naturalistic inquiry.* Thousand Oaks, CA: Sage Publications.

Lincoln, Y., & Guba, E. (2000). Paradigmatic controversies, contradictions, and emerging confluences. In N. Denzin & Y. Lincoln (Eds.), *Handbook of qualitative research* (2nd ed., pp. 191–216). Thousand Oaks, CA: Sage Publications.

Linder, F., & Bauer, D. (1983). Perception of values among male and female undergraduate students. *Perceptual and Motor Skills, 56,* 59–63.

Little, A. (2006). Life as we know it. *Atlantic Monthly, 298,* 54–55.

Lofland, J., Snow, D., Anderson, L., Lofland, L. (2006). *Analyzing social settings: A guide to qualitative observations and analysis.* (4th ed.). Belmont, CA: Wadsworth.

Love, K., Bahner, A., Jones, A., & Nilsson, J. (2007). An investigation of early research experience and research self-efficacy. *Professional Psychology, 38*(3), 314–320.

Luebbe, A., Radcliffe, T., Callands, T., Green, D. & Thorn, B. (2007). Evidence-based practice in psychology: Perceptions of graduate students in scientist-practitioner programs. *Journal of Clinical Psychology, 63*(7), 643–655.

Luszcyznska, A., & Sobczyk, A. (2007). Planning to lose weight: Randomized controlled trial of an implementation intention prompt to enhance weight reduction among overweight and obese women. *Health Psychology, 26*(4), 507–512.

Lynch, D., Teplin, S., Willis, S., Pathman, D., Larsen, L., Steiner, B., & Bernstein, J. (2001). Interim evaluation of the rural health scholars program. *Teaching and Learning in Medicine, 13*(1), 36–42.

Manicas, P., & Secord, P. (1983). Implications for psychology of the new philosophy of science. *American Psychologist, 38,* 399–413.

Manning, C., & Cheers, B. (1995). Child abuse notification in a country town. *Child Abuse and Neglect, 19*(4), 387–413.

Marsh, B. (2007). *Plagiarism: Alchemy and remedy in higher education.* Albany, NY: State University of New York Press.

Maslow, A. (1976). *The farther reaches of human nature.* New York: Penguin.

Mason, L. (2007). Introduction: Bridging the cognitive and sociocultural approaches In research on conceptual change: Is it feasible? *Educational Psychologist, 42*(1), 1–7.

Mason, S. (2006). Offering African-Americans opportunities to participate in clinical trials research: How social workers can help. *Health & Social Work, 30*(4), 296–304.

Mastel-Smith, B., Binder, B., Malecha, A., Hersch, G., Symes, L., & McFarlane, J. (2006). Testing therapeutic life review offered by home care workers to decrease depression among home-dwelling older women. *Issues in Mental Health Nursing, 27,* 1037–1049.

Matheny, K., & Edwards, C. (1974). Academic improvement through an experimental classroom management system. *Journal of School Psychology, 12*(3), 222–232.

Mayer, D. (2004). *Essential evidence-based medicine.* New York: Cambridge University Press.

McMillan, J. (2004). *Educational research: Fundamentals for the consumer* (4th ed.). Boston: Pearson.

McNaughten, D., & Gabbard, C. (1993). Physical exertion and immediate mental performance of sixth-grade children. *Perceptual and Motor Skills, 77,* 1155–1159.

Mendelsohn, E., & Nowotny, H. (Eds). (1984). *Nineteen eighty-four: Science between utopia and dystopia.* Boston: Reidel.

Mendenhall, W. (1983). *Introduction to probability and statistics* (6th ed.). Boston: Duxbury.

Merlo, L., Collins, A., & Bernstein, J., (2008). CIDCP-affiliated clinical psychology: Student views of their science training. *Training and Education in Professional Psychology, 2*(1), 58–65.

Merrell, K. (1999). *Behavioral, social, and emotional assessment of children and adolescents.* Mahwah, NJ: Lawrence Erlbaum Associates.

Messersmith, E., Garrett, J., Davis-Kean, P., Malanchuk, O., & Eccles, J. (2008). Career development from adolescence through emerging adulthood: Insights from information technology occupations. *Journal of Adolescent Research, 23*(2), 206–227.

Miles, M., & Huberman, M. (1994). *Qualitative data analysis: An expanded sourcebook* (2nd ed.). Thousand Oaks, CA: Sage Publications.

Milgram, S. (1963). Behavioral study of obedience. *Journal of Abnormal and Social Psychology, 67*(4), 371–378.

Milgram, S. (1974). *Obedience to authority: An experimental view.* New York: Harper and Row.

Minium, E., & King, B. (2003). *Statistical reasoning in psychology and education* (4th ed.). Hoboken, NJ: Wiley & Sons.

Mio, J., & Iwamasa, G. (1993). To do or not to do: That is the question for white cross-cultural researchers. *Counseling Psychologist, 21*(2), 197–212.

Moore, G. (1983). *Developing and evaluating educational research.* Boston: Little Brown.

Morawski, J. G. (1992). There is more to our history of giving: The place of introductory textbooks in American psychology. *American Psychologist, 47*(2), 161–169.

Murphy, L., Conoley, J., & Impara, J. (Eds). (1994). *Test in print IV: An index to tests, test reviews, and the literature on specific tests.* Lincoln: University of Nebraska Press.

National Institutes of Health. (1994). *Outreach notebook for the NIH guidelines on inclusion of women and minorities as subjects in clinical research.* Bethesda, MD: Author.

Nelson, M., & Neufeldt, S. (1996). Building on an empirical foundation: Strategies to enhance good practice. *Journal of Counseling and Development, 74,* 609–615.

Nezu, A., Ronan, G., Meadows, E., & McClure, K. (2000). *Practitioner's guide to empirically based measures of depression.* New York: Kluwer Academic.

Nystul, M. (1999). *Introduction to counseling: An art and science perspective.* Boston: Allyn & Bacon.

O'Bryant, S., & McCaffrey, R. (2006). Preliminary findings on the cross cultural test of face recognition. *Applied Neuropsychology, 13*(4), 223–229.

Odom, S., Brantlinger, E., & Gersten, R., Horner, R., Thompson, B., & Harris, K. (2005). Research in special education: Scientific methods and evidence-based practices. *Exceptional Children, 71*(2), 137–148.

Office of Protection From Research Risks. (1993). *Protecting human research subjects: Institutional Review Board guidebook.* Washington, D.C.: U.S. Government Printing Office.

Olvera, A., Stewart, S., Galindo, L., & Stephens, J. (2007). Diabetes, depression, and metabolic control in Latinas. *Cultural Diversity and Ethnic Minority Psychology, 13*(3), 225–231.

Onwuegbuzie, A., & Leech, N. (2005). On becoming a pragmatic researcher: The importance of combining quantitative and qualitative research methodologies. *International Journal of Social Research Methodology, 8*(5), 375–387.

Osborne, J., & House, R. (1995). Evaluation of counselor education programs: A proposed plan. *Counselor Education and Supervision, 34,* 253–269.

Padgett, D. (2004). *The qualitative research experience.* Boston: Thomson Brooks/Cole.

Pandiani, J., Banks, S., & Schacht, L. (2001). Consumer satisfaction and incarceration after treatment. *Administration and Policy in Mental Health, 29*(2), 145–155.

Parham, T. (1993). White researchers conducting multicultural research: Can their efforts be "mo betta"? *Counseling Psychologist, 21*(2), 25–256.

Park, S., Chang, S., & Chung, C. (2005). Effects of a cognition-emotion focused program to increase public participation in Papanicolaou smear screening. *Public Health Nursing, 22*(4), 289–298.

Parsons, R., & Brown, K. (2002). *Teacher as reflective practitioner and action researcher.* Belmont, CA: Wadsworth.

Patton, M. (1990). *Qualitative evaluation and research methods* (2nd ed.). Thousand Oaks, CA: Sage Publications.

Pineda-Olvera, A., Steward, S., Galindo, L., & Stephens, J. (2007). Diabetes, depression, and metabolic control in Latinas. *Cultural Diversity & Ethnic Minority Psychology, 13*(3), 225–231.

Pfeiffer, S., Burd, S., & Wright, A. (1992). Clinicians and research: Recurring obstacles and some possible solutions. *Journal of Clinical Psychology, 48*(1), 140–145.

Ponterotto, J. (1993). White racial identity and the counseling professional. *Counseling Psychologist, 21*(2), 213–217.

Ponterotto, J., & Casa, J. (1991). *Handbook of racial/ethnic minority counseling research.* Springfield, IL: Charles C Thomas.

Pottick, K., Kirk, S., & Hsieh, D. (2007). Judging mental disorders in youths: Effects of client, clinician, and contextual differences. *Journal of Consulting and Clinical Psychology, 75,* 1–8.

Preechawong, S., Zauszniewski, J., Heinzer, M., Musil, C., Keresmar, C., & Aswinanonh, R. (2007). Relationships of family functioning, self-esteem, and resourceful coping of Thai adolescents with asthma. *Issues in Mental Health Nursing, 28*(1), 21–36.

Pring, R., & Thomas, G. (2004). *Evidence-based practice in education: Conducting educational research.* New York: McGraw-Hill.

QSR International (1997). *Nonnumerical, unstructured data-indexing, searching, and theorizing.* Victoria, Australia: QSR International.

Raykov, T., & Marcoulides, G. (2006). *A first course in structural equation modeling.* Mahwah, NJ: Lawrence Erlbaum Associates.

Reid, P., & Finchilescu, G. (1995). The disempowering effects of media violence against women on college women. *Psychology of Women Quarterly, 19,* 397–411.

Richards, T., Richards, L., McGalliard, J., & Sharrock, B. (1992). *NUD*IST 2.3: Users manual.* La Trobe, Australia: Replee Pty/La Trobe University.

Robinson-Zanartu, C., Pena, E., Cook-Morales, V., Pena, A., Afshani, R., & Nguyen, L. (2005). Academic crime and punishment: Faculty members' perceptions of and responses to plagiarism. *School Psychology Quarterly, 20*(3), 318–337.

Roig, M. (1997). Can undergraduate students determine whether text has been plagiarized? *The Psychological Record, 47*(1), 113–123.

Roig, M., & Caso, M. (2005). Lying and cheating: Fraudulent excuse making, cheating, and plagiarism. *The Journal of Psychology, 139*(6), 485–494.

Rosaldo, R. (1989). *Culture and truth: The remaking of social analysis.* Boston: Beacon.

Rosenthal, J. (2001). *Statistics and data interpretation for the helping professions.* Pacific Grove, CA: Brooks/Cole.

Rossi, P., & Freeman, H. (1993). *Evaluation: A systematic approach* (5th ed.). Newbury Park, CA: Sage Publications.

Rousseau, D., & McCarthy, S. (2007). Educating managers from an evidence-based perspective. *Academy of Management Learning & Education, 6*(1), 84–101.

Sackett, P. (2000). Observational research in mental retardation. *American Journal of Mental Deficiency, 17,* 17–31.

Sackett, D. L., Straus, S. E., Richardson, W. S., Rosenberg, W., & Haynes, R. B. (2000). *Evidence-based medicine: How to practice and teach EBM* (2nd ed.). London: Churchill Livingstone.

Salkind, N. (2006). *Exploring research* (6th ed.). Upper Saddle River, NJ: Pearson/ Prentice Hall.

Sanders, J. (1994). *The program evaluation standards: How to assess evaluations of educational programs.* Thousand Oaks, CA: Sage Publications.

Sawilowsky, S., & Markman, B., (1990). Another look at the power of meta-analysis in the Solomon Four-Group design. *Perceptual and Motor Skills, 71,* 177.

Scriven, M. (1987). New frontiers in evaluation. In D. S. Corday and M. W. Lipsay (Eds.), *Evaluation studies: Review annual* (Vol. 11, pp. 54–91). Newbury Park, CA: Sage Publications.

Scriven, M. (1991). *Evaluation thesaurus* (4th ed.). Newbury Park, CA: Sage Publications.

Seignourel, P., Green, C., & Schmitz, J. (2008). Factor structure and diagnostic efficiency of the BDI-II in treatment-seeking substance users. *Drug and Alcohol Dependence, 93*(3), 271–278.

Sells, S., Smith, T., & Sprenkle, D. (1995). Integrating qualitative and quantitative research methods: A research model. *Family Process, 34,* 199–218.

Sexton, T. (1996). The relevance of counseling outcome research: Current trends and practical implications. *Journal of Counseling and Development, 74*(6), 590–600.

Sexton, T., & Whiston, S. (1996). Integrating counseling research and practice. *Journal of Counseling and Development, 74*(6), 588–589.

Sharpe, D., Adair, J., & Roese, N. (1992). Twenty years of deception research: A decline in subjects' trust. *Personality and Social Psychology Bulletin, 18*(5), 585–590.

Shearer, B. (2004). Multiple intelligences theory after 20 years. *Teachers College Record, 106,* 2–16.

Shimahara, N. (1988). Anthroethnography: A methodological consideration. In R. Sherman & R. Webb (Eds.), *Qualitative research in education: Focus and methods* (pp. 76–89). New York: Falmer.

Shore, B. A., Lerman, D. C., Smith, R. G., Iwata, B. A., & DeLeon, I. G. (1995). Direct assessment of quality of care in a geriatric nursing home. *Journal of Applied Behavior Analysis, 28,* 435–338.

Slegelis, M. (1987). A study of Jung's mandala and its relationship to art psychotherapy. *The Arts in Psychotherapy, 14,* 301–311.

Smith, K., Subich, L., & Kalodner, C. (1995). The transtheoretical model's stages and processes of change and their relation to premature termination. *Journal of Counseling Psychology, 42,* 34–39.

Sorin-Peters, R. (2004). The evaluation of a learner-centred training programme for spouses of adults with chronic aphasia using *Qualitative Case Study Methodology, Aphasiology, 18*(10), 937–949.

Spurling, L. (Ed.). (1989). *Sigmund Freud: Critical assessments*. London: Routledge.

Stake, R. (1994). Case studies. In N. Denzin & Y. Lincoln (Eds.), *Handbook of qualitative research* (pp. 236–247). Thousand Oaks, CA: Sage Publications.

Stake, R. (2000). Case studies. In N. Denzin & Y. Lincoln (Eds.), *Handbook of qualitative research* (2nd ed., pp. 443–466). Thousand Oaks, CA: Sage Publications.

Stangor, C. (2006). *Research methods for the behavioral sciences*. Boston: Houghton Mifflin.

Stenhoff, D., & Lignugaris-Kraft, B. (2007). A review of the effects of peer tutoring on students in secondary settings. *Exceptional Children, 74*(1), 8–30.

Stoltenberg, C., McNeil, B., & Elliot, T. (1995). Selected translations of social psychology to counseling. *Counseling Psychologist, 23,* 603–610.

Strasser, F., Binswanger, J., Cerny, T., & Kesselring, A. (2007). Fighting a losing battle: Eating-related distress of men with advanced cancer and their female partners. A mixed-methods study. *Palliative Medicine, 21,* 129–137.

Strohmer, D., Pellerin, M., & Davidson, K. (1995). Rehabilitation counselor hypothesis testing: The role of negative information, client disability, and counselor experience. *Rehabilitation Counseling Bulletin, 39,* 82–93.

Stufflebeam, D. (1991). *The personnel evaluation standards* (2nd ed.). Newbury Park, CA: Sage Publications.

Stufflebeam, D. (2003). The CIPP model for evaluation. In T. Kellaghan & D. L. Stufflebeam (Eds.), *The international handbook of educational evaluation* (pp. 31–62). Dordrecht, Holland: Kluwer.

Stufflebeam, D. (2005). CIPP model (context, input, process, product). In S. Mathison (Ed.). *Encyclopedia of evaluation*. Thousand Oaks, CA: Sage Publications.

Stufflebeam, D., Foley, W., Gephart, W., Guba, E., Hammond R., Merriman, H., & Provus, M. (1971). *Educational evaluation and decision making*. Itaska, IL: Peacock.

Stufflebeam, D., & Shinkfield, A. (2007). *Evaluation theory, models & applications*. San Francisco: John Wiley.

Sue, D. W. (1993). Confronting ourselves: The white and racial/ethnic minority researcher. *Counseling Psychologist, 21*(2), 244–249.

Szymanski, D., Ozegovic, J., Phillips, J., & Briggs-Phillips, M. (2008). Fostering scholarly productivity through academic and internship research training environment. *Training and Education in Professional Psychology, 1*(2), 135–146.

Tanenbaum, S. (2003). Evidence-based practice in mental health: Practical weaknesses meet political strengths. *Journal of Evaluation in Clinical Practice, 9,* 287–301.

Tashakkori, A., Teddlie, C. (1998). *Mixed methodology: Combining qualitative and quantitative approaches*. Thousand Oaks, CA: Sage Publications.

Tashakkori, A., & Teddlie, C. (2008). The evolution of mixed methods research. In V. Clark and J. Creswell (Eds.), *The mixed methods reader* (pp. 5–26). Thousand Oaks, CA: Sage Publications.

Taylor, S., & Bogdan, R. (1984). *Introduction to qualitative research methods: The search for meaning* (2nd ed.). New York: John Wiley.

Teddlie, C., & Tashakkori, A. (2008). *Foundations of mixed methods research: Integrating quantitative and qualitative techniques in the behavioral sciences.* Thousand Oaks, CA: Sage Publications.

Tedlock, B. (2000). Ethnography and ethnographic representation. In N. Denzin & Y. Lincoln (Eds.), *Handbook of qualitative research* (2nd ed., pp. 467–482). Thousand Oaks, CA: Sage Publications.

Thomas, S., & Quinn, S. (1991). The Tuskegee syphilis study, 1932 to 1972: Implications for HIV education and AIDS risk education programs in the black community. *American Journal of Public Health, 81*(11), 1498–1505.

Thyer, B. (2005). *Program evaluation: An introduction.* Belmont, CA: Wadsworth Publishing.

Todd, Z., Nerlich, B., Mckeown, S., & Clarke, D. (2004). *Mixing methods in psychology: The integration of qualitative and quantitative methods in theory and practice.* New York: Psychology Press.

Toothaker, L. Miller, L. (1996). *Introductory statistics for the behavioral sciences* (2nd ed.). Pacific Grove, CA: Brooks/Cole.

Townend, M., & Grant, A. (2006). Integrating science, practice and reflexivity cognitive therapy with driving phobia. *Journal of Psychiatric and Mental Health Nursing, 13*(5), 554–561.

Urbina, S. (2004). *Essentials of psychological testing.* Hoboken, NJ: Wiley.

Urdan, T. (2005). *Statistics in plain English* (2nd ed). Mahwah, NJ: Lawrence Erlbaum.

Verdonk, P., Harting, A., & Lagro-Jannson, T. (2007). Does equal education generate equal attitudes? Gender differences in medical students' attitudes toward the ideal physician. *Teaching and Learning in Medicine, 19*(1), 9–13.

Vespia, K., Sauer, E., & Lyddon, W. (2006). Counselling psychologists as scientist-practitioners: Finding unity in diversity. *Counselling Psychology Quarterly, 19,* 223–227.

Vierra, A., & Pollock, J. (1988). *Reading educational research.* Scottsdale, AZ: Gorsuch Scarisbrick.

Vosniadou, S. (2007). The cognitive-situative divide and the problem of conceptual change. *Educational Psychologist, 42*(1), 55–66.

Wampold, B., Goodheart, D., & Levant, R. (2007). Clarification and elaboration on evidence-based practice in psychology, *American Psychologist, 62*(6), 616–618.

Weikel, W., & Palmo, A. (1996). *Foundations of mental health counseling.* (2nd ed.). Springfield, IL: Charles C. Thomas.

Whaley, A., & David, K. (2007). Cultural competence and evidence-based practice in mental health services: A complementary perspective. *American Psychologist, 62*(6), 563–574.

Whyte, W. (1990). *Participatory action research.* Thousand Oaks, CA: Sage Publications.

Whiston, S. (1996). Accountability through action research: Research methods for practitioners. *Journal of Counseling and Development, 74*(6), 616–623.

Wholey, J., Hatry, H., & Newcomer, K. (2004). *Handbook of practical program evaluation.* San Francisco: Jossey-Bass.

Wiersma, S., & Jurs, S. (2005). *Research methods in education: An introduction.* Boston: Pearson.

Willig, C. (2001). *Introducing qualitative research in psychology.* Philadelphia: Open University Press.

Yin, R. (1984). *Case study research: Design and methods.* Beverly Hills, CA: Sage Publications.

Yin, R. (2003). *Case study research: Design and methods* (3rd ed.). Thousand Oaks, CA: Sage Publications.

Index

Abbott, M., 85
Abramson, M., 136
Academic honesty, 21–22
Academic Search Primer database, 18
Accessible populations,
    130, 137, 154 (table), 155
Accountability. See Program
    evaluation research
Adair, J., 94
Admi, H., 127
African American subjects, 92–93
Age, 44
Aggression modeling, 39
Alcoholics Anonymous (AA), 66
Alcohol use during pregnancy, 80
Alpha level of significance, 31
AltaVista search engine, 20
Alternate-form reliability, 169
Alternative hypothesis, 122
    alternative directional hypothesis, 122
    alternative nondirectional
        hypothesis, 122
Alternative research designs, 229
Alzheimer's disease, 174
American Counseling Association
    (ACA), 88, 89, 91
American Psychological Association
    (APA), 6, 88, 89, 91
American Psychological Association
    Code of Ethics, 95
American Psychological Association
    Presidential Task Force on
    Evidence-Based Practice, 82

Analysis of covariance (ANCOVA),
    35 (table), 36–37, 186, 187
Analysis of variance (ANOVA),
    34, 35 (table), 36
    factorial analysis of variance, 34
    repeated-measures analysis of
        variance, 34, 36
    See also Inferential statistics;
        Statistical methods
Anastasi, A., 168
Anderson, L., 64, 65, 66
Anorexia nervosa research, 40–41
Anshel, M., 36
Anthropology, 69
Apter, A., 40
Arcuri, J., 21
Art therapy. See Mandala drawing study
Ary, D., 44
Assessment:
    descriptive approach and, 5
    follow-up assessments, 159
    See also Evaluation; Instruments
        evaluation; Literature review
        evaluation
Aswinanonh, R., 58
Attributes, 44
Attrition, 153
Authority, 4
Autobiography, 71–72
Autonomy principle, 89

Baban, A., 86
Babbie, E., 5, 134

About the Author

Rick Houser is currently the Department Head in Educational Studies in Psychology, Research Methodology, and Counseling at the University of Alabama. He has been Associate Dean in the College of Education at the University of Massachusetts, Boston. Also, he was a professor and department chair for several years at the University of Massachusetts, Boston. Rick Houser has taught graduate-level research courses for more than 20 years. He received his doctorate from the University of Pittsburgh in rehabilitation counseling with a minor in research methodology. He conducts research in ethical decision making, stress and coping, and the use of virtual reality in counseling.